Wales' Unknown Hero: Soldier, Spy, Monk

THE LIFE OF HENRY COOMBE-TENNANT, MC, OF NEATH

Dedicated to the memory of

Winifred Coombe Tennant
'Mam o Nedd'

whose careful retention of Henry's letters made this biography possible.

Wales' Unknown Hero: Soldier, Spy, Monk

THE LIFE OF HENRY COOMBE-TENNANT, MC, OF NEATH

BERNARD LEWIS

First impression: 2021

© Copyright Bernard Lewis and Y Lolfa Cyf., 2021

The contents of this book are subject to copyright, and may
not be reproduced by any means, mechanical or electronic,
without the prior, written consent of the publishers.

The publishers wish to acknowledge the support of
the Books Council of Wales

Cover design: Y Lolfa
Cover image courtesy of the Coombe-Tennant family

ISBN: 978 1 912631 33 9

Published and printed in Wales
on paper from well-maintained forests by
Y Lolfa Cyf., Talybont, Ceredigion SY24 5HE
website www.ylolfa.com
e-mail ylolfa@ylolfa.com
tel 01970 832 304
fax 832 782

Contents

	Acknowledgements	7
1.	A New Messiah	9
2.	The Wise One	21
3.	Unhappy at Eton	32
4.	A Success at Cambridge	43
5.	The Welsh Guards	58
6.	Into Battle	68
7.	Prisoner of War	84
8.	Over the Wire	101
9.	On the Run	115
10.	Special Forces	140
11.	Behind Enemy Lines	153
12.	Advancing on Germany	177
13.	The Palestinian Mandate	203
14.	Inside Intelligence	218
15.	A Benedictine Monk	234
	Select Bibliography	253
	Index	256

Acknowledgements

I AM INDEBTED to Mark Coombe-Tennant, who kindly gave his blessing to my research into the life of his late uncle and provided me with much information. Thanks also to John Coombe-Tennant and Rosalie Hoffmann.

I would particularly like to thank my editor at Y Lolfa, Carolyn Hodges, for her championing of the work and her expert editing, which hugely improved the final manuscript. I must also thank the Y Lolfa Commissioning Editor, Lefi Gruffudd, for accepting my proposal for the book.

Once again, I am very grateful to the County Archivist for West Glamorgan, Mr Kim Collis, and his excellent team at the West Glamorgan Archive Service, whose expert advice and assistance never faltered, even during the Covid-19 pandemic.

I would also like to thank for assisting me in various ways: Stephen Beale, Charles Beer, Stuart Booker (Swansea University), the Books Council of Wales, Jon Cooksey, Professor Rory Cormac (University of Nottingham), Dr Luke Daly-Groves (University of Leeds), Dom Leo Maidlow Davis (Downside Abbey), Bruce Dennis, Marian van Dijken (Dutch Embassy), Jonathan Elms, Taff Gillingham (khakidevil. co.uk), Professor B G J de Graaff (Utrecht University), Jeff Griffiths (Dyffryn Clydach and Bryncoch Historical Society), Professor A G Hildenbergh-Bode (Utrecht University), Tony Howard (nomadstravel.co.uk), Joshua Insley (Eton College), Sally Jennings (Eton College), Dr Simon Johnson (Downside Abbey), Bert Keers (Ministry of Defence, the Netherlands), Steven Kippax, L. Sgt. Stuart Laing (Welsh Guards, Wellington Barracks), Robert Laker (Swansea University), the late A R

(David) Lewis (Proprose.co.uk), Greg Lewis, Barbara Lloyd, Paul Lucas, Dom Dominic Mansi (Downside Abbey), Nigel Marshall, Alex Marut, Patricia McGuire (King's College, Cambridge), Brian Mooney, Alison Morgan (www.trosol.co.uk), Brigitte d'Oultremont (President, Comet Line), Steve Parsons (Downside Abbey), Jeremy Racher (Cambridge District Scouts), Lee Richards (www.arcre.com), Charles Rollings, Mary Scott (Cambridge University), Aurel Sercu, Angelo da Silva Cosme, Jonathan Smith (Cambridge University), William Spencer (formerly National Archives, Kew), Sir Beville Stanier Bt., Helen Symington (National Library of Scotland), Dr Xiaolong Tang (University of Birmingham), Anita Teuwen, Paul Tracey, Dr James Vaughan (Aberystwyth University) and members of the WW2Talk forum.

And last, but by no means least, I must once again thank my wife, Elizabeth (Lib), for her enthusiasm and support for my endeavours regarding the life of Henry Coombe-Tennant.

Bernard Lewis
September 2021

Due to space restrictions, footnotes for this work are available as a free PDF download from the following site:

https://bernardlewisauthor.wordpress.com/

A paper copy has also been deposited with the West Glamorgan Archive Service at Swansea and can be consulted according to their usual terms and conditions.

CHAPTER ONE
A New Messiah

HENRY COOMBE-TENNANT OF Cadoxton, Neath had a truly remarkable life. He was variously a scholar, soldier, prisoner of war, escapee, Special Operations Executive agent, military intelligence officer, MI6 operative and Benedictine monk. However, the most astonishing fact about Henry's remarkable life is the one that seems to have had the least impact on him: he was born in accordance with a secret plan that was to see him become the 'New Messiah', bringing peace and reconciliation to a troubled world. Clearly, that plan did not come to fruition, but Henry's life was nevertheless very eventful.

He was born at Cadoxton Lodge near Neath on 9 April 1913 and was the fourth child of Winifred Tennant. Her husband Charles Coombe Tennant was the grandson of George Tennant, the man who had built the Tennant Canal that linked Aberdulais, near Neath, with an outlet to the sea at a location near Swansea that is still known today as 'Port Tennant'. The canal was opened in May 1824 and was in commercial use (transporting mainly coal and processed metals to the Swansea Docks) until the 1930s. Even after that time and, indeed, up to the present day, the canal remained in the ownership of the Coombe Tennant family and still provides water for local industries on a commercial basis. The Tennant family also had extensive land holdings in the Neath area, with the family home at Cadoxton Lodge on the outskirts of the town being at the centre of estate affairs.

Charles Coombe Tennant, Henry's father, was born in London in 1852 and had received his education at Harrow and Balliol College, Oxford, where he graduated with a BA. A law student, he was called to the Bar in 1882 and subsequently practised on the South Wales circuit, where he also became a Justice of the Peace for the county of Glamorgan. Charles' mother, Gertrude, hosted a famous London salon, where she became an intimate friend of some notable people including W E Gladstone, John Bright, Joseph Chamberlain, Lord Balfour and David Lloyd George. His sister, Dorothy Tennant, married the famous explorer Henry Morton Stanley, of "Dr Livingstone, I presume?" fame.

In 1895, Charles Coombe Tennant married Winifred Margaret Pearce-Serocold, who was over 20 years his junior. Winifred had been born in 1874 and was the daughter of Lieutenant George Pearce-Serocold, RN and Mary Clarke Richardson, who came from a well-known Swansea family. A friend of Lloyd George, Winifred would become the first female delegate sent by the British Government to the League of Nations Assembly in 1922. Though a non-Welsh speaker, Winifred played an active role in local life and devoted a lot of time to the National Eisteddfod, where she was given the bardic name of 'Mam o Nedd' ('Mother of Neath') and became Mistress of the Robes. She was also a great supporter of local artists, advancing the careers of Evan Walters, Kyffin Williams and several others, and advised the Swansea Corporation for many years on its purchases for the Glynn Vivian Art Gallery (in conjunction with Mr W Grant Murray, Principal of the Swansea School of Art and curator of the gallery).

After marriage, Charles and Winifred moved into the family home at Cadoxton Lodge, Neath – an imposing property that required the services of six servants to ensure its smooth running, as indicated by its 1911 census return. The union eventually produced four children. The firstborn was Christopher (George Christopher Serocold Tennant, to give him his full name), who arrived in October 1897. After attending the West Downs School at Winchester, Christopher, or 'Cruff', as the family affectionately called him, progressed to Winchester College. Further plans for study were interrupted by the outbreak of the Great War and in 1916 Cruff volunteered for service with the Welsh Guards. As befitting a Welsh Guard, he stood at 6' 2" in height when he enlisted, though he weighed only 9st 6lb. His career at the front (near Ypres) proved to be tragically short, and he was killed by a shell splinter in September 1917 as he was leaving the front line to commence a few days' leave in Paris.

Sadly, though he was the eldest child of the family, he was not the first to die. Daphne was the second child of the marriage but had only reached the age of 18 months when, in 1908, she contracted pneumonia with fatal results. The third child was Alexander, who in adult life became a partner in the investment firm of Cazenove. The fourth and final child of the marriage was Henry, the circumstances of whose conception and birth were very unusual. To understand the background to that situation, we need to look at the interests and beliefs of his mother, Winifred.

Winifred's sister-in-law was Eveleen Tennant, who, in 1880, had married Frederic William Henry Myers, a Fellow of Trinity College, Cambridge who had returned there as a lecturer in Classics in the late 1860s. Myers had become interested in psychical research and was keen to prove by careful scientific experiment that the human spirit survived the death of its earthly body. He was a founding member of the London-based Society for Psychical Research and became its president in 1900. The Society took the issue of psychical research very seriously and was far removed from the strain of mediumship that asked questions along the lines of "Is that you, Granny? Where did you hide the money?"

Winifred grew to like and admire Myers and briefly joined the Society for Psychical Research. With the tragic death of her infant daughter Daphne in 1908, her interest in the survival of the human spirit was rekindled, in the hope that someone with 'access' to the spirit world – a psychic medium – could reassure her that Daphne still existed in another form, beyond the gaze of those who were left on Earth.

To that end, Winifred tried the services of a well-known psychic medium, but became frustrated at the apparent lack of firm evidence regarding the survival of Daphne's spirit. With help from her contacts within the Society for Psychical Research, she discovered with surprise that she herself could apparently contact the spirits of the departed via a process known as 'automatic writing', where the hand of the medium was guided in writing down words and sentences by an unseen spirit. By this method, she came to believe that she was indeed personally in touch with the spirit of her late daughter Daphne, as well as the spirits of Frederic Myers and other, by then deceased, former acquaintances.

Winifred began participating in a long-running series of seances that were of great interest to the members of the Society for Psychical Research and became known as the 'Cross-Correspondences', where the automatic writings ('scripts') of several geographically separated mediums (including Winifred) were brought together. The scripts were closely analysed in an attempt to identify and understand the cryptic clues that seemingly tied them together. The subsequent analysis was believed to prove that the spirits of deceased psychic researchers were indeed communicating with the psychic mediums across several continents – one medium was based in New York, while another lived in India – and providing hints and clues that linked the material together in a manner that allowed no possibility of fraud or collusion.

Winifred adopted the name of 'Mrs Willett' when sitting as a medium, in order to retain her anonymity in psychic matters, and her involvement was kept secret from all except a close-knit circle. Sittings usually took place in the presence of a

A New Messiah

living psychic researcher who assisted her during the session, sometimes writing things down when Winifred delivered a spoken message and at other times suggesting possible questions for her to pose to her 'spirit guide'. Sometimes this researcher was Sir Oliver Lodge, but there were also others. Winifred became the key conduit for what seemed to be the spirit of Mary Lyttleton, a lady who had been very close to the prominent British politician Arthur Balfour, before dying of typhus in 1875, aged only 24.

As the automatic writing sessions developed, Winifred came to believe – much to her surprise – that suggestions were being made from beyond the grave encouraging her to become pregnant again. Indeed, she believed that the spirit of Frederic Myers was telling her that a child delivered of her would have the huge benefit of being guided in life by the spirits of Myers himself and other deceased and previously eminent psychic researchers. She was assured that the child's future would be mapped out and assistance rendered from behind the veil of death so that the infant could grow up to become 'The New Messiah', bringing peace and hope to a troubled world. That child was destined to be Henry Coombe-Tennant.

This idea may well appear very far-fetched to the modern reader, though it is worth remembering that world history is peppered with the names of those who were thought – by themselves or others – to have Messianic qualities. And Winifred and others in her circle of confidants sincerely believed that 'The Plan' to produce a Messianic child was quite realistic, even if a virgin birth was not practical. It was decided that the child would be conceived in the normal manner, though, as it happened, Winifred's husband Charles, who was unaware of 'The Plan', was not to be the biological father. That role fell to Gerald Balfour, an eminent British politician who was the brother of the former British Prime Minister, Arthur Balfour. How was it that Gerald Balfour, a stranger to Winifred not long before, was chosen to be the father of her future child?

In December 1910 Sir Oliver Lodge had told her that Balfour, also a psychic researcher, wished to meet her. She travelled to Balfour's home at Fisher's Hill, Woking on 4 February 1911 and confided to her diary that she found him:

> ...intensely attractive, like a Greek head or an old ivory, snow white hair, a most beautiful voice – the most beautiful I think of any speaking voice I ever heard.

Winifred's spirit guides encouraged her to sit with Gerald for a 'daylight impression', a psychic event where a spirit spoke verbally through Winifred rather than guiding her hand in automatic writing. Though initially reluctant, she visited Fisher's Hill again in June 1911 and once more sat with Gerald. He visited her at her Cadoxton home in July 1911, where sittings were held and psychic matters and the sad death of her daughter Daphne discussed. Her diary noted: 'I have grown to feel a great affection for him', and on his departure she recorded, 'I shall miss him.' By September 1911, after further letters and meetings, the relationship had matured and Winifred warmly recorded:

> Gerald arrived at tea time, unexpressibly [sic] dear and beautiful. The joy of seeing him and the pain, too, of love that has to be our secret instead of the acknowledged centre and spring of life. We had a long talk after tea, alone, sitting hand in hand.

The relationship, which was still at this time probably platonic, suffered a setback in November 1911, after Gerald told Winifred that his wife, Betty, was pregnant and the child would be born in June 1912. This was disconcerting news, as it was clear that Gerald (who was then 57) had had sexual relations with his wife after commencing his romantic relationship with Winifred. Though her reaction to this news was at first philosophical, it soon resulted in a flurry of letters between the two, in which each confirmed the pre-eminent importance of the other in their lives. Winifred was eventually mollified by Gerald's declaration that he loved her '…first and best, loves me as he has never loved any woman… I come first.' On 19 January 1912, the couple met at Woking and Gerald gave Winifred a belated Christmas present, a gold ring, in a symbolic act of marriage.

They began to meet more regularly, their common interest in psychic matters providing them with a plausible excuse and allowing time for the relationship to blossom. As well as assisting Winifred with her psychic episodes, Gerald was also able to discuss the scripts of other mediums with her. Both tried to make sense of what often appeared to be inconsequential sentences that might nevertheless harbour important, if somewhat obscure clues. It was hoped that those clues – once 'deciphered' – would help confirm that the communications truly came from the spirit world and were not simply the work of some psychic charlatan.

On 1 March 1912, Gerald told Winifred that he had ceased having sexual relations with his wife, who at that time was three months away from producing what would be the final child of the marriage. Betty, Gerald's wife, seemed to be aware of the growing relationship between her husband and Winifred but, much to Winifred's surprise, expressed no great annoyance at the fact. Indeed, after the birth of her daughter on 6 June 1912, Betty suggested to her husband that Winifred be asked to be the child's godmother, and that was agreed. Winifred's diary is largely silent about her husband Charles' knowledge of her romantic entanglement, though it seems likely that if he did have any suspicions, he took no overt action. In fact, on 7 July 1912, he asked Gerald Balfour to become the guardian of his children, Christopher and Alexander.

On 18 April 1912, Winifred was able to tell her diary:

> I realised today as never before what Gerald's love for me has grown to be – how completely I fill his life, how outside everything else is, how I am all to him, how he adores me – in a word how

completely I have become to him what he is to me... My beloved is mine and I am his. Perfect love and perfect trust.

On 4 July 1912, Gerald Balfour arrived at Cadoxton Lodge and stayed for a week. At the end of July, it became apparent to Winifred that she was pregnant, the child having been conceived during Gerald's visit. 'The Plan' of Winifred giving birth to a 'chosen one', as advocated by entities from the spirit world, was now on its way to fruition. In December 1912, prominent members of the Society for Psychical Research were informed in confidence of the pregnancy.

Winifred's pregnancy was problem-free, though the birth itself was beset with difficulty. The child arrived on 9 April 1913 with Winifred believing that the spirits of deceased psychical researchers Frederic Myers, Edmund Gurney and Henry Sidgwick were in attendance, as – somewhat surprisingly – was the spirit of her late daughter, Daphne. The family doctor feared that the child would not survive the birth, but eventually a son was delivered – though at first he did not cry, being stupefied by chloroform.

Winifred did not doubt that the birth had been assisted by benign, unseen forces, recording in her diary entry for 9 April 1913, 'This day was born my dear son, Augustus... At last I lay, Augustus born, perfect in limb and symmetry and vigour, by the mercy of God and of Daphne's companions.' On the following day, a telegram was sent to Gerald Balfour, advising him of the birth. He was on the point of departing for Denmark, hence his reply was somewhat slow. On 2 May, his response finally reached Cadoxton and was probably well worth waiting for: it ran to 41 pages, reflecting the depth of his relationship with Winifred.

By 16 April 1913, names for the newborn child had been decided on. He was to be called Augustus Henry Serocold Tennant ('Coombe' would be added by deed poll later in his life). Given that the spirit-driven Plan aimed to guide the child into a Messianic role, it seems that Augustus was chosen with reference to the mighty emperor. It was hoped that the child would also become a great leader of men, with some help from the spirit world. Despite the imperial nature of the first name that was chosen, the family nevertheless called him Henry in everyday life. Winifred stated that Henry was used as a mark of respect to the late psychic researcher Henry Sidgwick, while Serocold was her maiden name.

Winifred took Henry to visit Gerald Balfour at Fisher's Hill on 9 June 1913 and also met his new daughter (and her godchild) Kathleen for the first time, finding it a strange experience. At Fisher's Hill, while snatching kisses with Gerald during private moments together, she also found time to have a long conversation with Betty, who showed 'perfect sympathy and nobility on her part'. Betty Balfour indicated that she fully understood and accepted the situation, seeming to put the happiness of her errant husband above her own. She told Winifred, "He belongs more to you now than to me."

In September 1914, Christopher, Winifred's eldest son, was at Winchester College. His younger brother Alexander wrote to him (with a little adult help) to wish him a happy birthday. The letter was signed by Alexander ('Danda') and by an adult who signed on behalf of little Henry, using the name the family had begun calling him by – a name that reflected the ability and potential that Winifred hoped and thought was already being observed in the toddler. It was signed 'Wise One'. That name was still in use within the family when Henry was a battle-hardened soldier some 40 years later. Indeed, Henry often signed his letters to his mother as 'Wise One' or 'W.O.'

Given her belief in the spirit-world's involvement in Henry's conception, Winifred was particularly keen to record the minutiae of his life as he hopefully progressed towards greatness. In December 1916 she had typed up (probably for the benefit of the nursemaid) the details of his daily routine and diet, headed 'Wise One's Day'. At the risk of overwhelming those charged with Henry's care during the day, Winifred went on to lay down several other rules that needed to be followed to ensure the Wise One's health and happiness.

In February 1918 Winifred was staying in London and, while there, visited Mrs Leonard, a noted psychic medium, with Sir Oliver Lodge. Mrs Leonard had apparently assisted Lodge in contacting the spirit of his son, Raymond, who had been killed during the Great War. Winifred's identity was concealed from Mrs Leonard and the sittings, spread over several weeks, were judged to be a great success as contact was supposedly made with the spirit of Christopher, who had also been killed a few months earlier. Winifred's diary for 8 February 1918 recorded, 'The whole thing was so wondrous and oh! so comforting. My living son. It is not the past I must turn to but the present. I am deeply impressed by this sitting.' On 11 February she wrote: 'I believe it brought me as near to Cruff as it did him to me. God bless him. This has been a wonderful experience.'

Christopher's death had had a traumatic effect on Winifred. She was determined that the memory of his life would not be allowed to fade away and had him commemorated in several locations in both Britain and France. She also worked closely with Sir Oliver Lodge in producing an admiring biography of Christopher's short life, something that ultimately damaged her relationship with Gerald Balfour. Having asked him to write a foreword to the book, his less than effusive praise of her son led to strained relations between the two. They remained in contact until Balfour's death in 1945 – he was still Henry's godfather and took an interest in his progress – but the passion of their early relationship was very much a thing of the past from late 1917 onwards.

Perhaps because Winifred expected great things of Henry, she was always pleased to hear encouraging remarks about his intelligence and development and it seems that he was quite a gifted little boy – as his subsequent academic progress would confirm. Miss Tavender, the children's governess, told

Winifred, '[He] amused Bessie and myself by telling us a long yarn. His vocabulary is wonderful. His ambition now is to become a knight! ...Mr Tennant came in while he was working [on the blackboard] and was very surprised at what he could do.' Henry was also a sensitive young lad, as his older brother Christopher had been. In February 1918, Miss Tavender told Winifred that while Henry had been 'talking about Christopher last evening, he asked me if everything was beautiful where he was and I told him yes, it was. He is a very thoughtful child and is always burning to know.'

Efforts were made to record Henry's progress as his skills developed. Most events, many of them fairly inconsequential, were nevertheless scrupulously noted by Miss Tavender, with Winifred later having them typed up to serve as a lasting record. Aged only five, he began to display a precocious outlook. After his father had made some comment, Henry bluntly told him, "That's colloquial English. You wouldn't write it like that." When Miss Tavender struggled to understand a point he was trying to make, he retorted, "That's King's English and I can't help it if you don't understand it."

He ended one letter in a manner that must have been open to very few small children, asking his mother, 'How is the Prime Minister?' At that time Winifred was in London, where she met and dined with several prominent Liberal Party politicians as well as meeting the Prime Minister, David Lloyd George, at both 10 Downing Street and his country retreat, Chequers. At Chequers, they discussed the Irish problem and she offered him her opinion on the matter. During her time in London she was told that she had been chosen to be a Coalition-Liberal Party candidate at the next Parliamentary election.

Not all Henry's writings took the shape of a formal letter, however, and his childish outlook still shone through. In one apologetic note to members of the Cadoxton Lodge household he wrote, 'I promise not to touch the weights or chains on the cuckoo clock.' This was signed (erroneously, as he mixed up his initials) 'A.S.H. Tennant' and was solemnly witnessed by Miss Tavender. This was followed sometime later by a promise not to: '1. Unlock front or garden doors. 2. Touch oak room shutters. 3. Blow out maid's candles. Signed} I will promise that I will not do these things. W.O. 24 Jan 1921.' Rather more alarmingly, he also signed an undertaking to never 'try and open a door of a railway carriage when the train is moving.'

On 14 August 1922, Winifred Coombe Tennant received an invitation to act as one of the members of the British delegation to the League of Nations Assembly at Geneva. On acceptance, she would become the first female representative selected by the British Government for such a role. Her attendance would be required for about a month, starting on 2 September. In the event, she remained abroad for seven weeks, enjoying her time at the Assembly and working and speaking on the problem of the illegal traffic in women and children. After a month at the League of Nations Assembly, she spent three weeks sightseeing, for two of which she was joined by her husband. While she had been alone in Geneva, Charles had written to her affectionately, even if he stiffly signed his letters 'C.C.T.', rather than the more intimate 'Charlie' of their earlier days together. He told Winifred, 'You have apparently got well into your work – and all recognise your ability. It is wonderful to see how you can do all you do; and master so many subjects. I know no one man or woman who in the time could do what you do – and do it so well.'

In relation to Henry and his brother, Alexander, Charles commented, 'The 2 dear Emperors are happy. I do all I can for them to my own delight. They have their little ups and downs – but are well and enjoy their walks and expeditions by car.' No doubt Winifred was always anxious to receive news of her beloved children and she would have been especially keen to hear of Henry's progress, given the special future that she thought awaited him. The next step on his path to greatness would be taken when he started preparatory school.

CHAPTER TWO

The Wise One

WINIFRED HAD WRITTEN to Lionel Helbert, Principal of the West Downs School at Winchester, as far back as 7 May 1913, just a month after Henry's birth, to put his name down for the May 1923 intake. In the event, the date of his departure to the boarding school was brought forward to May 1922. The West Downs School had been founded by Helbert himself in 1897. He had died in 1919 and by the time that Henry started, it was under the stewardship of Kenneth Tindall, who would remain Headmaster until 1954, supported by his wife.

Whilst it was all new for Henry, his brother Alexander had been attending West Downs since 1920. He therefore knew the ropes and was consequently not as apprehensive as was his younger brother, who would be staying away from home for the first time. Alexander had obviously briefed his sibling on the school's teachers, with the result that Henry was somewhat fearful of Mr Benson, a teacher prone to shouting. Other tips included the advice 'not to join in games unless you are invited, especially with bigger boys', to keep up with the other boys during a walk, to obey the seniors quickly, not to go outside the school gates without permission and to 'avoid Boyle minor and any gang he gets up.' Alexander ended his note by stating, 'The whole of the first month keep quiet, watch what everyone does and do the same.'

Henry soon found being away from home a great trial, telling his mother:

> Just a line to tell you that I love you very much, and each day
> I wish more and more to have a cold, so that you might come
> and see me! And then if I was very bad… you'd take me home to
> Cadoxton…

Mrs Tindall provided soothing words for a concerned Winifred, telling her that Henry seemed to be settling down and was enjoying cricket and, oddly, going to bed early because it was so much quieter in the dormitory than in the noisy classrooms and corridors. She said she thought that he would 'be a great addition to West Downs', before concluding with the news that he was so far ahead of his classmates academically that he had already been moved into a higher form.

His academic progress soon featured in his letters home, and he told his mother that he could well be the top pupil in Latin, though his English needed a little more work. His essay on theatres in Shakespearean London was adjudged by his tutor, Mr Gibson, to be the best 'by far' of his class. He enjoyed a visit by his godfather, Gerald Balfour, though he implored his mother by letter to 'REMEMBER TO TRY AND COME AND SEE ME BEFORE THE END OF THE TERM!!!' His hopes were not realised, however, partly because Winifred was kept busy in canvassing as a candidate for the Forest of Dean in the Gerneral Election held in November 1922. She came third, attracting almost a fifth of the votes cast.

Henry, only nine years old and far from home, was not averse to a bit of mischief. With Winifred busy on other matters, she despatched Miss Tavender, who was still in the family's employ despite the boys now being away at school, to West Downs School in late June 1922 to make a full report on Henry's academic progress. Miss Tavender began her report with the bad news:

> W.O. had a midnight expedition with a very noisy ending, and he
> has promised Mr and Mrs Tindall and me that it will be the VERY
> LAST. He got out of bed to see the stars and he put his stool on

the chest of drawers and another stool on that and stood on it – of course ending by the stool tumbling over and just before midnight everyone in the dormitory and the sister heard this noise, of stools falling over, glass being broken, etc. He broke the glass of GF's [godfather's] portrait and a tumbler and he has to pay for the latter.

He had made a great many friends at West Downs and everyone was impressed by his honesty and conscientiousness. After each 'midnight revel' he habitually went to Mrs Tindall and promptly admitted his guilt, happily accepting the minor fines imposed and on one occasion even counting the drops of gravy he had spilt and offering to pay a fine for each one.

On 18 July Mr Tindall wrote to Winifred to outline his concerns about Henry. It did not make pleasant reading. Henry had been 'continually disobedient and troublesome in the Dormitory and seems to have no conception of what is meant by school discipline.' He regularly continued talking after lights out and was prone to walk about amusing himself, disturbing the other boys. Even a mild slippering by Mr Tindall had no effect on his behaviour.

One thing Henry certainly was happy about was the piano lessons that had been arranged for him so that his aptitude could be improved upon. He later told his mother that he was popular with the other boys because he could play the piano for them. This was a talent that Henry would deploy throughout his life.

Henry's growing talent for the piano led to Mr Tindall arranging extra tuition for him with the music teacher, Dorothy Playsted. She told Winifred by letter that she found Henry 'unusually promising, he has a gift for improvisation, and the musical way in which he attacks his work makes him a delightful pupil.' Henry was able to proudly tell his mother, 'Yesterday was the first time I was asked to play the piano before company! I was asked to play the Moonlight Sonata before the boys and masters at a "sing-song"! I got a loud applause, too!'

Sadly, Henry's time at West Downs would soon come to an unhappy end. He regularly suffered from colds or influenza while he was there and, on returning him to the school in April 1923, his ever-vigilant mother had warned Mrs Tindall that he was suffering from a very rapid pulse and she wanted the school to take his temperature regularly. It seems that although Mrs Tindall had passed these instructions on to the school nurse, they were forgotten about, with the result that Henry's condition worsened.

When made aware of Henry's illness, Winifred collected and conveyed him to Gerald Balfour's home at Fisher's Hill, Woking, where a doctor was summoned. She promptly complained to the Tindalls: 'I have formed an unfavourable opinion of the sister from much that I have heard and have not repeated and I am convinced she is not the right stamp of woman and that you will find in the long run that I am right...'

Winifred's dissatisfaction grew when it emerged that the nurse had apparently attacked two pupils with a toasting fork while they were in the sick bay, causing them to cry. With the Tindalls, in Winifred's view, not taking the matter seriously enough, she determined to take action. On 27 May 1923 Winifred wrote to tell Mr Tindall that, as regarded Henry, 'After much consideration we have come to the conclusion that he would do better in a smaller school and in one where the pace is less strenuous than it is now at West Downs.' Henry would not be going back.

Pinewood School, near Farnborough, was chosen for Henry after Winifred visited it in May 1923 and formed a favourable opinion of it, its Headmaster and staff. Nevertheless, after the experience at West Downs, several references were also taken up before a final decision was made. The school had been established by the Reverend F F Brackenbury at Maiden Erleigh in Berkshire in 1875, relocating to Farnborough in 1883.

The Headmaster in 1923 was Colonel W Shirley, only the third Headmaster since the founding of the school. The school was 'a comfortable modern country house, and quite ideal for its purpose – the drains are excellent, the accommodation is ample and well arranged, and the walls are washable. The School has its own chapel, kitchen garden, laundry, and farm, a covered play-shed 70ft. by 35ft., a theatre and library of about 1,000 books… and 12 acres of ground (exclusive of farm) ENTIRELY devoted to the use of the boys. This includes the playing field…' Additionally, it had a 'competent Staff of YOUNG men, and the Care and Management of our boys is in charge of [Mrs Shirley], who is past-mistress of her work, and has the support of a Governess and TWO matrons – all three gentlewomen, and the two latter fully trained hospital nurses with many years' experience of nursing children.' Including Colonel Shirley, the school had eight masters and could accommodate up to sixty pupils.

Henry's arrival at Pinewood was delayed by yet another bout of influenza, but by 1 July 1923, he had settled in so well that he was able to tell his mother, 'I am enjoying myself extremely and am almost as happy as if I was home!' His piano-playing was already attracting attention, with various masters encouraging him to play well-known pieces as well as improvisations.

Henry received an end-of-term report on 31 July 1923. His results were no doubt affected by his switching schools and then arriving later than planned at Pinewood due to illness, and he was also one of the youngest boys in his form. He came an unhappy 11th out of 11 boys. Colonel Shirley rounded off the report – which must have caused Winifred great concern – by stating, 'He is an intelligent boy and I am quite sure could do extremely well if he could and would concentrate and be more conscientious. I think he is under the impression that there is no necessity to apply himself to anything but music.' Henry's subsequent school reports fell into a familiar pattern, which highlighted his undoubted gifts but also underlined his frequent failings. The ability was undoubtedly there, but it was often let down by outright carelessness.

The issue of Henry paying too much attention to the piano was tackled head-on by Winifred, who drew up a simple agreement that read: 'It is agreed between Henry Tennant and his mother that his ration for music (piano, pianola, compositions) shall be – 1 hour and a half per day. Also, that no piano playing shall take place before 9.30 a.m. nor after 6.45 p.m.' Both parties duly signed the agreement. It seemed to be important to spell out the acceptable boundaries to a strong-willed Henry.

With the autumn 1923 term underway, Henry was quite happy at Pinewood, telling his mother that he had identified a couple of boys who also came from Wales, a fact that pleased him immensely. Table tennis and tiddlywinks were all the rage at the school, while he was enjoying reading the *Si Fan Mysteries* by Sax Rohmer, a series of books that featured the oriental villain Fu Manchu. Indeed, Henry took a great interest in facts about China and the Chinese language. One highlight of the early autumn was returning home to Cadoxton Lodge in September 1923 at the same time that it was graced with a visit by David Lloyd George. Henry had his photograph taken with family members and the by-then former Prime Minister and his party.

At Colonel Shirley's request, Winifred had a detailed discussion with Henry on 10 November 1923, during which she tried to impress upon him the need to make more effort with his school work, as well as to behave better. This seems to have had a useful effect as Colonel Shirley was soon able to report that 'Henry is making a real effort and I thought it would please you to know that he had taken to heart all you had said.' Henry was also busy in gathering information in advance of the December 1923 General Election, canvassing the other boys regarding their political allegiances and telling his mother that the breakdown of party support at Pinewood revealed 11 Liberals, 37 Conservatives and just one Labour supporter. The election produced a hung Parliament and as the news filtered through to Henry, he feared the worst for the family fortunes, telling his mother:

> As far as I can gather Labour have beaten Liberal and are quite likely to beat Conservative too! I hope and pray they don't! 'Cos if they do, why, we shall have to give up running the car, we shall have to give up part of the grounds, and it will generally ruin us! Things are beginning to look black!!

The impact of Winifred's November pep-talk had resulted in an immediate uplift in her son's efforts at Pinewood. The report on Henry drawn up in December 1923 was a marked improvement on the July effort, with him moving from bottom of his class to top. Colonel Shirley was also complimentary about the change in Henry's results and behaviour, telling Mrs Coombe Tennant that 'Where I had two or three complaints every day about Henry up to half-term, I have not heard a single word against him since [you] spoke to him on 10th of November... he has done just about his very best.' However, Henry being Henry, Colonel Shirley was compelled to add a handwritten footnote to his typed comments, saying:

> I wrote the foregoing on Saturday, 15 Dec; that very afternoon Henry climbed over the railing round the stove in the changing-room – I do not know how he managed to squeeze his body in between the stove and the railing, but he did it – and burnt his shorts. Of course, they were brand new shorts – they would be! ...Well – one escapade in 6 weeks isn't bad – is it?

Even though Henry's behaviour was showing signs of welcome improvement, he was still not averse to making his views known in a quite direct manner, informing his mother:

> It strikes me that I am now just in the developing stage, and that I intend to grow up 90 per cent our way, and 10 per cent my own. I entirely agree with your way, except in one or two things of which I will tell you. You say I am free; but am I free?

I will give you an example of 2 things which I violently object to, the last much more than the first. First of all, I dislike being put to bed at seven. It does no good. Perhaps you think it makes me go to sleep earlier. On the contrary it makes me go to sleep LATER. Here, I go to sleep pretty late anyhow, but I have more to think of here, and besides, I do not get so tired. But if you put me to bed later at home, I am convinced that I should go to sleep earlier, because I should be more tired. The second thing, would you believe it, is that I appear to not be allowed to go to any shop or anything by myself for fear, I suppose, that I should be run over in the street... I quite agree to any sensible restriction, but when I am subjected to restrictions like that, and especially the last one, there is only one word to say and that is CAPTIVITY.

In November 1924, he was awarded his colours after playing in the first team for rugby and Colonel Shirley was pleased to tell Mrs Coombe Tennant that Henry's improved behaviour was continuing, adding, 'His outlook on life is now completely altered. He is really willing to please, really anxious to get on at work and games as well as in the general sense. He used to think that there was nothing in life worthy of any attention but his music and even there was unwilling to face the drudgery of the necessary technique... He is now beginning to learn that there is NO royal road and that "hard work and a dashed deal of it" is the only road to success.'

In music he was now under the supervision of Roy Wakeham, who found that on the piano 'His power of interpretation far surpasses his technique. If he will give to the latter continual attention, I am confident that the future holds much in store for him.' A piece of music that he had composed was so highly thought of by Mr Wakeham that he sent it off to the Royal College of Music to seek an opinion on its merits.

The opinion duly arrived, in the form of a letter from Sir Hugh Allen, Professor of Music at Oxford University and Director of the Royal College of Music in London, a man described as being the 'acknowledged but unofficial head of the music profession in [Great Britain]'. Allen said of Henry's talent, 'It is certainly precocious and undoubtedly promising. He has the feeling for pianoforte writing – but whether he does so with his muscular memory or with his musical wits, it is perhaps hard to tell as yet. I should be interested to see the child if you were willing to bring him here one day...' That 'one day' arrived in July 1925 when Mr Wakeham accompanied Henry – now 12 years old – to the Royal College of Music for an interview with Sir Hugh Allen. Wakeford subsequently confided to Winifred by letter that:

> Sir Hugh Allen has as I know, so brusque a manner that I feared Henry might be rather taken aback, but he acquitted himself wonderfully well...
>
> He played his 'Contented' by Schumann from memory and was then asked to play it again in a different key without music – most difficult – but he did it very creditably. He also played the Fantasia of Mozart with much soul... Sir Hugh's criticism was that he has the music all right, that it is being brought out well and that he should be given every scope... [Sir Hugh] is pleased that Henry hopes to go to Eton for there: 'he will get atmosphere' and he has asked me to keep in touch with him so that he may write to the Music Master there and say that he has 'a composer' coming to him.

It was not only Henry's skill at the piano that was drawing attention. He had often produced poetry, its subject matter frequently harking back to his home in Wales or to his deep love for his mother. He produced a poem ('Ode to a Lark') that so impressed Colonel Shirley that he promptly sent it off to 'two critics of whose literary acumen I have the highest opinion.' The critics agreed that 'Henry's verses are "marvellous" and that there is in them "...a touch of real genius"', opinions that the Headmaster entirely agreed with. He was given permission by Mrs Coombe Tennant to print it in the next school magazine.

During 1925, Henry had also begun to teach himself Chinese using self-teaching books on the subject (one of which he promptly lost!), and he was able to give a fellow student lessons in the language. He had, for some unknown reason, developed a great interest in all things Chinese, telling his mother, 'I can't explain what I feel about the Chinese. Have you ever felt that your imagination is stretched so far that it is bound to snap if you stretch it anymore? Because that is what I feel now...' He later added, 'I can never make any sort of a man unless I have to put up with trials now. After all, it is only a preparation for my work in China.' A young Henry saw his future 'work in China' being of a missionary nature.

Henry began 1926 at Pinewood in a buoyant mood, telling his mother that 'I am very happy here indeed.' He was quite friendly with Mr Jourdain, the French tutor, and had visited his home, where he found Jourdain's wife 'very intriguing'. She had subsequently written to Henry, calling him affectionately 'The Sphinx', presumably due to the fact that she found him rather impassive.

Henry's confirmation in the church was set for 23 March 1926 at St Mark's Church, South Farnborough, a mere five minutes from Pinewood School. His excitement grew as the day approached and he told his mother that he looked forward to soon having to 'fend for myself, and get away from the protection of other people.' With both Winifred and Charles being unable to attend the ceremony, Henry invited Gerald Balfour, his godfather and biological father, who happily accepted. As Henry later told his mother after the ceremony:

> I could almost feel the Holy Ghost entering me as I felt the Bishop's hand on my head and heard his voice. As he said 'amen' I got up and returned to my place, and prayed a while and thought of you and dear Chrissifor [Henry's older brother]... I went to bed feeling considerably older and very much wiser.

The school reports on Henry for April and July 1926 were filled with the familiar criticisms of his lack of attention to detail and carelessness across all topics, although Colonel Shirley noted with obvious warmth:

Henry is... most friendly, anxious to please, willing and conscientious, and he has a high moral sense. He is also brilliant in many things and over-anxious to advance in all things but he is apt to be forgetful and unpractical, and he fails to recognise that the foundations of success and happiness can only be well and truly laid by solid grind and methodical progress... I do not know when I have loved any boy so much.

Henry's work on the piano continued to improve, though he was inclined to forge ahead, losing some of the nuances. His tutor, Mr Wakeham, noted, 'In losing Henry I lose a pupil whom it has given me the greatest pleasure to teach...' Mr Wakeham would be 'losing' Henry since his mother had already arranged for him to be admitted to Eton College in September 1926, where the Master of Wotton House said Henry would be very welcome.

CHAPTER THREE

Unhappy at Eton

BY THE SUMMER of 1926, Henry was 13 years of age. Eton typically took boys between the ages of 10 and 14 as 'Oppidans', dependent on results in the Entrance Examination, with boys usually boarding in single rooms in Masters' houses. The Headmaster at the time was Cyril Alington.

The autumn of 1926 saw Henry take his second trip abroad with his mother, father and brother. His first had taken place in September 1925, when the family had gone to Rouen in northern France. They had in particular visited the cathedral, where Winifred had placed a statue of the Madonna in remembrance of Christopher. The family had visited several other places of interest and also took a boat trip on the Seine. Henry had thoroughly enjoyed himself, noting on his return to Britain, 'When we landed at England, I felt so flat! What a horrible place England is after France, to be sure!'

For Henry's second sortie abroad, the party left London on 1 September 1926 for Dieppe. Once again, a key part of the trip was a visit to the cathedral at Rouen. Henry attended Mass with his mother, finding that he 'was most impressed by the Mass, which I think much more beautiful than the Church of England services. I liked the incense very much.' They also made a visit to the castle at Arques. Henry kept a careful account of his spending on the trip, recording that he had spent around 35 francs – of which almost 10 francs was given to poor people that he had encountered on his travels.

Unhappy at Eton

With the French sojourn completed, Henry was ready for his exciting – if daunting – admission to Eton College. He was medically examined on arrival and was recorded as being 5' 4" tall and weighing 6st 11lb. He was unflatteringly described as being 'a tall, slightly built and not very robust looking boy. He holds himself badly, with round shoulders, flat chest and prominent abdomen. He is not as sun burnt, in comparison with other boys, as one would like to see him.'

By the end of term in December 1926, his Housemaster Leonard Todd told Winifred, 'Personally, I like Henry very much and he is always friendly and cheerful... He is, I am sure, absolutely straight, honest and sound in essential matters – at the moment he is rather overburdened by the cares and worries of school life, but I hope he will find things easier next half.' In contrast, his mathematics tutor found him 'rather incompetent... he frequently forgot to bring his work or his books into school and often did the wrong sums... However, he is not weak at the subject and should be able to do himself better justice...' Other tutors found him to be 'an excellent boy' and 'certainly the best of my Fourth Form pupils.'

Despite his limited attendance at class due to illness in the early part of 1927, Henry still managed to form sharp opinions on his new tutors, committing them to paper and sending them to his mother for her enlightenment. Some of the things they did would set alarm bells ringing in a modern-day school. Of Mr Todd, his Housemaster, he wrote:

> Picture to yourself a short, and rather stout man, sly, jovial, with plenty of bonhomie, but a capacity for seriousness, and you have Leonard Todd, Esq, B.A. etc.
>
> He comes to see me in the evening, and the method of procedure of this interview is nearly always the same. I hear a creaking tread on the passage and my door opens, and in comes m'tutor.
>
> 'Well, creature,' he croaks, by way of a beginning, 'how is it?' Then without any warning he suddenly twists my head under his

arm and proceeds to slap that unfortunate member vigorously for about half a minute, after which he begins to tickle me. He then suddenly drops his jovialness and with a serious air says, 'Hurry up into bed, creature, I'm coming to turn out the light in a few minutes.' When he comes in again he says, 'In bed, object? Ye-e-es, that's right. Good night creature!', and out goes the light.

Henry seems to have spent some time away from Eton, probably to improve his health, with a period spent in Switzerland in late 1927 or early 1928. Dr Attlee, the college physician, said in March 1928 that he had 'never seem him look so well before', his height now 5' 8½" and his weight 8st 6lb. His concentration levels, however, still needed attention and he was given 440 lines after completely forgetting to attend one class. Happily for Henry, the Headmaster, Mr Cyril Alington – who had succeeded the Revd the Hon. Edward Lyttelton in 1916 – remitted a large part of the punishment in return for assistance in moving books up some stairs to another room. Even better, the Headmaster's butler provided fruit, milk and cake for the errant pupil as he toiled at his task.

A new academic year, commencing in September 1928, brought with it new tutors for Henry. The most interesting was probably Dr T C Porter, who taught science and of whom Henry said that he '...is generally considered quite mad... He had a house once, but had to give it up because everybody smoked and did what they liked!' Indeed, Dr Porter ('Daddy'), was a little too easy-going in some respects. He seemed oblivious to the antics of one of his appointed House Captains, a young lad who was wildly in love and in the habit of exiting his bedroom window at night to visit his lady friend in London. Another tutor, William Hope-Jones ('Hojo'), provided his pupils with a talking point after being taken before the Bournemouth magistrates for bathing on the beach in the nude.

In mid-October 1928, Henry fell out with his housemaster, Mr Todd, after a tailor was sent by Winifred to see her son at the college for a fitting. The tutor took exception to this unapproved visit and a shaken Henry informed his mother that 'I have never seen Todd so furious before. He was excessively rude and said it was none of your business to invite people to his house. It isn't certainly any of his business to be so jolly offensive...' Things didn't improve in the short-term; some days later Todd spotted a translation of a Greek text on Henry's table: a commercially published 'crib', designed to aid the student in his work. Todd took great exception to this, calling it 'immoral' as its use was intended to make life easier for the pupil. Henry told his mother that he regarded Todd's reasoned arguments against the use of cribs to be 'gibbering drivel.' Nevertheless, he was made to promise his tutor that he would not use them again. An incensed Henry later went to the trouble of typing up a five-page justification of the use of cribs, though for whose eyes it was intended is unclear.

A far more concerning matter then came to the forefront of Henry's mind, however. The health of his 'father', Charles, had been giving much cause for concern. At the same time that the Eton Headmaster was warning parents that there had been a case of poliomyelitis at the college (though he was satisfied that the risk of further cases had passed), Henry was writing to his mother to express his distress at news of a relapse in his father's health. His concerns were justified and Charles Coombe Tennant died at Cadoxton Lodge on 5 November 1928, aged 76. The cause of death was an intestinal obstruction with a secondary feature being a carcinoma of the intestine. He was cremated at Pontypridd and his ashes were interred in a vault at Highgate Cemetery in London. The *Cadoxton-juxta-Neath Parochial Magazine* noted:

> For 50 years, or so, he had read the Lessons at Cadoxton Church, and by his kindness and simplicity had become a part of the life of the place. Cadoxton will never be the same place without his genial presence. Perhaps he was never appreciated as much as he deserved... In his mother's house he had come into contact with some of the foremost statesmen and literary men of that day...

But to us he was the simple friend who was always the same unassuming gentleman. He could talk with the humblest.

With the death of her husband, Winifred's thoughts soon turned to the financial provisions for her two sons. She had some concerns about too much money reaching Henry's hands before he reached the age of 25, telling her probate advisers that 'Henry is a very brilliant boy of a happy-go-lucky nature, with very little idea of the value of money, whereas Alexander is a thoroughly solid person who will keep things together. It is fortunate that he is the elder of the two.' Her view of Henry's potential for frittering money away was reinforced by the comment that '...in regard to the respective incomes of these two boys... it is my wish as it was my husband's that Alexander should be considerably better off than Henry as the eldest son.' As a result of bequests from their father and provisions made by their mother for them after her death, it was estimated (in 1929) that Alexander would eventually have an income of roughly £4,320 per annum and capital assets valued at £49,200 while for Henry the figures would be at least £3,375 and £49,500. It is possible that, at that time, Winifred gauged Henry's future employment prospects, given his rising academic excellence, as better than those of his older brother.

It was understandable that a Henry distracted by the illness and eventual death of his father would struggle at Eton, and his tutors no doubt made some allowance. Nevertheless, his next report must have made very hard reading for Winifred. Some of the comments were sympathetically phrased but remained quite scathing. At the end of the December 1928 term, Mr Todd wrote and told Winifred that:

> The truth is, I think, that he is too self-centred, thinks too much of himself and not enough of others and does not see that his may not be the only point of view. People here, I mean the masters, must criticise and correct – no one likes doing it but it must be done for the welfare of the boys and there is something wrong if the boys

resent it. I sometimes think that Henry must hate me when I 'tell him off' as I have to at times, and it is a great joy when he greets me with his old friendly smile which shows that I am forgiven! He is also still terribly un-business like, leaves his things about and loses them, and is then inclined to say that others have taken them.

Mr Streatfield wrote that as regards his Latin exercises, 'They have never been good and at times are simply disgraceful, full of careless mistakes and suggesting a downright ignorance which he emphatically does not possess. His behaviour too is at times silly and unworthy of his real character and his undoubted talent.' The only bright spot was Henry's performance in music, where 'his keenness is rewarded with considerable success.' Indeed, he was awarded a prize for his musical talent, a pleasing outcome bearing in mind that his mother had paid an extra five guineas over the term for private lessons.

While at Eton, Henry regularly gave piano recitals at school concerts. At a concert given at Westminster School, he played 'Night in May' by Palmgren, while during an informal concert at Eton he played two Schumann compositions. For the latter, the *Eton College Chronicle* noted that 'Coombe-Tennant tackled big works, and if he did not quite bring them off, he showed promise and distinction, and must be thanked for playing such lovely Schumann.' Of another concert where Henry played in a two-piano work, it was reported, 'Coombe-Tennant and Rowe in the Bach Concerto were splendidly together, well contrasted and harmonious; they were, in fact, almost better than the orchestra – which in this case is saying a great deal.'

Following the death of her husband in 1928, Winifred began to contemplate a life away from South Wales. It was clear to her that her remaining children, Alexander and Henry, would be pursuing their careers away from Neath, meaning that she faced the prospect of spending her later years largely alone. The Tennant Estate had also had to pay heavy death duties twice in ten years; once on the death of Charles' mother, Gertrude, in 1918 and again on the death of Charles himself in 1928.

Estate land had been sold in 1920 to meet the first demand and further land sales were inevitable following Charles' demise.

Alexander was set to pursue a career in finance in the City of London, while although Henry's plans were not quite as advanced, it was obvious that his future interests would eventually carry him away from the family home that he still loved dearly. Winifred therefore agreed with Alexander when he advised that the best option for the family was to sell Cadoxton Lodge and relocate to London. Leaving would be a wrench and Winifred regretted that she would have to sever her ties with the local bench of magistrates as well as the Swansea School of Art and the Glynn Vivian Art Gallery, where she had worked happily in cooperation with the curator Mr W Grant Murray in recommending artwork for purchase by the Swansea Corporation. Her interest in the Eisteddfod, at least, could continue by way of annual visits to the event. Momentous change was unavoidable, however, and in November 1931 some of the contents of Cadoxton Lodge were advertised for sale. The lots included mahogany and satinwood bedroom furniture, feather beds, Axminster carpets, a grand pianoforte in a burr walnut case, chests of drawers, gate-leg tables, wardrobes, Hepplewhite and Chippendale chairs, china, glass, miscellaneous books and three safes.

There were also other family issues to contend with. Henry had changed his surname from 'Tennant' to 'Coombe-Tennant' by deed poll in April 1929, combining his late father's middle name with his own surname. While Charles had been a plain 'Coombe Tennant', Henry inserted a hyphen between the names, as did his brother Alexander.

By the middle of September 1931, Henry had for some reason become disenchanted with his studies at Eton. He asked his mother to 'think over whether it would be possible for me to leave at the end of the half. I am prepared to stay on but really do not feel I can face this place for another year and could spend my time more profitably elsewhere...' It is not clear what had led Henry to take this viewpoint, though he does seem to have suggested to his mother some areas where he thought his talents could be put to better use. Winifred was unhappy at this prospect and discussed the issue with Gerald Balfour, who was Henry's godfather. When Henry was advised of their hesitation in agreeing to his suggestion, he fired off a testy response:

> Well either I decide to remain, or you two do. In the latter event, it is plainly useless to continue this argument. If it is impossible for you and GWB [Gerald Balfour] to comply with my request, it is absurd for you to 'advise' me to 'stick it out' for you are, in effect, compelling me to stick it out willy nilly...
>
> But at the moment I would rather take a job as stoker on a tramp steamer than stay in this place 24 hours longer than necessary... I am prepared to go against the excellent judgements of you and GWB because I know the whole thing from INSIDE... I hate quarrelling, but I do not see myself kept here by force without putting up a pretty efficient resistance. Of course, I may change my mind, though frankly I think it extremely unlikely.

However, it seems that Henry's plans were eventually scuppered by an obligation that he had entered into with Mr Beasley-Robinson, his Housemaster at the college at the time. Henry had been appointed House Captain and when Beasley-Robinson revealed himself to be not best pleased at Henry's plan to abandon his House Captain role as well as the college itself, Henry's strong moral compass prevented him from merely walking away from the agreement. He was dismissive of his mother's gratitude in the matter, telling her bluntly, 'I am here as a prisoner, and it is as a prisoner that I am remaining. So please let us have no cant about it.' Two months later he was still bemoaning the situation he found himself in, writing to Winifred to say, 'Life goes on here – the daily round, the common task – the important trivialities of house politics – the little dramas, joys and sorrows that mean so much. I shall be glad to look back on it all as a bad dream.'

At the end of term in December 1931, Henry and Alexander embarked on the *Arandora Star* cruise ship. As Christmas approached, the young men were nearing Gibraltar. In letters home, Henry was his usual outspoken self and very much a young man of his time and class. He told Winifred, 'The ship is full of the most frightful people you could imagine. Terrible, vulgar young men and terrible, vulgar young women, with flashy clothes and an accent you could cut with a knife... like the people who used to come to the Esplanade Hotel [in Porthcawl] on Saturday afternoons. If they are representative of the class in England who have money – as presumably they are – all I can say is God help England!'

His letters provide an insight into his relationship with his brother Alexander, who was over three years older. Henry stated in a letter home that while he himself was trying to get away from his mother's apron-strings, Alexander, by way of contrast, seemed overly keen to cling on to them, and needed to be dissuaded from that path for his own good. Henry reported that he himself was playing deck tennis, the piano and smoking too much, the latter point being a revelation that would have alarmed his mother, who always worried about his health.

It is unsurprising to find that young ladies did not feature much in Henry's life at this time. Being closeted away at an all-male college for most of the year and spending holidays in the company of close family members inevitably limited his contact with members of the opposite sex. Around this time he does seem to have attracted the unwelcome attentions of a gentleman named Swaffield, with whom he had had some discussions regarding future employment opportunities in the diplomatic service. Winifred sensed that Swaffield's feelings for Henry were more than just platonic, leading Henry to reassure her in no uncertain terms of his lack of partiality for men.

Another of Henry's interests was chess. He played competitively at Eton, winning the Eton Cup for chess in both 1928 and 1931. His mother was persuaded to provide him with a trophy which presumably he could display with pride in his room. Henry was less happy to have both his winning years inscribed upon it on it as that would tend to highlight the fact that sandwiched in between his victories were two years where he had come up short in the competition. His interest in chess extended far beyond the confines of Eton and in 1932 he began corresponding with Mr A C Bottomley, a gentleman who claimed to be a former president of the Cambridge University Chess Club. Sadly, Mr Bottomley was at that time an inmate of the Park Prewett Mental Hospital near Basingstoke, a fact that did not dissuade Henry from commencing a game of postal chess with him and facilitating his involvement by kindly sending him 30 stamped, addressed envelopes.

He also found time to play rugby, though it seems that he was never especially adept at the sport. He did leave his mark in an unintended manner, however, when in 1932 he took part in a match where the team numbers were made up by some of the Eton College tutors. Mr Van Oss attempted to tackle Henry and both fell to the ground, with the result that the teacher's leg was broken in two places. Henry visited him in hospital, where he 'looked pale and smelled strongly of ether' and would clearly be unable to undertake any teaching duties for some weeks. It was absurd, noted Henry, to have allowed a game of rugby to proceed on a pitch that was as hard as a brick. He also tried his hand at boxing, though he was beaten by a promising-looking fighter in the first round of the competition.

The disappointment and unhappiness caused to Henry by his family's reluctance to allow him to leave Eton appears to have receded over time. He soon seemed to be working hard to improve his occasionally melancholy outlook on life. In a letter of May 1932, he told Winifred:

> I realise that happiness depends much less than I supposed upon circumstances. The routine and the restrictions of Eton life are irksome to me, and yet I am happy – happy with that deep and wholesome contentment that springs largely from within, and

is sustained by hard exercise and intellectual interests. Such happiness is worth infinitely more than the feverish and precarious elation which is the only reward of the lido type, and the type that depends upon cocktails, bright lights and emotional excitement for its happiness. I hope I am not arrogant about this, but it has pleased God to help me to see the truth in these things.

If Henry was now a little more settled at Eton, his mother was already looking further down the academic path that lay before him, as she saw it. One person who offered Winifred some advice was the Welsh journalist, Gareth Jones. Jones had left Cambridge in 1929 with a first-class honours degree in French, German and Russian. He obtained a position as foreign affairs adviser to David Lloyd George before working in public relations for a New York City firm, travelling extensively in the Soviet Union and then returning to the employment of Lloyd George, where he helped the former Prime Minister with the preparation of his war memoirs. He had met Alexander Coombe-Tennant at Cambridge University and soon became a family friend.

In June 1932 he accompanied Winifred to a grand dinner at the Clothworkers' Hall in London. In a subsequent letter, Jones advised Winifred against pushing Henry onto a degree course in which he had little interest, suggesting instead that he be encouraged to pursue his fascination with the history and language of China, an economic area that was of some interest to Great Britain. There would be a need for more trained people in future years to assist with trade dealings and other activities connected with China. As a casual aside, Jones ended his letter to Winifred by stating that he had received an invitation to accompany a politician during the last few days of an election campaign. The politician was Adolf Hitler and Jones duly accompanied the future German Chancellor (and various of his henchmen) in his private aeroplane. The Coombe Tennants knew some interesting people.

CHAPTER FOUR
A Success at Cambridge

GARETH JONES' ADVICE for Henry to focus on his Chinese interests when at Cambridge University proved problematic. Winifred made enquiries of tutor J R M Butler, who told her that Cambridge did not provide the sort of course or tuition that would enable Henry to eventually obtain a suitable Civil Service post as a student interpreter in the Far East. Butler's advice was that Henry should concentrate on getting a good honours degree, the subject of which was not particularly important, while improving his language skills by living abroad during the university vacations. He thought that economics or history might fit the bill, though moral sciences was also a contender. Henry eventually decided to pursue the Moral Sciences Tripos under the supervision of C D (Charlie) Broad – a man who, as well as being prominent in philosophical circles, showed an interest in psychic affairs; a fact that must have intrigued Henry's mother, given her own involvement in such matters.

Before going up to Cambridge, Henry had a two-month visit to Canada to prepare for and enjoy. The trip was organised by the Schools' Empire Tour Committee, a body that arranged educational visits to other countries for pupils of prominent public schools such as Eton. The 30 or so students who made the trip were in the care of Lieutenant Colonel J D Hills of the 60th Rifles, assisted by Lord Nigel Douglas-Hamilton. The tour party left Liverpool on 30 July 1932, sailing for Canada on the Canadian Pacific Railway steamer, *Duchess of York*.

The itinerary involved visits to Montreal, Ottawa, Vancouver and Toronto, while His Royal Highness, Edward, the Prince of Wales, extended an invitation to the group to visit his ranch near Alberta. Such tours sought to build strong educational, business and social links between different parts of the British Empire. It was later reported that:

> The boys saw Canadian life from many angles – public, home, farm, prairie, ranch, lumber camp, forest, and mine – and they had formed some good friendships... A memorable event was the private luncheon that Mr Bennett, the Prime Minister, gave to the party... Mr Henry Coombe-Tennant, recently a house captain at Eton, who is shortly going up to Cambridge, said that after seeing something of the size of Canada the railway journey from Liverpool to London made England look like a garden in comparison, and British rolling-stock seemed to be of miniature dimensions in contrast with that of Canada.

In early October 1932 Henry arrived at Cambridge University and soon described himself to his mother as having 'settled in'. After some initial doubts, he was quite happy that he had chosen the correct path and had attended some lectures.

He had attended the Freshman's Trials for rugby, though he was frustrated that the chaotic organisation of that sport within the college meant that he had subsequently only played one game so far. He was, however, maintaining his physical fitness by almost daily visits to the gymnasium, where he undertook strenuous exercise that included physical jerks, work on the parallel bars and some ju-jitsu. On the non-physical side, he was playing six games of chess by letter and was planning to approach the college chess club regarding membership.

He found his supervisor, Charlie Broad, to be 'an amazing man, small, cherubic, meek, placid, unemotional, authentic and profoundly sceptical. He has a first-class brain...' Others at Cambridge University were subjected to the occasional bite of Henry's tongue and in one letter home he told his mother

A Success at Cambridge

that: 'I don't really think much of Whitney Straight. He is a fearful lounge-lizard and though superficially brilliant, I don't think there is much behind it.'

In November 1932 Henry dined with the Master of Trinity College, Mr Joseph John Thomson, a distinguished physicist who had discovered electrons and isotopes and won the 1906 Nobel Prize in Physics for his work on the conduction of electricity in gases. Henry pithily described Thomson as 'grunting and shuffling about like an old walrus, and a daughter – an extraordinary female, with a vacuous grin and a sort of helpless, despairing way of talking – like a dying swan: she wrapped herself round me and talked a lot of nonsense.' He did add, though, that Thomson 'gave me the impression of being half a minute ahead in time of anyone else. He obviously has a brilliant brain.' Unbeknownst to Henry, he had made a big impression on Thomson's daughter, Joan, which would cause him difficulties in the future.

Christmas 1932 was spent in the Swiss Alps, where Henry found the group he was with somewhat dull, though the snow was good and easily accessible after a bit of enjoyable climbing. He had quickly passed a skiing test and was able to climb to 1,000 feet in an hour, with the descent taking less than ten minutes.

Winifred appears to have become concerned that Henry's high moral tone, his varied work and social interests and his apparent emotional detachment possibly concealed the fact that he was becoming depressive, a claim that he hotly disputed. He told his mother:

> You are wrong to suppose that my standard of values and ethical code is in any way depressing me. My attitude to emotion is that it is primarily an aid to socially useful action and that to indulge in inactive emotions, particularly when they are of an obsessive type, is a demoralising waste of time. If to eschew inactive emotions is to be emotionally starved, I can only hope by the grace of God to remain in a perpetual state of emotional starvation.

It seems likely that the highly intelligent student must have appeared a 'cold fish' to many of his acquaintances. He also seemed to be very precise in matters that interested him (he even took the time to pointedly correct his mother's incorrect spelling of several words in one of her letters to him), but less so in other areas – as his occasionally absent-minded behaviour demonstrated.

In May 1933, Charlie Broad pronounced himself pleased with Henry's work and recommended him for an exhibition (an award), which would enable Henry to retain his existing room at Trinity College. He could maintain his progress by completing a minimum of two hours of work a day until he undertook another trip to Canada, this time having been appointed by the Royal Institute of International Affairs as an Assistant Secretary to the British Group at the Fifth Biennial Conference of the Institute of Pacific Relations. The conference was to be held in Banff in Canada from 14–28 August 1933. Henry had been assigned the task of arranging the accommodation for the British party as well as making sure its baggage was efficiently transported. He had been given the temporary use of an office at Chatham House in London, the home of the Royal Institute of International Affairs, to facilitate his work. Better still for Henry was the fact that, after the Banff conference, he was to accompany Archie Rose, a former diplomat who had survived the siege of the Foreign Legation in Peking during the Boxer Rebellion of 1899–1901, on a fact-finding trip to China. Given Henry's keen interest in China and the Chinese, this was a mouth-watering prospect. He was to be allowed a leave of absence from his studies at Cambridge in order to gain the experience offered by the trips to Canada and China.

At the Banff Conference, Henry was kept busy with a deluge of administrative tasks, though he did manage to find some time for personal enjoyment. He told Winifred that he and Archie would sail to China from Vancouver. Their first stop was to be Japan and by 9 September Henry had settled himself into the Imperial Hotel in Tokyo, having spent a couple of days at Yokohama. He told his mother that the journey by sea had been largely uneventful, though the duo's passenger ship had been caught in the tail end of a typhoon and had had to contend with some mountainous seas.

After arriving, he had seen the local people at work and play, before motoring to Tokyo along what he considered substandard roads, where Japanese drivers had apparently shown little concern for other road users. The idea was to spend perhaps two weeks in Tokyo, where Archie Rose was planning to conduct some business, before setting off for Shanghai on board the *Empress of Japan*. Archie's business involved meeting various high-ranking Japanese officials and discussing aspects of Japan's policy towards its neighbours and the wider world. He interviewed the Japanese Prime Minister, cabinet members of the Japanese Government and several military leaders. Henry found the Japanese to be 'a delightful people, all of them, from duke to dustman, but they are also a fine people, with a terrific patriotism and an obvious desire to be the hub of the world.'

The trip continued into Manchuria, with visits being made to Dairen (Dalian), Mukden (Shenyang) and Harbin. The countryside was not without its dangers:

> It was most interesting travelling, as our train was the one that had been held up by bandits a fortnight ago, and was full of armed guards... Harbin is rather a terrible place, I thought, full of demi-monde women. (It is famous for night-life, of which we saw a fair sample.) Harbin is supposed to be full of bandits, so we were not allowed to walk about alone, but were always attended by an armed bodyguard, which amused me quite a lot.

Hsinking (Changchun) was the next place on the itinerary, where once again Archie and Henry met several important officials for an exchange of views. As Archie had further matters to attend to in Mukden, Henry departed on his own for Peking (Beijing). After arriving in the capital, Henry visited the Summer Palace and the Forbidden City, before travelling to Kalgan (Zhangjiakou) for a look at the Great Wall.

He told Winifred that he was very busy and only had a chance to write up a diary for her information while travelling by train. He did find the time to do some thinking about his future career (he was now 20) and the probable futility of his long-standing desire to perform missionary work in China. Having had the chance to visit the country at last, he now began to doubt that he could perform any useful work there and his idea of a career in the diplomatic service also seemed less attractive to him than it had.

After his return from China, Henry's post-university career was still under consideration and by the beginning of 1934 he seemed to have finally discounted the prospect of becoming a civil servant in the diplomatic service, though the possibility of joining the secret intelligence services held some attraction for him. Joining the Royal Naval Volunteer Reserve was another option that was of interest. But his mind was not yet made up and soundings of well-placed persons were taken regarding his options, with the assistance of his mother's contacts.

Henry was still immersed in activity at Cambridge, finding the time to establish a university group of the Toc H organisation, a body that had been formed in the town of Poperinge, Belgium, during the Great War by the Revd P B (Tubby) Clayton. He was able to tell Winifred that it only took up two hours each week and would not affect his studies.

He had also been elected as secretary of the Moral Sciences Club at Cambridge University and was playing rugby ('inefficiently but with pleasure'), writing for the university's *Granta* magazine (he was later invited to join the editorial board) and had joined the university ski and mountaineering club. He also seems to have spent some time as an Assistant Scout Master with the 53rd Cambridge Scout Troop, where he would have worked with James Plowden-Wardlaw, a barrister and Church of England priest. It is possible that Henry would have played a part in the Rover Scout movement, whose activities included assisting at training camps for unemployed men, a role that he certainly took a later interest in. All in all, Henry Coombe-Tennant was a busy young man.

Over time, he seems to have developed a closer relationship with Trinity Master J J Thomson. The friendship between Henry and Thomson's daughter Joan took a downward turn, however, when Henry realised that she thought rather more of him than he did of her. It seems that even Winifred was advising caution in what must have been a purely platonic relationship before Henry stated his view on the situation in a typically robust letter, in which it is clear that Henry is keen to disentangle himself from Joan's unwelcome attentions:

> I feel somewhat troubled by it all: we know that Joan is almost half-witted, cannot see more than one move ahead, and is quite capable of taking important steps in her parents' name without having consulted them. We assume that she is either infatuated with me or at any rate taken with me in some way. She has already put me once in a very unpleasant position, and may easily do so again. It would be fatal to offend her; but it would be equally fatal to give her parents the idea that there was any sort of 'understanding' between us.

In the summer of 1934 he had other matters to pursue. A key one was his intention to attend a University Unemployed Camp in County Durham in the north of England. Camps of this sort were established during the inter-war years (primarily under the auspices of the Ministry of Labour, though several universities were also involved) to 'recondition' younger men who had suffered a prolonged period of unemployment. It was thought by Government officials that such men:

> ...have become so 'soft' and temporarily demoralised that it would not be practicable to introduce more than a very small number of them into one of our ordinary training centres without danger to the morale of the centre on which the effect of training depends...

It is obvious, therefore, that the class of whom I am speaking cannot be considered by our local officers for transfer until they are hardened.

Henry arrived at Tow Law Camp on 18 August 1934, only to find to his dismay that it had recently been moved to a new location some 12 miles distant, near Consett. It was rather romantically named 'The Windswept Camp'. After a frustrating hour trying to locate it, he found it contained around 100 unemployed men, mainly from the areas of Durham, Berwick, Cockermouth. He told Winifred:

> We are very under-staffed, having only 11, and everyone has to do two men's work. I am a tent-leader, and also secretary. The men are divided into 9 tents, and each unit has a tent-leader. In the morning work of various kinds is done about the camp site, in the afternoon there are games, evenings are free, with hobbies etc. and there is usually a sing song after supper.

The tent used by the staff of the camp had a modest supply of beer and whisky, for the use of the staff only. The whisky was probably especially welcome as the camp lived up to its name of 'Windswept', being situated at a height of 750 ft, though Henry found the weather bracing and the outdoor life much to his liking. The men in his tent were:

> ...all Durham [men], and most of them old enough to be my father. I find them rather uphill work, as they are a trifle surlier than the devil, and probably regard me as a bloated aristocrat, but the ice is breaking by now, and I think they are quite fond of me in their own odd rough way. The Durham people are notoriously difficult, I believe.

Unlike other camps Henry had heard about, the Tow Law Camp accepted men over a very wide age range, with attendees from 18 to 60 years old. This brought with it certain problems: the older men were less inclined to accept camp discipline than the

A Success at Cambridge

younger men. Only two hours of work was expected each day and though it was anticipated that useful or enjoyable hobbies could be pursued in the men's spare time, a lack of instructors severely hampered that objective. The focal point of the camp turned out to be the mess tent, where meals were taken during the day, but the lack of an on-site social hub meant that many men simply drifted off to Consett in the evenings for a beer or two. There was no camp padre, a fact that pleased Henry as 'There were no daily prayers, and (thank God!) no singing of hymns to "bring the evening to its official close". I felt strongly that an emphasis on "the religious side of things" – whatever that means – would have been totally out of place... During the last week we started having Camp fires (query – why not sooner?), which were on the whole a success, though the men showed a universal preference for the most drippingly sentimental ballads about their silver-haired mothers and blue-eyed sweethearts, which I found a great strain.'

Despite these issues, Henry gradually warmed to the men in his care, believing that while they may not have learned much from him, he had learnt a great deal from them. He recalled that his first attempts at conversation were roughly rebuffed so he resorted to simply acting as a servant and odd-job-man to the men, initially getting no thanks for his efforts. Gradually, though, they came around and began offering him cigarettes, showing him family photographs and discussing philosophical issues. They began helping him rather than the other way around and, overall, the total experience appeared to have a profound effect on Henry as he became more familiar with the men's morale-sapping experiences of prolonged unemployment in this period of the Great Depression. As he recorded:

> The Camp is the happiest month I can remember, and it has been in some ways a very unsettling experience. I learnt, with considerable surprise, that wood-chopping is more satisfying to the whole man than logic-chopping. It is possible to talk a lot of nonsense about getting down to the soil... but I suppose the

fact is that manual labour is allied to creative and artistic work, and that it affords a means of self-expression in a way in which intellectual labour most definitely does not. The Camp has been my first introduction to a new kind of life, and the first effect it has had is to make me radically dissatisfied with the old life to which I am now returning. Part of this dissatisfaction is doubtless due to the feeling of boredom and being at a loose end which is the natural reaction at the close of an interesting month; but when all due allowance has been made for this, I think there is no doubt that I have been 'well shaken', and I cannot yet tell which way the sediment will settle.

Difficult choices on his future career still concerned Henry, and his mother. The advice of another family acquaintance – Henry's old travelling companion, Archie Rose – was sought in the autumn of 1934. He advised the young Coombe-Tennant that military training might be the best way forward, and Henry promptly signed up for the Cambridge University Officer Training Corps. His decision was endorsed by Charlie Broad, who told Henry that he had never envisaged him in the role of a university don, seeing him instead as a man who could excel in dealing with other men in the wider world. Entering the Officer Training Corps meant that he would have to take part in a number of parades each year, as well as attending a two-week summer camp.

Henry was still in contact with J J Thomson, having tea at his home in October 1934 – while trying to steer clear of his daughter, Joan, lest her unwanted affections be inflicted on him once again. He was as direct as ever in letters home, bluntly telling Winifred that the experience was 'Very dull – Lady T like a constantly running tap'.

By early December 1934, a minor crisis occurred when Henry's packed schedule led to his exhaustion. The Christmas vacation offered the chance of a visit to Switzerland, which his tutors at Cambridge thought could only do him good. He was still undecided on what direction his future career might take, though Charlie Broad thought he was probably wise in

A Success at Cambridge

deciding to leave university as soon as his degree was secured. Broad seemed to think that Henry had a restless intellect that caused him to quickly become bored with routine and rendered him desirous of regular change and new challenges to tackle.

In Switzerland in December 1934, Henry found that he had retained his skiing skills and was soon making confident runs, even if the occasional fall was unavoidable. The clear air and lack of everyday cares and concerns seemed to help him crystallise the future plans that he had earlier discussed with his mother and Alexander. He planned to build on his Cambridge University Officer Training Corps experience and enter the Army, telling his mother with his usual breezy confidence:

> I have ruminated on things in general, and feel confident that my decision to go into the Army for a few years is wise, but that it must be regarded, amongst other things, as a part of my education in the most literal sense. I am certain in my own mind that the Army will not be my profession, any more than Pinewood, or Eton or Cambridge... I still think that I have been rescued from Cambridge just in time. It is dangerous to be a star performer of mental gymnastics if one has other gifts as well. At Cambridge it has not been difficult for one to gain academical distinctions and to inspire with awe persons of lesser intellectual powers... I believe what I needed was to be shown a slice of real life and to find someone of my own age whom I could admire with good reason, as a change from being surrounded by people who admired me for no good reason at all. The Camp gave me both in strong doses and caught me on the rebound into the bargain. Given these conditions, what has happened has been inevitable and most fortunate...

And so it was that, after a great deal of uncertainty, the Army was decided upon as the short-term career path for Henry. It was planned that he would join the Welsh Guards, the regiment in which his older brother Christopher had served (and died) during the Great War. This must have come as a great relief to all involved and – coupled with the holiday in Switzerland – must also have helped relieve his evident mental exhaustion.

He had been accompanied to Switzerland by Alexander, who was probably asked by his mother to keep a close eye on his troubled younger sibling and to report back. With Winifred often travelling in the pursuit of her own interests, Alexander building a career in the city and Henry at Cambridge, regular meetings between the trio were often hard to arrange, though letters flowed frequently in all directions. Alexander was able to report that Henry seemed well and was enjoying the holiday. He added, 'I see so little of him usually – I am not able to follow him (and you) into the higher realms of philosophical argument, but here in skiing we can do a Thing in common and together, and I have been extremely happy.' In another letter he told her, 'I am glad to have had a few days alone with him [Henry]. He is on the whole very silent, but I glean interesting pieces of information about himself. I can see that Archie [Rose] has had a tremendous influence on him, and... I think that that influence has been a good influence. H certainly is a very interesting person. I have to guard against being antagonised by the wide differences in outlook between us. I think these differences are more in the superficial than in the fundamental things. But I don't feel that I am 100% Jno [John] Bull, and H with his pipes and claret does strike me as such at times.'

Mentally refreshed, Henry returned to his academic work at Cambridge. As secretary of the university's Moral Sciences Club, he again arranged for various speakers to deliver papers on matters that were of interest to Society members. The topics covered included 'The Inductive Basis of Some Judgements of Perception', 'Is the Self a Substance?' and 'The Nature of Authority', amongst others. While at Cambridge, Henry inevitably came under the influence of Ludwig Wittgenstein, a giant of philosophical thought who lectured at the university in the 1930s and 1940s. It was the noted economist J M Keynes who had invited Wittgenstein to Cambridge and such was the latter's perceived status that, after meeting him off the train,

A Success at Cambridge

Keynes told his wife, "Well, God has arrived. I met him on the 5.15 train." Wittgenstein had very strong views on philosophy and came to dominate the meetings of the Moral Sciences Club to such an extent that Charlie Broad stopped attending them. Henry nevertheless admired Wittgenstein, noting that he 'was the only genius the twentieth century has produced'.

Part of Henry's time was dedicated to ensuring that his path into the Army was as smooth as possible. He learnt that his mother was due to dine with an officer of the Welsh Guards – W A L (Billy) Fox-Pitt – and he cautioned her, 'I advise you not to praise me – I shan't deserve it, and they won't believe it. I only say this because I know how enthusiastic you are over your own children – draw it mild, Mrs Tennant, draw it mild!' At the same time, Henry himself had written to Fox-Pitt requesting a meeting with another officer of the regiment, Merton Beckwith-Smith, who commanded the 1st Battalion, the Welsh Guards.

In the summer of 1935, Henry completed the examinations for the second part of the Moral Sciences tripos (having completed the first part by the Easter term in 1934), specialising in metaphysical and ethical philosophy. He gained First Class passes in both parts of the tripos and graduated in December 1935. With academic affairs receding, his attention switched to martial matters. As a member of the Cambridge University Officer Training Corps, he was eligible for attachment to a regular Army unit and Captain Kirby-Smith, the Officer Training Corps adjutant, provided detailed information to those who were about to be so attached. The University had a reputation to protect and it was important to prevent any military *faux pas* on the part of its students. As well as advice on the various items of uniform kit that were required, information on the supply of a sword, binoculars and compass was also provided. For off-duty hours, it was recommended that students should take with them a dinner jacket, tail coat, a good suit, grey flannels and plus fours as well as sporting kit

55

of various descriptions. Bedding, towels and soap would also have to be taken.

In July 1935 Henry's appointment to the General List of the Territorial Army was announced in *The London Gazette* and he was soon in Pirbright Camp near Aldershot, on attachment with the Welsh Guards – an assignment that would run from early July to late September 1935. He told Winifred that he now had no doubt that the Regiment would, in time, prove to be his spiritual home. He was still on the parade-ground, drilling with a squad of recruits and learning about regimental routine as well as the unavoidable book-keeping aspects of military work. Most importantly, he was enjoying himself. Battalion-level training commenced in August 1935 and it was planned that the unit would soon relocate to Clanfield Camp, near Petersfield in Hampshire. That involved a tough 40-mile route-march, which had to be completed within two days.

In October 1935, an assessment of Henry's performance while serving with the Welsh Guards was compiled. In response to a series of set questions posed by the adjutant of the Cambridge University Officer Training Corps, the officer commanding the 1st Battalion, the Welsh Guards (Lieutenant Colonel Fox-Pitt), provided his opinion of the prospective recruit. He reported that Henry possessed a great deal of personality and had quickly adapted to the life of the camp. He was found to be reliable, energetic and tactful. Even during the attachment, while still getting to grips with a new environment, he had started to show considerable powers of leadership, an ideal quality in a candidate for an officer's role. While listening carefully to the advice proffered by experienced non-commissioned officers (and even to the sometimes dubious advice cheerfully offered by men from the ranks to a novice officer), he nevertheless did not hesitate to assert such authority as he held where the circumstances required it. He had a grasp of the basics of soldiering despite his relatively limited experience, and Fox-Pitt opined that a little more drill work would soon help

A Success at Cambridge

build up his physique. When asked, 'Would you be prepared, if there were a vacancy, to accept him as an officer under your command?', Fox-Pitt answered, 'Very decidedly.' He concluded his report by saying, 'This young officer is very much above the average in intelligence. He thoroughly entered into the life in camp and, in my opinion, is very much above the average, in every way, of the officers of his age in the Battn.' In the light of such an encouraging report, Henry's smooth passage into the Army was assured and a new chapter in his life was about to begin.

While on attachment with the Welsh Guards, Henry had heard of the death of his grandmother on his mother's side. The family had already been saddened by the death in China of Alexander's old Cambridge friend, Gareth Jones. He had gained fame as the journalist who had broken the story in the Western press of the 1932–33 famine in the Ukraine that resulted from Stalin's policies. The report had not been well received in the Soviet Union and Jones had been officially informed that he was banned from ever visiting the country again. In late 1934 he had travelled to the Far East on a fact-finding tour. While in Manchukuo (a puppet state controlled by the occupying Japanese), he was captured by bandits and 16 days later was killed by them. There were suspicions that the Russian Secret Services had been complicit in his death, though that remained unproven.

With those sad episodes having been weathered by the Coombe Tennant family, the next stage of what Winifred believed would be Henry's progression to greatness was about to begin.

CHAPTER FIVE

The Welsh Guards

IN THE FIRST part of 1936, Henry Coombe-Tennant entered the Army as a Second Lieutenant (with seniority backdated 18 months), assigned to the 1st Battalion of the Welsh Guards at Pirbright Camp near Woking. As was Henry's custom, he approached his new position with great enthusiasm, as his company commander – Alexander (Sammy) Stanier – told Winifred: '...how <u>very</u> pleased I am in having Henry in my Company and am only too pleased to do what I can for him as he is so terribly keen on anything he takes up and so very pleased to have a shot at anything.'

One of Henry's early duties was to act as Picquet Officer, inspecting the cookhouse, bathhouse, latrines and Mess kitchen, among other areas. He also oversaw the serving of meals and was ready to deal with any complaints regarding the quality of the fare, though none were actually received. By August 1936, the adjutant of the battalion reported that Henry 'Thinks things through on his own, yet very receptive to advice and instruction. Could be smarter on parade, but is showing steady improvement.'

Henry also compiled musical programmes for the battalion choir and soloists, for occasional concerts in Pirbright Village Hall and the Wellington Barracks in London. He was able to visit Cambridge University, where he found his old tutor, Charlie Broad, 'unchanging, cracking the same old jokes, mostly about other dons – I can't tell you the horror that came to me as I thought suddenly of my own narrow escape from that living death – there but for the Grace of God etc.' He again visited Trinity Master J J Thomson and was cordial towards his daughter, Joan, though she was left in no doubt that he was not interested in her romantically and that, regrettably, even a simple friendship was out of the question. It seems that he found her unwanted attention stifling and, in his usual direct manner, wanted to have done with it.

The end of August 1936 found Henry and his comrades enduring the hardships of serious military training. There were long marches, irregular meals, little sleep and a host of other discomforts. The one redeeming factor was that the weather was fine. He had been enrolled for a three-week course on the use of gas in warfare, a reminder of the horrific use of gas during the Great War, and there was also a tempting possibility that he would become the battalion's Intelligence Officer. He enjoyed horse riding and was pleased that he was to be temporarily attached to the Horse Guards for an exercise that would involve up to 60 miles in the saddle.

Those plans did not come to immediate fruition, however, as Henry contracted a form of jaundice at the start of September 1936 and required treatment at the Cambridge Hospital, Aldershot. Winifred was always alarmed when any of her children became ill and soon visited her ailing son in the hospital. She was appalled at what she observed there and wasted no time in drawing the matter to the attention of the authorities. Never one to do things by halves, her 'report' on Henry's treatment – or lack of it – and the substandard running of the ward ran to nine pages. She forwarded copies to various people and was promised that improvements would be made. Happily, Henry was allowed out after a three-week stay and suffered no lasting ill-effects.

December 1936 saw Henry enjoying his by now customary Christmas break in Grimmialp, Switzerland. He was in a troubled state of mind, as he told his mother in a letter home.

Once again it seems that his tendency to become bored when faced with a routine that involved no major challenges was playing on his mind. He had been unwell for several days at his Alpine hotel and, while recovering, he had used the free time to consider his current circumstances very carefully. He now thought that he might be better suited for a career in politics, a yearning that had probably been awakened by his experience at the University Work Camp he had attended some time earlier. At that time, he had been struck by the demoralising effect of prolonged unemployment on men and obviously thought that politics would give him the opportunity to improve the lot of those so affected. His plan now was to busy himself in other areas until the age of 30, at which time he would be mature enough to seek election as a Conservative Member of Parliament. What Winifred, a friend of Lloyd George and a Liberal Party supporter, thought of that seems not to be have been recorded. The question that he was now grappling with was how to fill the time before he reached his chosen age.

In words that probably stunned her, he told his mother, 'Before I joined the Brigade [of Guards] I thought I might remain in it for good. After I had been gazetted a few months, I put it at 5 years at the most... [In fact] I don't think I can put up with the Brigade for more than a year or two, unless in a v. good cause.' In pursuit of his newly discovered political ambitions, he sought advice from a number of prominent people including George Hennessy, vice-chairman of the Conservative and Unionist Party. Henry had already submitted the relevant paperwork to possibly become a prospective Parliamentary candidate and hoped to be given a seat to contest (preferably in the Midlands) at a future election.

He discussed the matter with his commanding officer, Billy Fox-Pitt and, unsurprisingly, was bluntly told that he was making a great mistake. That bluntness was tempered by Fox-Pitt adding that, were he to stay with the Brigade, he had a good chance of advancing to the role of Adjutant, an unexpected prospect that excited Henry greatly. He regarded the role of Adjutant as 'a real job, and not simply a clothes-peg or pen and ink one. If I could be sure of getting it, I would consider putting off entering politics until I was 35.' He had renewed his interest in Army affairs when the news arrived that he was to be sent on a three-month signalling course at Catterick and would then replace the existing Signalling Officer at battalion headquarters, a role that came with an Austin Seven motor car thrown in for use on manoeuvres. With his military prospects looking brighter, Henry's restlessness was soothed, at least for the time being.

He was soon performing the duties of a Signalling Officer, and told his mother, 'I am very lucky to have got this job so soon. The work concerns every department of communication by line and visual instruments in the field of battle, including instruction in cable laying, operating of telephone [equipment] and the various rules of procedure for the transmission of messages.' At this time, he received an unexpected communication from Joan Thomson after a long period of silence. Henry accepted that the muddle between them was down to him: he had made friends with an older woman [Joan] and had failed to see the warning signs that she was becoming infatuated with him until it was too late. He did not wish to hurt her but, as far as he was concerned, the friendship was over. He was unsure as to how to deal with her latest overtures and sought advice from his mother. He pleaded, 'Perhaps you can suggest something. I hesitate now to take any steps on my own: I don't understand women and I certainly don't understand Joan Thomson.'

He was still fretting over his future plans and whether they would involve him staying in or leaving the Army. He was nevertheless getting unavoidably wrapped up in the regimental routine of the Welsh Guards, being served with a leek to eat by the Colonel of the Regiment, William Murray Threipland, DSO, on St David's Day, 1938 and acting as temporary Adjutant to the battalion when the regular incumbent of the post was on leave – the role not having permanently become his as had been hinted at earlier. He began to ponder a career in farming – an occupation in which he had never expressed any interest – and asked his mother to find out more for him from her contacts. On being asked about his plans for the future, Henry said he had told one of his senior officers, 'I would not do another two years' jay walking in London, and he said he would see what jobs were available outside the Regiment. I am all for looking around carefully before deciding to go, but it is obvious that the best jobs will only be available to those who declare their intention of going to the Staff College and making the Army their career, and this I cannot honestly do.'

In the first half of 1938, European affairs were dominated by the political crisis that resulted from the demands for a greater degree of autonomy by ethnic Germans who lived in the Sudetenland area of Czechoslovakia. These demands were tacitly backed by Adolf Hitler amid rising fears that Germany might invade Czechoslovakia, an action that could trigger a wider conflict within Europe. While there was widespread anxiety over this situation, Winifred had further concerns that were unique to her. Her work in psychic research meant that she believed in the survival of the human spirit after death and when her eldest son Christopher had gone to serve in the Great War, she had concluded a 'pact' with him as to what would happen if he were killed in action. The pact was that one way or another, Winifred and Christopher would resume contact despite the veil of death having descended. Indeed, Winifred was convinced that this did happen after Christopher's death in 1917, as her diary recorded that she was soon in contact with him in what she believed to be his new state of existence in another place.

With a potential European war looming, Henry already in the Army and Alexander probably subject to conscription if he did not volunteer, Winifred was keen to extend this pact to her two surviving sons. She discussed the matter with

Alexander and he passed her views on to Henry, who informed his mother:

> I do not count on surviving the death of my body, although I should not be surprised to find that I did. Whichever is the case, I regard the prospect of my own death with indifference. If you or Alexander were to die, I should know that all was well with you, whether you survived or not. If we do survive, we will surely meet on the other side. If we do not, we are finished and it doesn't matter. Either way there is no cause for alarm or despondency.

With that issue pragmatically dealt with, Henry attempted to help his mother understand his sudden interest in farming as a possible long-term career. He explained that he thought he had made a 'poor business' of the first 20 years of his life: being unhappy at Eton, finding much of interest at Cambridge, but deciding to spurn academia after the unsettling experience of the unemployed workmen's camp. He had chosen a career in the Army, 'being slightly tipsy' at the time, but soon realised that 'soldiering has nothing more to give me'.

He did add that, despite his developing plan to leave the Army, he was not actually in a desperate hurry to do so. That was just as well since, some eight months later, he found himself not ploughing fields in Britain but performing garrison duty on the Rock of Gibraltar. In April 1939, the 1st Battalion, the Welsh Guards were split over two locations on 'The Rock', with Henry being deployed to the South Barracks. There was uncertainty as to just how long the battalion would remain on Gibraltar, with the political situation in Europe becoming more unsettled as German agitation over the city of Danzig led to renewed worries of an armed conflict, this time between Germany and Poland. On the upside, Gibraltar was a pleasant assignment, the April weather being warm with a pleasant breeze and the sea views from the barracks impressive. Mornings were taken up with the inevitable drilling of the men, while the afternoons were usually free for the pleasant pursuits of polo or tennis.

Henry managed to enter Franco's Spain from Gibraltar, and played polo in a Spanish town on a day when a celebration was taking place and the town was full of soldiers, with flags fluttering from every window. Back in Gibraltar, he attended a 'mammoth' party with champagne-cocktails much to the fore and spent a lot of time visiting other officers and receiving guests, as well as going aboard a number of naval destroyers that had entered the harbour. He was quite happy, though he found garrison life to be artificial and generally unappealing. It was, however, part of the job and thus had to be endured.

With the international situation still fraught with tension, the decision had been taken in London to form a second battalion of the Welsh Guards. This would be partly achieved by depleting the ranks of the 1st Battalion to form the nucleus of the new battalion. Gibraltar was at that time a quiet posting and it was decided that the number of Welsh Guards officers stationed there could safely be reduced, with the others being transferred to the new battalion. Henry and another officer, H J Moore-Gwyn, were pencilled in as possible transfers, a prospect that did not please the young Coombe-Tennant in the slightest: 'I don't fancy the idea of the 2nd Bn and I don't at all want to return to England until the autumn, but I don't want to find myself stuck here for 18 months, and Cop [Lieutenant Colonel F A V Copland-Griffiths] thinks that the 1st Bn will certainly stay here until next summer. On balance I have decided to raise no objection to being sent home, though it is a difficult decision and a gamble either way.'

Major Sammy Stanier had already been extracted from the Gibraltar garrison and instructed to help form the new battalion in Britain, starting off with just two other men at the Chelsea Barracks in London. Other officers from the 1st Battalion – including Henry – soon joined him. Henry had set sail from Gibraltar for Great Britain on 11 June 1939, some other regiments had provided experienced men, and raw recruits were sent up from the Guards' Depot. By August, the number in the new battalion – augmented by a batch of Reservists who had reported for three months' training – had risen to almost 400 and outgrown the barracks at Chelsea, necessitating a move to the Tower of London, where they upset the ancient routine of the Beefeaters (and, indeed, the Beefeaters themselves) by constantly training within the grounds and inconveniently taking over certain rooms. Henry was actively involved in training the men.

A R (David) Lewis had enlisted in Welsh Guards in the late 1930s and experienced the harsh reality of military life for a green recruit. He noted, 'you were not just a nobody, but a non-person doomed to continuous fatigues of sweeping the roads, cleaning toilets, working in the cookhouse... All outside training, marching, arms drill, saluting, were the NCO's responsibility. All activities in the barrack room; cleaning of equipment, the barrack room itself, were the job of [a] trained soldier, plus the teaching of military history of the Welsh Guards... plus all the drill movements, both with and without weapons, all the various parts of your rifle, all had to be absorbed. Even the method and drill of your walking out cane (all Guardsmen carried a swagger cane in uniform and off duty), was quite an elaborate performance.'

In London, Henry had his bull terrier Queenie with him. This resourceful animal managed to escape on one occasion from the confines of the Tower of London to pursue her master as he headed off to perform guard duty at Buckingham Palace. She was 'arrested' en route and returned to her barracks. David Lewis recalled that the Buckingham Palace guard duty was 'considered to be the best one. The sentries, pre-war, patrolled outside the gates and railings, and were in touch with the public. This led to some strange meetings. The worst nuisance was that of model girls, starlets, etc, with their photographers and agents trying to get a picture to enhance their clients' careers... Sometimes a pretty girl would pop a note into the barrel of your rifle. Occasionally, so did strange old men. The pretty girls of course got a smile and a wink, the strange men got the shock of their lives: the sentry springing to attention, taking a sharp step forward, the big army boots crashing down on his toes.'

Henry went to Paris for Bastille Day, 14 July 1939 and took part in a parade of some 10,000 men on the Champs Élysées; an event that also featured a fly-past by several squadrons of British aircraft. It was a display of military power no doubt primarily intended for the attention of Herr Hitler in Berlin. The watching crowd was estimated to exceed 1,000,000, but the show of military strength by the comrades in arms of Britain and France did little to dissuade Hitler from his expansionist ways and, within two months, war had been declared.

At first little changed as the so-called 'Phoney War' developed in the latter part of 1939 and into 1940, though Poland had by then already fallen to the attacks of both Germany and its previously sworn enemy turned ally, Russia. On 14 February 1940, His Majesty, the King, Colonel-in-Chief of the Regiment, presented the 2nd Battalion, the Welsh Guards with its first Colours at a ceremony held at the Tower of London on a bitterly cold day.

The preparations for war continued within the battalion, though the date on which active service would actually commence remained shrouded in mystery. Routine guard duty at the Tower of London was undertaken by battalion members dressed in wartime khaki rather than the traditional redcoats, and much was made of the important role of guarding the Crown Jewels – though in fact the jewels had been secretly spirited away to the safer location of Windsor Castle.

In early April 1940, the battalion was put on alert for possible embarkation for Norway, which the Germans had recently invaded. Commanding Officer Sammy Stanier was aghast, telling his superiors that his new battalion was not ready since much of its equipment had yet to reach it, while its field training had been restricted to platoon-size exercises in Richmond Park, a hopelessly inadequate preparation for warfare in a snow-covered landscape against a dangerous enemy. The news that the skis that his men would need in Norway would soon arrive did little to placate him, especially as none of his men had received any ski or winter warfare training. Happily for Sammy Stanier – if not for Great Britain and Norway – his men were not called on to partake in the Arctic warfare for which they were totally untrained.

On 11 April 1940 a telegram reached Henry, telling him that he had been promoted to Captain. He was busy at the time with regimental duties as well as the absorption of lessons that were being learned by the British Expeditionary Force (BEF) in France, where it awaited any move by Hitler against France and the Low Countries. He was studying pamphlets such as *Notes on Concealment and Camouflage*; *Front Line Duties and Patrolling* and *Joining the B.E.F.*, the latter covering areas such as discipline, billets, rations and messing, traffic discipline, sanitation and hygiene, amongst other things. Having fended off the unwanted attentions of the War Office over the Norwegian affair, Sammy Stanier took the opportunity to remind his superiors that the men under his command had not had a day's leave in over six months. By the time that his observation had filtered through the layers of command, the battalion was in training at Camberley, though agreement was soon forthcoming that the men of the 2nd Welsh Guards could indeed proceed on leave at the end of the current exercises. To that end, special trains were laid on for 10 May 1940 to take most of the men away, while others motored off to their destinations. Hardly had the special trains left the railway station than the War Office ordered the immediate recall of all ranks in the light of the German attack on Holland and Belgium that had taken place that very morning. For Henry Coombe-Tennant and his comrades in the 2nd Battalion, the Welsh Guards, the war was about to begin in earnest.

CHAPTER SIX
Into Battle

ON 10 MAY 1940, German forces crossed the Dutch and Belgian borders to begin their long-anticipated offensive in the West. The British Expeditionary Force was in position to the left of the French 1st Army near Dunkirk and Bailleul and had spent much time between September 1939 and May 1940 in preparing field defences on the border. As Belgium had previously declared itself neutral, any move by French or British forces onto Belgian soil could only take place after an invitation from the Belgian Government had been received and could only be triggered by Nazi aggression, or it would have been viewed as a provocation in Berlin. With the German invasion, the Allied forces began to move into Belgium to meet the oncoming enemy, leaving behind them the protection of the fortifications that had seen so much time and effort devoted to their construction.

In Holland, German air attacks were aimed at various military airfields and shortly afterwards paratroopers began to land in an attempt to capture landing strips so that reinforcements could be more easily flown in. An attempt by German airborne troops to capture The Hague was repulsed, though a similar attack on Rotterdam was more successful and several key bridges fell under the control of the invaders. Alarm grew in London at the developing situation in Holland and the British War Cabinet decided to send two Army battalions over by sea to support its ally and try and stabilise the position.

Into Battle

On 10 May 1940 the urgent order came through from the 20th Guards' Brigade Headquarters to stop all leave. As the soldiers of the 2nd Battalion, the Welsh Guards were on their way home that day, the special leave trains were halted and brought back where possible, and telegrams hastily despatched to all members of the unit. Those Welsh Guards personnel who happened to be readily available were driven to the Agricultural Show Ground at Tunbridge Wells, where they were joined by members of the 2nd Battalion, the Irish Guards.

Welsh Guardsman Syd Pritchard was at Cardiff, on the way to his home in Aberdare, when he became aware of the leave cancellation order. He promptly abandoned the train that would have taken him home and went over to the platform that served trains to London. There he met some comrades who pragmatically decided that a bit of long-awaited leave took precedence over an unexpected recall to duty – and, after all, who in authority would be able to prove that the recall order had actually reached them? They all simply continued on their journey homeward, occasionally hiding in the train toilets to avoid detection. Leave completed and enjoyed, they all returned to camp and awaited orders. At Tunbridge Wells, it became apparent that there were big gaps in the ranks of both the Welsh and Irish Guards battalions and that it would be necessary to form a composite battalion comprised of men from both if the urgent War Office requirement for a full battalion to be despatched to Holland was to be met.

Eventually, several officers and about 200 other ranks of the 2nd Battalion, the Welsh Guards, under the command of Captain Cyril Heber-Percy, helped form the composite battalion which, containing mainly Irish Guardsmen, was placed under the command of Lieutenant Colonel J C Haydon of the Irish Guards, with Major G St V J Vigor of the Welsh Guards as his second in command. On 12 May, the composite battalion, known as Harpoon Force, left Tunbridge Wells by train for Dover with Captain Henry Coombe-Tennant acting as second

69

in command of the company of Welsh Guardsmen. It took with it (on separate trains) all of its requisite day-to-day equipment for active service, while the higher command indicated that further stores should be available at Dover. These extra stores were to include 1,000 hand grenades, 200,000 rounds of small arms ammunition, 10,000 rounds of tracer bullets, 600 rounds of high explosive 3" mortar rounds, enough normal rations to supply the force for 14 days, 1,500 emergency rations, water sterilising kits and other miscellaneous items. This was considered to be adequate provision for two battalions, though the quantities were liable to be reduced in the event of only one battalion actually going across to Holland.

A force of some 200 Royal Marines – with rations for only three days – had already been sent to The Hook of Holland to secure a safe landing place in advance of the arrival of the composite battalion, which would itself consist of about 650 men. As the train containing the Welsh Guards trundled towards Dover, a great amount of planning was ongoing at the port and elsewhere. It was recognised that time was of the essence and that it might be necessary to cut corners to give the mission the best chance of success. The plan had envisaged two battalions being sent over to The Hook, though in the event, only the composite battalion (with Henry in it) actually made the trip. The objective was to 'give heart to the Dutch, to resist attacks by German parachute troops at The Hague.'

The composite battalion was also to cooperate with the local Dutch commander at The Hague in his attempts to safeguard the members of the Dutch Government and to try and restore order in the area. Major Mitchell of the Royal Marines had landed at The Hook of Holland with his 200 strong force on the night of 11–12 May and he was told to expect the composite battalion early on the 13th, but was also warned: 'This is too small a force to restore a bad or deteriorating situation but by its moral rather than its military effect might tip the scales if situation is nearing restoration by the Dutch.' After viewing the situation at first hand, Mitchell starkly advised his superiors that he was 'of [the] opinion that one composite force in support of my force would not have any material effect without aircraft support being considerably strengthened.'

The British high command recognised that the additional airpower thought necessary by Mitchell would not be forthcoming but the composite battalion was nevertheless despatched from Dover in two ships, the SS *Canterbury* and the SS *Maid of Orleans*, with an escort of four British destroyers. At 3.30 a.m. on 13 May, they landed at The Hook, from where fires could be seen blazing inland. Captain Heber-Percy's company promptly moved across a railway line and took up defensive positions, even before much of the kit and supplies had been unloaded. German reconnaissance aircraft were observed overhead and enemy parachutists were later seen being dropped inland from the defensive perimeter. Harpoon Force was required to acquaint itself with the situation by liaising with Major Mitchell as well as the local Dutch commander. It would defer to the Dutch commander and act as directed by him – though Lieutenant Colonel Haydon, the force commander, was to refuse to perform any action that, in his opinion, would entail a futile sacrifice of his men. Ideally, Harpoon Force would be able to advance towards The Hague, dealing with any isolated enemy forces that it encountered as it moved forward. In the event that the Dutch Government extricated itself from The Hague, Haydon was to withdraw his men to The Hook and await re-embarkation for Britain, his mission essentially completed.

Though Haydon's secret orders did not specifically mention it, it became apparent that Harpoon Force might indeed be able to assist in the evacuation of the Dutch Queen and her Government if The Hague became untenable as a result of the German advance. The Military Attaché at The Hague managed to contact Haydon at his headquarters and request that every effort be made to keep the harbour clear and the road from

The Hook to The Hague open for vehicles. Haydon had already realised that the situation was beyond recovery and an advance to The Hague was unlikely to restore any semblance of order. No motor transport had been brought over with the composite battalion as it was planned to use transport provided by the Dutch Army or hired from local contractors. To move his men and a substantial amount of military stores any distance without transport would be difficult in the extreme. In the circumstances, he was content to hold the perimeter around The Hook and try and keep traffic moving from the direction of The Hague until the situation became clearer and he received precise instructions from his superiors.

Much time on 13 May was spent in digging out and then camouflaging basic field fortifications on the edge of the town. At around midday, Haydon was surprised to see a convoy of black cars come down the quayside before one man exited his vehicle and announced the arrival from The Hague of Queen Wilhelmina, the Dutch monarch. Haydon sent one of his officers onto HMS *Malcolm*, a British destroyer moored at the quay and advised the captain that his next passenger was going to be the Queen of the Netherlands and her entourage. "Nonsense," the captain replied, "she left yesterday!" After it was explained to him that he had mixed up Princess Juliana (who had indeed been evacuated the day before) with the Queen of the Netherlands, he promptly allowed the Royal party to board and set sail from the harbour. At 6 p.m. members of the Dutch Government came through the defensive perimeter, intent on getting a passage to Britain, and it became clear to Haydon that he was supporting a lost cause. He advised his superiors of his gloomy assessment of the situation.

At 7.20 p.m. on the 13 May, German aircraft began bombing the quayside and harbour installations, an action that continued until 9 p.m., causing several casualties, primarily among the Irish Guards. Throughout the day, a steady stream of Dutch refugees passed through the defensive cordon set up

Into Battle

by Harpoon Force, while enemy armoured vehicles could be seen moving in the distance. The War Office finally responded to Haydon's request for further orders in the changed situation. He was informed that in the light of the evacuation of Queen Wilhelmina and her Government, steps would now be taken to also evacuate Harpoon Force.

Henry and his comrades stood to in their defensive positions until 4 a.m. on 14 May, in case the Germans launched a dawn attack. At 9 a.m. German aircraft began bombing Harpoon Force positions, while enemy machine-gun fire also came into play. It was now clear that the evacuation of Harpoon Force from The Hook could not be long delayed. Orders were given shortly before noon for the Welsh Guards contingent to begin withdrawing to the quayside at the double, bringing with them as much kit and equipment as was possible in the difficult and dangerous circumstances. News also filtered through that the Dutch Army General Headquarters was cut off and armed resistance to the invaders was likely to cease in the very near future. The situation was hopeless. The Welsh Guards reached the storage sheds on the quayside and set about destroying petrol and other stores to prevent them falling into the hands of the enemy, before embarking onto a destroyer. The embarkation was harried by enemy bombing attacks but was eventually completed, with the force arriving back at Dover at midnight on 14 May, followed shortly afterwards by a small rearguard under Captain Heber-Percy. Despite the traumatic experiences at The Hook, casualties were thankfully light. Two Welsh Guardsmen had been killed, while the Irish Guards' fatalities could be counted on the fingers of two hands. Each loss was a tragedy, of course, for the families of the fallen.

The composite battalion was moved by train from Dover to the Old Dean Common Camp at Camberley on 15 May and immediately commenced training in trench-manning and withdrawal procedures. There would, however, be little time to review and absorb the lessons learned in Holland because, before the Welsh Guards (and their Irish comrades) had had time to properly rest and reorganise, they were earmarked to be pitched into another desperate situation.

While Henry had been trying to hold The Hook of Holland with the rest of his comrades, the invading Germans had been bursting through the Allied defences in France and Belgium. Spearheaded by the Panzer divisions, the advance passed quickly over the hard-fought-over battlefields of the Great War before reaching the English Channel at Noyelles on the evening of 20 May. This meant that most of the British Expeditionary Force, the French 1st Army and the remaining Belgian forces were surrounded, with their backs to the sea, cut off from Allied comrades in the as yet unconquered southern part of France. Allied units in this 'pocket' were falling back towards the English Channel, where the ports of Boulogne, Calais and Dunkirk remained in Allied hands and offered some hope of evacuation if the situation could not be stabilised. On 21 May the 2nd Battalion, the Welsh Guards, received fresh orders, placing them on two hours' notice of a move.

The 2nd Battalions of both the Welsh and Irish Guards were ordered to the port of Boulogne. The situation at Dover was chaotic though the SS *Biarritz* was ready to begin embarking men and materials for the trip to France. Though Henry and his comrades managed to board, the all-important weapons, ammunition and stores were still on the road. With time running out, some of the equipment needed was eventually taken on board, but the ship's captain then announced that the vessel was overloaded and nothing else could be brought on. The Welsh Guards company commanded by Captain Heber-Percy was ordered to disembark and board the SS *Mona's Queen*, which was also making the trip to Boulogne. With difficulty, given the total darkness necessitated by the risk of an enemy air raid, the company loaded the stores that still lay on the quayside and the *Mona's Queen* set sail for Boulogne four hours after the *Biarritz*.

Into Battle

The *Biarritz* got the battalion into Boulogne in pouring rain at 10 a.m. – having passed a burning oil tanker a few miles from the harbour, obviously a victim of a German bombing raid. The men were disembarked promptly with No. 2, No. 3 and Headquarters Companies taking shelter in the dockside sheds to await further orders, while No. 4 Company (with Henry second in command to Captain J H V Higgon) started the arduous task of unloading the battalion stores. This was made more difficult by the haphazard arrival of some of the hastily requisitioned transport, since the vehicles that had been promised before the battalion left Britain had failed to materialise. The quayside was thronged with refugees, troops of various units and wounded men awaiting evacuation, hampering the movement of those unloading the stores. A chain of men was established, however, and the stores were passed off the ship and along the line as quickly as possible. Even as the work was in progress, somewhat unnervingly for the newly arrived Welsh Guards, members of the Royal Army Medical Corps began bringing aboard wounded men as well as a few dead bodies. As the unloading was nearing completion, an air raid began, forcing the SS *Biarritz* – essentially a sitting duck while moored in the harbour – to steam away with no time to retract her gangways, so they were left dangling down the side of the ship. The melee of jostling humanity on the quay made the carrying of weapons even more dangerous than usual and a guardsman had his thumb accidentally blown off by a bullet. There would be far worse to come.

While the unloading was underway, the commanding officer of the battalion, Lieutenant Colonel Sammy Stanier, had gone off to liaise with the 20th Guards Brigade commander, Brigadier W A F L Fox-Pitt. Stanier was given his orders, and they were uncompromising. There was a major risk that the German forces that had reached the sea to the south of Boulogne would soon turn north and advance up the coast towards the town and, after that, towards Calais and Dunkirk.

If those ports were lost to the enemy, substantial elements of the British Expeditionary Force and some units of its allies would be unable to be evacuated back to Britain. The Welsh and Irish Guards were therefore ordered to hold Boulogne for as long as possible. Every hour gained would help the retreating Allied forces reach the evacuation ports and improve the chances of rescue. The Welsh Guards were detailed to hold the ground to the north-east of Boulogne while their Irish Guards comrades were to secure the area to the south-west. It was instantly apparent to Stanier that the perimeter that his men were expected to defend was too long, while men from other units retreating through the defence line were typically in no condition to assist the defenders. He did, however, utilise the services of some stray Royal Engineers, who helpfully used explosives to crater some of the roads approaching Boulogne so as to slow down the expected enemy advance.

Henry and his comrades were fatigued even before they left the quayside sheds and started for their assigned positions. Having had little sleep and no real food on an overcrowded ship, they filled their packs with bully-beef and started to push their way through the jostling crowds on the quayside – singing as they did so, to the astonishment of onlookers. The road out of the town was partly blocked by soldiers of other units, as well as civilians travelling by various modes of transport, making progress difficult. The confidence of the guardsmen was not helped by the sight of numerous Allied barrage balloons being released from their moorings in the distance. Intended to impede enemy aircraft as they attacked, it was apparent that their groundcrews were freeing up the balloons before hastily heading for a hoped-for evacuation back to Britain.

Henry's company arrived at their assigned position to the south of St-Martin-Boulogne in the early afternoon and immediately started digging trenches for shelter from the expected enemy attacks. They did not have to wait long. At around 8 p.m., after an ineffective attack by German aircraft, enemy armoured vehicles appeared and attacked Henry and Jim Windsor-Lewis' companies while an artillery barrage passed overhead and battered the streets of Boulogne. Happily, Sammy Stanier had made certain that several anti-tank guns had been manhandled onto lorries and brought to the front lines. Once offloaded, however, the anti-tank guns were essentially stuck wherever they had been placed. The enemy tanks showed no real determination to press forward at this time and soon moved out of the sight of the guardsmen. There was no doubt, however, that they would soon return.

As dusk fell and under cover of the darkness, Henry and two guardsmen went out on a reconnaissance patrol but only encountered fleeing French civilians, some of whom Henry spoke to in French regarding what they had seen of the enemy. As was usual, the guardsmen stood-to in their fox holes at 3.30 a.m., in case of an enemy attack as dawn drew near. As the morning progressed, Second Lieutenant Peter Hanbury took up a new position at a crossroads where the road from St Omer to Boulogne crossed the road from Calais in the north, only to find that an enemy sniper was making a nuisance of himself. It became apparent that he was hidden in a nearby church tower and Hanbury ordered two Bren guns to pepper the tower with bullets, which stopped the sniper's firing.

Things now became far more serious as German tanks could again be seen approaching and it was apparent that No. 3 Company, under Jim Windsor-Lewis, had been hit hard by the enemy. A couple of anti-tank shells were fired (missing the target) before the gun-crew fell back with several men wounded. Much to Hanbury's surprise, in the midst of the battle, Henry Coombe-Tennant suddenly appeared to issue new orders. Hanbury moved his men towards the shelter of some slit-trenches as instructed by Henry but, as they crossed an open space, tank shells wounded several men and blew him into a sewage-filled ditch. Climbing out, he saw several wounded men falling back, one of whom was missing an arm.

Hanbury and his men entered the suburbs of Boulogne as an enemy air-attack took place. They sought refuge in the cellar of a nearby building which was being used as a makeshift wound-dressing station and, as the sound of explosions rumbled nearby, he was pressed into service by an overworked French nurse. Of one of the wounded soldiers, he noted:

> He had been shot through his insides, and the nurse said he would not live more than a few hours, but was in no pain as she had filled him with morphia. He asked me to get the photograph of his girlfriend out of his pocket, which I did and propped up his arm on his chest so he could die looking at it...
> Another soldier had had his jaw shot away and his tongue cut off. He kept swallowing the stump and choking. The nurse thrust her fingers down his throat and pulled the stump back. She suggested I did this. I don't know whether I could have, but thank God, we got new orders.

In Boulogne, Sammy Stanier's units had no wireless sets with them and he was forced to depend on reports arriving or being sent by motorcycle despatch riders. It was an unsatisfactory situation, made worse by several riders not returning. Some men who were sent to the harbour to find out what had happened to the battalion stores found themselves being herded unwillingly onto Britain-bound transport by an over-zealous embarkation officer. Stanier also had to guard against activity from enemy fifth columnists – Germans or their sympathisers who adopted false personas to sow confusion among the Allied forces. He became suspicious of a lady who seemed to be very active with a bright lamp, even though she offered an innocent explanation, while a man was observed to be signalling from a church tower. He was stopped by a well-aimed anti-tank shell. A 'priest' with a notebook under his cassock was found to be writing down things of a decidedly untheological nature that would benefit the enemy and it was apparent that he was, in fact, an enemy agent rather than a man of God. He was unceremoniously thrown into the harbour, where he drowned.

Into Battle

By 23 May, enemy attacks were gradually forcing the Welsh Guards and their Irish comrades back into Boulogne. All companies had been under attack and it became important to reduce the size of the defensive perimeter and attempt to block the approaches to the harbour, which represented the only chance, however slim, of getting men back to the safety of Dover.

Shortly after 6 p.m. the Welsh Guards were ordered to fall back to the quayside. Messengers were sent by battalion headquarters to the last known location of each Welsh Guards company to order them to withdraw to the harbour at once. This proved difficult, as several platoons were actively engaged with the enemy. Sammy Stanier decided that he was personally well-placed to pass the order on to Jim Windsor-Lewis and his No. 3 Company. As he noted:

> ...I undertook to go to No 3 Company myself. They were in a white house in the middle of the town. When I got there, they were under heavy fire as I was myself. I banged on the door of the house, which was locked, but nobody came to open it and all my efforts to attract attention were unavailing. Eventually, I couldn't stay there any longer. There were too many bullets flying around.

Understandably, Windsor-Lewis had not been expecting visitors and had had the house barricaded against the enemy. When a guardsman drew his attention to the loud banging on the door, he ordered that a window be uncovered so that the identity of the caller could be established before the door was opened. By the time that had been done, Stanier, with bullets whizzing all around him, had given up and left the street. The upshot was that Windsor-Lewis did not receive the all-important order to withdraw.

No. 4 Company, Welsh Guards, under Captain Higgon, with Henry as his second in command, managed to work their way down to the harbour – being shot at by enemy fifth columnists as they went – where they were upbraided by the Guards

Brigade Commander, Billy Fox-Pitt, for being late! They were directed into a large shed on the quayside and found it filled with members of various military units, each man waiting hopefully for his turn to be embarked for a crossing to Dover. Two destroyers, HMS *Keith* and HMS *Vimy* were taking men aboard while under fire from the enemy – the captain of one of these vessels was killed by German small-arms fire while the other was mortally wounded. The destroyers, both damaged, left the harbour despite still having room aboard for more evacuees. HMS *Whitshed* then entered the harbour, followed by HMS *Vimiera*, and both began to embark those still waiting.

Once they had departed the harbour, HMS *Wild Swan* and HMS *Venomous* sailed in to take their places. When HMS *Venetia* started to enter the harbour, the Germans made a concerted effort to sink her in order to block the entrance and trap all the ships within it. Heavily damaged, she was unable to assist further in the evacuation and retired. On the up side, each of the destroyers was able to engage enemy targets with their sizeable naval guns at a range of only a few hundred yards, scoring direct hits of devastating effect on at least one German tank and demolishing several machine-gun positions.

At around 10.30 p.m. HMS *Windsor* succeeded in bringing out another 600 or so men. Even then, not all Allied personnel had been rescued. Around 600 men of the Auxiliary Military Pioneer Corps (AMPC), under Lieutenant Colonel D J Dean, VC, had been dutifully guarding some roadblocks and had not reached the quayside in time to be taken off. Dean finally made his way into the port area around 1.30 a.m. HMS *Vimiera* arrived and was rushed by a desperate crowd of AMPC, French and Belgian soldiers, as well as some fleeing civilians. In all, around 1,200 personnel were crammed aboard as she set sail, although a further 200 or so were unavoidably left on the quayside. The destroyer evacuations had brought over 4,000 men – and a small number of women and children – back to Great Britain.

Into Battle

Henry and his comrades, however, had not been evacuated. They had tried to reach the departing destroyers earlier in the evening but got caught up in the crush of displaced persons and when they reached the quayside, were told by an officer that the last ship had already left. Captain Higgon had therefore decided that, with no obvious remaining prospect of evacuation, the only option was to strike south and attempt to get past the German lines in order to reach the French territory to the south that was still in Allied hands. It is possible that the 'officer' who had given the misleading information was in fact a fifth columnist, or it may simply have been a genuine misunderstanding. In any event, in the early hours of 24 May, Higgon led his men off into the darkness, heading south through the battered streets of Boulogne.

They reached the suburb of Outreau, where they came under machine-gun fire and had to disperse and take cover in damaged houses, though not before Captain Higgon had silenced one machine gun by firing into a house through a shattered window. In the confusion, a number of guardsmen decided to return to the quayside and were fortunate enough to get on board a destroyer they had not expected to see. Henry, however, had no such luck and settled down for the night with a number of guardsmen in an abandoned house. Second Lieutenant Peter Hanbury did likewise with his comrades in a house across the street. In the morning, food was scavenged from adjacent houses while German tanks trundled down nearby streets, oblivious to the fact that around 50 heavily armed Welsh Guardsmen were so close to them. Organised resistance to the invader had now ceased and the Germans were consolidating their grip on the town.

The situation was obviously very grave, though Higgon's plan was to continue the withdrawal to the south at the first opportune moment. Efforts were made to maintain morale amongst the men and they were encouraged to wash and shave, as well as ensuring that their weapons were clean and ready for action. At some point during the morning of 25 May, a German soldier on a bicycle rode past the house that contained Henry and his party. The enemy soldier presented a very tempting target and a Welsh Guardsman promptly shot him, an action that precipitated the rapid conclusion of Henry and his comrades' campaign in France.

The gunfire attracted the attention of nearby Germans and shortly afterwards two German tanks proceeded cautiously down the street towards the houses occupied by the Welsh Guardsmen. A number of shells were fired into Henry's house and Captain Higgon ordered his men to retreat into the cellar. This provided only a temporary respite as German infantrymen soon entered the house and threatened to throw hand grenades down the stairs, an action that would have had devastating consequences in such a confined space. Having run out of options, Captain Higgon reluctantly ordered his men to lay down their arms and surrender. The guardsmen in the house opposite had little choice other than to do the same. Second Lieutenant Hanbury was forced by his captors to stand with his hands in the air for a prolonged period. He recalled:

> Weary minutes in which we were searched until our arms almost broke, then they let us put them on our hats. The four [Welsh Guards] officers [including Henry] were put against a wall, and the tank turret turned to point a machine-gun at us. At that moment, a German officer arrived and shouted at the tank crew, and we were returned to the men... One of the German soldiers tried to pull off my signet ring, but it was too tight.

Henry was now a prisoner of war and, on 26 May, he and his comrades were marched from Boulogne to Desvres, a distance of about ten miles. The next part of the journey took the prisoners from Desvres to Montreuil, a gruelling trek that saw at least one man pass out while another was blown up by a piece of rogue explosive ordnance. Much of the march was carried out under pouring rain and food was in short supply, though a compassionate Frenchman did hand the passing Peter Hanbury bread, an egg and a slab of chocolate. As night fell, the men were consigned to sleep on the wet cobbles of a town square while the officers had the dubious pleasure of a night's rest on the filthy floor of a local café.

Thankfully, as May gave way to June 1940, transport for the captives was provided in the form of lorries and trains through Beauraing, Trier and Mainz. In the latter part of the journey, food was supplied on a more reliable basis and beds with straw padding were provided along the route. In addition to Henry's group, hundreds of other British and French captives were being concentrated together. Questionnaires were distributed amongst the men, but Henry and the other guardsmen refused to fill them in as to do so would provide the enemy with potentially useful military information. This commendable stance provoked some nervousness when a large number of men who had filled in the form were moved elsewhere, leaving the non-signers in an exposed position. Jack Higgon and Henry waited under guard in a building for the next stage of the process. Higgon noted that Henry seemed relaxed and was busy writing on a scrap of paper. When asked what he was writing about, the reply was, "I'm composing a symphony." As had so often been the case with Henry, his music came first.

Interrogations began, with the Germans keen to discover exactly which Welsh Guards battalion their prisoners were from. When Peter Hanbury refused to answer, he was told he could be shot, though having bravely called his accuser's bluff, he was allowed to return safely to his comrades. Eventually the group's immediate future was made clear when they entered the prisoner-of-war camp at Laufen on 13 June. Captivity for Henry Coombe-Tennant and his comrades was set to continue.

CHAPTER SEVEN

Prisoner of War

BACK IN BRITAIN, Winifred Coombe Tennant had no idea that her son had been taken prisoner by the Germans. The daughter of another Welsh Guards officer had told her that Henry's battalion had recently left Britain for an unknown destination and the news later filtered back that it had been involved in the fighting at Boulogne. Though the information received from various sources was fragmentary and often contradictory, it became apparent that elements of the battalion had subsequently returned to Britain – but of Henry there was no firm news. On 25 May information was received by telegram to say that Henry had been reported missing, which, while very worrying, at least did not indicate that he had been killed. Having already lost Christopher during the Great War, Winifred's anxiety over her youngest son's fate can only be imagined.

No other information was forthcoming until, on 5 July, Winifred received a printed card from Henry himself, telling her that he was a prisoner of war. Later in August, the management of the hotel in the Swiss Alps that Henry and Alexander had regularly visited in the 1930s for skiing holidays told Winifred that they had heard (with no information as to the source) that Henry was 'well, [a] prisoner [in] 506 Oflag VII-C/H Germany [the camp at Laufen]. Wants tobacco, chocolate, cigarettes and biscuits.' At this very welcome news, Winifred sprang into action, sending letters to various bodies including the Welsh

Guards' Regimental Headquarters, the British Red Cross and the War Office, as well as writing to Henry himself and also thanking the Swiss hotel.

Winifred then turned her attention to Henry's welfare in his prisoner-of-war camp, as well as that of Allied prisoners of war in general. Henry was sent the things he had requested, as well as a collection of books and other items that included a complete works of Shakespeare, works by Boswell, a prayer book and a pocket chess set. She also seems to have very kindly sent books to other prisoners of war, including Henry's fellow guardsmen A J Williams and Victor Davies. Winifred had always fretted over Henry's frequent periods of childhood ill health and she had despatched to him a range of medicines, 'just in case', including quinine tablets, Carter's Liver Pills, Andrew's Liver Salt, Chalk Powder and Empirin Compound.

On 11 October 1940 she had a letter published in *The Times* that advised the relatives of prisoners of war that it was possible to send their loved ones a sum not exceeding £2 per month. This money could then be used to buy local items that would improve their comfort in the camp. A letter from Henry dated 6 August arrived some weeks later and Winifred would have been greatly relieved to read:

> No news from you yet but I am not worried as I feel sure War Office or Red Cross have notified you I am a prisoner. The days pass quickly. We have made a sort of University out of this place, and there are courses going all day long in every conceivable subject. There are plenty of schoolmasters, poets, economists, scholars, farmers, stockbrokers, doctors, parsons, lawyers, etc among the officers, of whom we now have 1500 here. It all helps to keep us from getting bored. We have plenty of books. In case any of my earlier letters have gone astray [they had], as soon as you can send me a private parcel I want pipe tobacco, chocolate, biscuits, butter or margarine, tinned meat, fish, etc., and any sustaining food you can think of... Warm winter clothes we may get, but by all means send them. Flint cigarette lighter useful.

Winifred soon began to realise that the forwarding of parcels to Henry was fraught with difficulty and often hampered by inefficiency amongst the British officials who were charged with the task. It was not permissible for parcels to be despatched directly to prisoners of war by their relatives and food and tobacco for prisoners could only be sent from Britain under the auspices of the British Red Cross and the Order of St John. In theory, the Prisoners of War Department of the British Red Cross sent a 10lb parcel containing food and tobacco to every prisoner once a week. The reality was that the number of British servicemen captured in France had simply overwhelmed the system.

There were also strict rules for families back home about how letters could be sent to British prisoners of war. While the letters could be sent postage-free, there were precise requirements on how a prisoner was to be addressed on the envelope. A letter should not exceed two sheets of paper, a trying restriction for Winifred and Henry, who were conditioned to write lengthy missives to each other. No information that might be of use to the enemy could be included in a letter and the presence of any other material in an envelope inevitably meant the packet would be inspected by the German authorities and thus delayed in transit.

Winifred began to apply her considerable abilities and energy to the job of improving the parcel distribution system by constant scrutiny and, where necessary, criticism of those she judged to be at fault. On 22 October, she placed an item in the Personal column of *The Times* that asked those who were desirous of improving the present system of parcel distribution to raise the issue with their Member of Parliament. She signed it simply 'A Mother' in order to protect her identity. Similarly, on 30 October she placed an item in *The Times* again, this time drawing attention to the fact that in many prisoner-of-war camps, no Red Cross parcels had been received since 10 September, some seven weeks earlier.

The matter was escalated in November when Winifred, never short of a string or two to pull, had the issue raised in the House of Commons. The Government had entrusted the despatch of parcels for prisoners of war to the British Red Cross partly because they and their parent organisation, the International Red Cross in Geneva, were seen as unconnected to the British Government and could thus anticipate more cordial relations with the German authorities. In answer to a Parliamentary question, it was stated that while the general treatment and housing of British prisoners of war gave little cause for concern, the camp rations issued to prisoners were well below an acceptable standard. The strain imposed on the British Red Cross parcel distribution system had led to its collapse after the fall of France and efforts to rebuild the system so as to meet new demand levels had been hampered by transport issues in France following the German invasion and occupation. It was, however, stressed that the British Red Cross was doing its utmost in very difficult conditions.

Letters sent to Winifred by Henry were also caught up in the administrative chaos. A letter from Henry dated 17 September did not reach her until the end of November, though it was gratefully received by a mother anxious for any news of her beloved son. If Henry's letter seemed a little tardy in arriving, very few of Winifred's letters had reached him at all. He told her that he was longing for pipe tobacco and was keeping himself busy in the camp at Laufen. He was lecturing other prisoners on metaphysics and his piano-playing skills were much in demand as a means to lift the gloom of camp life. He said that he was not totally depressed by his circumstances and told Winifred, 'I think this experience will be very valuable. It has left me completely unmoved deep down. It is a good thing to have one's strength tested and I am pleased to find mine unaffected.'

With the British Red Cross seemingly in chaos, Winifred also sought methods by which she could bypass that organisation in getting comforts to Henry in his prisoner-of-war camp. She made contact with an enterprising lady in Portugal who was prepared to send Henry a small parcel of items on a weekly basis, while refusing to accept Winifred's offer of reimbursement. Winifred also got in touch with a Mrs Barclay, the wife of the military attaché at the British Legation in Budapest, who was sending almost 30 parcels a week to various British prisoners of war. Parcels were also being sent to the camps from Geneva and Bucharest. Even these efforts were destined to become problematic as Hungary and Romania joined the Germans in the 1941 invasion of Russia, while the advent of rationing in Switzerland had a marked effect on the availability of food items for prisoner-of-war parcels.

Continuing public criticism of the prisoner-of-war parcels situation led Sir Philip Chetwode, chairman of the British Red Cross executive, to appoint a new managing director for the Red Cross parcels department in February 1941. The man chosen, Mr Stanley Adams of Thomas Cook and Sons, had the right background to achieve an improvement in parcel distribution due to his experience in the travel and transport business. His main aim was to speed up the delivery process by creating reserves of pre-packed parcels at strategic railway depots. The packing departments of several major West End stores would also be used to streamline the packing process. If these seemingly simple changes could be quickly brought into play, as well as improving the lot of those captured, public criticism of the system's failings would be likely to decrease.

Despite these promised improvements, Winifred kept up her agitation on behalf of Henry and Allied prisoners of war in general. Her opinions of officials could be caustic. When Mr R K Law MP (the son of former Prime Minister Andrew Bonar Law) left his post of Financial Secretary to the War Office in July 1941, she annotated a press cutting that included a photograph of him with the remarks, 'This is the miserable skunk whose hostility to prejudice against British Prisoners of

War should never be forgotten. He... obstructed every effort for their welfare, shielded Chetwode and Clarendon of the British Red Cross and when both were lying to next of kin of prisoners of war... [he] showed bitter antagonism to [the] next of kin...'

Henry naturally knew little of his mother's unceasing efforts on behalf of himself and other prisoners of war and was simply making the best of it in Oflag VII-C/H at Laufen. The camp at Laufen contained mainly prisoners of officer rank and was in Bavaria, near the Austrian border. It was centred on a fifteenth-century palace, originally built for the Archbishop of Salzburg. The prisoners had arrived in the clothing that they had been wearing when captured. Their physical condition had been worsened by their journey, which for some had included transport by barge, crowded horse-wagons and marching, with little in the way of food and water and barely any sanitation. As one told his family back in Britain, 'I arrived here with nothing except what I stood up in – no greatcoat or hat or raincoat or blanket or change of clothing. I've bought some essential washing and shaving kit, but warm clothing cannot be bought here and if it could, the cost would be prohibitive.' Another wrote that, after capture, 'I have only got my battledress, shirt, vest, drawers, socks, boots and tie.'

Thankfully, the prisoners were not subjected to ill treatment and the food that was provided was passable, though hunger was at first ever-present. As one officer recorded, 'Days pass reasonably, lectures, rumours, walk around yard 9 times to make a mile. Meals. Coffee breakfast. Half a litre soup midday and tea with potatoes at least once... Soup is sometimes meat, but usually barley, sago and cornflakes. Bread 2 loaves for 9 days. We save potatoes for breakfast and supper... Have no cooking facilities or hot water.' Another prisoner – unaware that in the early days of captivity letters to Britain seemed to vanish into a dark void – wrote home to say, 'Will be glad when food parcels start arriving and some essential clothes. You would laugh to see us, scarecrows with ragged clothes and all rather lean, with shaven heads. I lost one and a half stone...' Conditions were cramped, with one officer saying he was sharing a space the size of a modest drawing room with more than 80 others, sleeping in tiered bunk-style beds.

Many letters home pleaded for extra food to be sent out to supplement the meagre rations. Another problem was that even in summer the climate was chilly at times, so warm clothing was another regular request made by the prisoners. On the plus side, for what it was worth, the camp was located in an almost idyllic location, as one prisoner noted:

> My room is at the top of a four-storey barracks and at the S.E. corner, with one window looking out in each direction. It is the best room in the building, having magnificent views in clear weather. Close past the ground flows a smooth fast river, discoloured with snow water... Eastward, beyond the village, are rolling green fields and further away are hills thickly covered with conifers. Upstream are very high mountains, which look their best in the early morning or late evening light. The river valley between them is wide and flat and thickly wooded. Rising out of it is a picturesque looking town.

Under the terms of the Geneva Convention of 1929, officer prisoners could not be required to perform any work by their captors, which meant that time would weigh heavily on the minds of the captured if steps were not taken to fill it with diverting activities. As well as Henry's classes in metaphysics and entertaining at the camp piano, many other activities were provided by the prisoners. Card games of various types (especially bridge) were played, while a multitude of study classes was available – including law, German, French, Italian, poetry, farming, forestry, economics and shorthand, amongst others. Concerts were staged, books were read and sunbathing was possible when the weather allowed.

As Winifred well knew, the parcel delivery situation to prisoner-of-war camps remained a constant problem. One officer stated that on 23 July 1940, 'We got some parcels from the Swiss Red Cross once, each parcel of 10lbs containing everything one wants, but we shared each among 8; if we could get one each periodically life would be Heaven! The Red Cross also sent some clothes which we drew for. There is talk of getting more clothes from the ordnance dumps we left in France. A parcel and letters once a week would make life very bearable here.'

Winifred was made privy to a letter sent in reply to another person who had complained about the parcel delivery problems. Lord Revelstoke (formerly Rupert Baring of the banking dynasty) had overall responsibility for the prisoner-of-war parcel packing centre at Park Lane, London and he had told the enquirer that he was very conscious of the problems surrounding the system. By way of explanation, he stated that the number of parcels packed had increased from a starting point of only 13,000 to around 46,000 a week in December 1940. Some of the issues had arisen because once the parcels had left the packing centre, they became the responsibility of the postal authorities in the countries through which they passed by land: Portugal, Spain and the unoccupied part of France. It soon transpired that the land routes through Spain and unoccupied France were problematic, resulting in delays. Arrangements had therefore been made to move the parcels from Lisbon by sea transport to the French port of Marseilles, cutting out Spain completely in an effort to speed things up. From Marseilles the parcels were taken by lorry to Geneva, from where they were conveyed to the prisoner-of-war camps under the direction of the International Red Cross. Lord Revelstoke hoped that the benefits of the streamlined transport system would soon be evident in the camps. Despite this explanation, Winifred's regular badgering of officials and politicians seems to have continued without pause.

To that end, she contacted her old friend David Lloyd George, Clementine Churchill (the wife of the Prime Minister) and, amongst others, the MPs Sir Alfred Knox and Sir William Davison, to highlight her concerns regarding prisoners of war. The latter two promised to raise Winifred's concerns in the right quarters, as well as asking questions in Parliament. Less helpful was the Under-Secretary of State for War, Lord Croft, who merely suggested that she take her 'rather strenuous criticisms' directly to the Red Cross itself. Leslie Pym MP told Winifred, 'there is certainly a general stir going on the question, largely owing to the interest you have taken in it, and it is certain that those responsible have been put on their metal [sic].'

In the autumn of 1940 Winifred was further agitated by discrepancies in what food and clothing the Red Cross could send to a prisoner of war, since the information printed on pro forma postcards sent back to Britain by Henry seemed to indicate that a greater allowance of such items was permissible. Another of her concerns was as to whether the prisoner-of-war camps were being inspected by the Red Cross and, if so, why no completed reports had been made publicly available. She would have been pleased to read that in late October 1940 Henry had returned cards to the British Prisoners of War Auxiliary Service (Geneva branch of the British Legion), indicating that two parcels sent to him by that body had been safely received. A further six or so parcels were in transit, so things were definitely improving on what had gone before.

Laufen Prisoner-of-War Camp was not escape-proof, as was proven in September 1940 when six men escaped via a tunnel. One of the escapees was Pat Reid, who later became famous as a successful escapee from Oflag IV-C, the notorious Sonderlager – or 'special' camp – for recalcitrant prisoners and VIPs at Colditz. The Laufen escape tunnel had been completed with the aid of a hammer, two nails, a stone and some other minor tools and it took 11 weeks of toil to extend it to a sufficient length to clear the camp perimeter. It surfaced in a wooden shed outside the camp walls and Reid made his exit from Laufen with two others, dressed as a woman. The three of them were soon apprehended, while another group boarded a train only to find it was headed in the wrong direction, a fact that necessitated a dangerous double-back. With that difficulty successfully overcome, they had the misfortune to be arrested on suspicion of being burglars while on the road to Switzerland. The six were initially threatened with execution for stealing bicycles that were the property of the Third Reich, for possessing a compass and for cutting up a German Army blanket. Happily, wiser counsel prevailed amongst their captors and all were subsequently sent to the supposedly more secure Colditz Castle.

Letters from Henry continued to reach Winifred on an intermittent basis as 1940 gave way to 1941. A period of silence was broken by the arrival of a postcard from Henry dated 25 February 1941, in which he stated that, though he was to remain at Laufen, about 600 men were about to be moved to a different camp. In April Winifred despatched a personal parcel to Henry containing leather shoes, handkerchiefs, socks, khaki shirts, pyjamas, pants, vests, caps, soap and razor blades. Henry duly acknowledged the safe receipt of the parcel but added that he was continually short of tobacco and that some chocolate would be very welcome. In July 1941 he cryptically told his mother that he was 'very sad at losing his job', a reference that Winifred initially took to mean that he was no longer playing the piano in camp concerts. A further letter indicated that he had tried to explain to her in a cryptic manner that he had actually been deprived of a chance to escape by the Germans discovering a partly dug tunnel.

In September 1941 Winifred wrote in large print in the notebook in which she recorded the actions she had taken regarding prisoners of war, 'God be thanked.' The reason for her joy was the news that Lord Clarendon was no longer chairman of the British Red Cross Prisoner of War Department. She added waspishly, 'reasons "health" – ha! That will take in nobody who knows the Devilish record of this man in relation to P-of-War... well, thank Heaven!' It was also apparent that the chaos in parcel distribution that had dominated Winifred's thinking in 1940 was now much reduced, an improvement that she credited to Stanley Adams and his work since taking up the role of director of the parcel organisation at the British Red Cross. In his praise, she penned a six-verse poem to the tune of 'Rule Britannia', one verse of which read:

> Tis thou dost speed the ships, the train,
> Thy traffic doth with commerce shine,
> Nor shall Geneva dare again
> Deflect a parcel that is thine.
> Rule o Adams, for thou our woes hath halved,
> Prisoners never never never will be starved.

On 11 October 1941, Henry was moved from Laufen to Oflag VI-B Prisoner-of-War camp, near Warburg in Westphalia. The camp was situated on a high, desolate plateau and had a perimeter of about one mile in total. Unusually, a narrow road ran through the camp, linking Dössel to Menne, though the exit and entry points were closely guarded. In October 1941, the camp became home to about 2,500 British officers plus another 450 other ranks. Conditions in the camp were never very good, though things did improve slightly as time went on. It was reported that:

> During the first weeks of the camp's existence no canteen or common room existed, the huts had no latrines in them and P/W were locked in their sleeping huts from sunset to sunrise. Huts were, in the main, divided up into 10 large rooms and 4 small ones. The rooms measuring roughly 7 metres by 4 metres, in this confined space anything from 12 to 16 officers being lodged. Bunks in the rooms were double tiered.
> Meals in October 41 consisted of hot vegetable soup once a day and an issue of bread, margarine, and jam. Fortunately, there was a large quantity of Red Cross parcels in the camp which kept the

P/W going. Without these parcels they would have been on extremely short rations.

In the camp's early stages, fleas, mice and rats were very prominent and no means existed to dispose of them.

When the Warburg camp became fully operational in October 1941, the 3,000 prisoners of war who had arrived at its gates were all in a reasonable state of health, allowing for their recent ordeals. It is therefore telling to note that the camp infirmary saw every one of its 84 beds continually filled from October through to the end of December 1941, with poor conditions at the camp being a major contributing factor to the ill health of the captives. Happily, new brick buildings were under construction by the end of 1941 and eventually eased some of the worst over-crowding while, during January 1942, a concerted attack was launched on the flea, mouse and rat populations, with pleasing results. Nevertheless, in early 1942 there was an outbreak of bronchitis and 11 cases of diphtheria in the camp, though no fatalities occurred.

The food had improved, though heating and lighting in the huts was still inadequate. On a number of occasions, small groups of captives were transferred to other camps, thus easing the pressure on the facilities at Warburg. A camp library existed and contained a remarkable 4,000 books, and there were three netball pitches and a cinder football pitch, factors that helped improve morale a little. An 'exchange mart' named 'Foodacco' – a conflation of the words 'food' and 'tobacco' – was set up in the camp so that items not required by a particular prisoner could be exchanged with another. The currency unit was one English cigarette. In May 1942, a tin of bully beef could be had for 90 cigarettes and 1lb of butter for 120 cigarettes. Prices were subject to fluctuation.

The camp commandant proved to be quite friendly in the circumstances and the camp security was somewhat relaxed about the possibility of escape attempts. It seemed that failed attempts would thankfully not provoke retaliatory measures of too harsh a nature and those recaptured could expect merely to be confined to a punishment cell for a couple of weeks, together with a temporary forfeiture of the limited privileges that were available in the camp.

A camp Escape Committee was formed under the chairmanship of Brigadier Henry C H Eden (later replaced by Major Kenneth Wylie), with several other officers under him who were responsible for various aspects of escape-related activity. One officer designated as 'G' dealt with plans, while another referred to as 'I' handled intelligence and security. A third officer rejoiced in the designation of 'Q' and was in charge of gadgets, an amusing but unknowing reference to a character in the yet-to-be-written James Bond books. Indeed, by a strange quirk, Desmond Llewelyn, the actor who played the role of Q in the early James Bond films, had himself been held in the Laufen and Warburg camps after being captured in 1940. He played an active role in the camps' dramatic productions.

The camp layout lent itself to being divided into five 'battalions', or sections. Henry was in 2nd Battalion, and each had its own designated 'Q' officer involved in the clandestine preparation of maps and other items. Parcels arriving at the camp were discreetly scrutinised by Lieutenant C B Gilroy and a small team of prisoners. Over time, items that might be useful in an escape attempt were included in what appeared to be perfectly innocent parcels sent from Britain by concerned relatives. In reality, the British security services in the form of MI9 were involved in such despatches. Boxed games and tobacco tins proved to be useful in the concealment of banned items and wire cutters, maps, compasses and dyes were all smuggled into the camp by this method. The camp 'parcels team' became very proficient at sniffing out parcels that looked as if they had not simply been sent by the relative or friend of a prisoner, putting them discreetly to one side for careful examination by the camp Escape Committee to see if they contained well-hidden escape materials.

Prisoner of War

On arrival in the camp at Warburg in October 1941 it was obvious to the prisoners that their stay might well be a lengthy one. One of the first matters to be considered by senior British officers at the camp was the formation of a camp entertainments committee, with sub-committees to deal with music and theatre. As early as 18 October, within a week of the prisoners' arrival at the camp, a variety show entitled *Kick Off* was staged, with a programme that included a singer accompanied by a guitarist, a magician, a violin solo and, amongst other items, a piece of theatre that went by the name of *The Play's the Thing*. The event was a great success, bringing enjoyment to the captives at a difficult time. A week later on 25 October Henry appeared in a revue and a drama, while on 14 December he was at the piano, playing works by Handel and Brahms. He had a major role over the Christmas period since on Boxing Day evening a musical work that he had composed was premiered in a Christmas pantomime that received a 'wonderful reception' and saw more than 4,000 tickets issued, with some prisoners attending more than once.

While Henry was busying himself with helping provide musical entertainments, his mother was still active in corresponding with fellow activists to promote the interests of prisoners of war, in badgering Government departments and officials and in writing regularly to her son. Indeed, the energy she applied to keeping in touch with Henry led to a slap on the wrist from the Postal and Telegraph Censorship Department of the Ministry of Information. On 18 December, the Chief Postal Censor wrote to Winifred about her letters to Henry:

> It is noted that, in order to ensure that your news reaches him, you are in the habit of sending letters in duplicate and I am to point out that this practice increases the already enormous bulk of mail to be handled and tends to delay the despatch of your letters...
>
> It will help the work of this Department and save delay to your own correspondence and that of other relatives of Prisoners of War if you will refrain from any unnecessary duplication.

In February 1942 theatrical entertainment was temporarily banned by the Warburg camp authorities following the discovery of certain items that were probably linked to covert escape activities. Use of the No. 2 Dining Room was still permitted, however, and Henry and Lieutenant Saunders were able to give a piano recital. A concert comprised of entirely original material, written or composed by prisoners, was staged on 22 March, during which Henry performed his *Suite for Horn and Piano* and his *Piano Sonata in E Major*, while in April he performed *Music in Manhattan* in a revue show that was said to contain 'a wealth of orchestral and musical talent.' He told his mother that the slow movement of his piano sonata had been compared favourably to the work of Elgar by a prisoner who was also a talented musician.

It was planned that the revue would be staged over several nights but that possibility was brought to an abrupt end when the camp guards discovered a couple of airmen hiding under the Dining Room floor, a discovery that put paid to theatrical activity until May. Efforts to provide entertainment at the camp suffered another blow in June 1942 when several shovels and a pair of pliers – all useful items for escape attempts – went missing from the camp stores, much to the annoyance of the authorities. For a period, no tools whatsoever were allowed into the camp, as the risk of them being purloined by light-fingered captives was rated as being too high.

With a number of talented pianists in the camp (including Henry), two additional pianos had been ordered on behalf of the prisoners so that more practice time would be available. One piano eventually turned up at the camp, though the other fell victim to an RAF bombing raid on Cologne. Henry had certainly helped provide a varied programme of entertainment to help relieve the drudgery of camp life. In addition to his performance of classical works he had also taken the opportunity to occasionally perform more modern swing music, a treat for the ears that sadly seemed to be lost on many of his more conservative fellow captives. Much of his time in camp was spent in reading or performing music, though he was also walking about five miles a day. With the arrival of the summer months of 1942, however, Henry's interest turned to other matters.

If the camp guards at Warburg did not adopt too severe an attitude to escape-related activity, care still had to be exercised at all times. Major Robert Scott-Moncrieff, Royal Artillery, was in Warburg after having been captured in April 1941 while aiding in the defence of Greece. In May 1942, he was looking out of the window of his prison hut when:

> I saw a German sentry, who was in charge of a Russian working party digging a sump-pit about 200–300 yards away outside the camp, raise his rifle and fire at our hut. I heard the bang and immediately afterwards from the adjacent partition of our hut a shout of 'fetch the doctor', and it transpired that Lieutenant YOUNG had been shot through the ankle...
>
> Subsequently I heard that one of the British prisoners of war had thrown some cigarettes over the wire to a party of Russians passing. This sentry who fired the shot was in charge of a different party of Russians and was not one of our camp guards. The action of throwing the cigarettes to the passing Russians was the apparent reason for this guard firing the shot.

Lieutenant Young had been lying on his bed when the bullet struck him – though it was not all bad news for the unlucky officer since, as a result of the wound, he was eventually repatriated back to Australia. In the immediate aftermath of the war's end in 1945 a number of enquiries were made of witnesses to this incident in the hope that the culprit could be identified and brought to account. However, given that the offender was not a guard at the camp and had only been seen at some distance, evidence of identification proved to be insufficient for a case to be brought and the matter was reluctantly filed away.

Though it was not a duty, it was considered 'good form' for British prisoners to attempt to escape and to generally make life as frustrating as possible for their captors. Steps were taken by the camp Escape Committee to ensure that escape plans that were proposed did not conflict with each other, and they also had the final decision on which plans should actually proceed. Security and self-discipline were paramount concerns for the captives. Early attempts at escape from Warburg were ill-fated. One tunnel that had been commenced in November 1941 progressed satisfactorily until March 1942, when it was affected by flooding and collapsed before use could be made of it.

An escape attempt made in May 1942 had the character of a pantomime performance. Captain M E Few crawled into a trailer that was attached to a tractor, a transport combination that often left the camp only to later return. Shortly after he had concealed himself, Few and his trailer were ferried outside the camp by unsuspecting guards but, on arriving at Warburg Railway Station, he found that he was unable to safely get out of the trailer due the constant presence of other people in the area, with the result that he was disappointingly towed back into the camp a little later. His absence had been noted by the guards at the morning roll call, however, and he had already been posted as 'missing', having presumably escaped. He consequently remained in the camp as a 'ghost' prisoner, avoiding roll calls and often in hiding, until he was rediscovered at the end of August when the camp was closed down and the prisoners moved elsewhere. As it happened, August 1942 would prove to be a momentous month for Henry, while the ensuing months would cause his mother, Winifred, great worry and distress.

CHAPTER EIGHT

Over the Wire

ON 15 AUGUST 1942, Winifred Coombe Tennant received a letter from Henry that had been written on 9 July. Despite his involvement in camp entertainments and his reading and musical composition activities, he still found time for some thoughtful reflection on his life so far. He told his mother, 'I have got myself more or less sorted out and straight after 12 months of conflict – and that has brought an inner peace and a true balance that I have not hitherto known – all the sweeter because I feel I have honestly earned it, though it cannot be more than a stage on the road. There are very few "ends" for the complete man, and they are all attainable; it is in our choice of means that we are limited, each in his different way.' Winifred must have read those words with a sense of relief and joy. Perhaps Henry, at last, had some idea of what to do with the rest of his life once he was out of the Army even if, at present, he was prevented from striving to reach his new goals by the barbed wire of the camp perimeter fence.

Winifred's joy proved to be short-lived, since towards the end of September 1942 she received the disconcerting news that the camp at Warburg had been closed and the prisoners moved to destinations that were at present unclear to the British authorities. She wrote in her notebook, 'Oh, my wise one – I do not know where you are...' She continued to write letters to Henry at Warburg but was unsure whether they were actually being forwarded on. As usual, she tried to enlist the help of her wide range of contacts and also made personal approaches to various officials by letter, even pitching up at the War Office at Curzon Street in pursuit of any news.

Her worries were compounded when British newspapers mentioned an Allied commando raid on the German-occupied island of Sark in the Channel Islands. During the raid, which took place over the night of 3–4 October 1942, several German soldiers were captured and had their hands tied in preparation for their transport back to Britain for interrogation. After one prisoner had escaped and tried to raise the alarm, the others were taken quickly to the beach, where another escape attempt took place. In the confusion it was unclear whether the German captives had managed to untie their hands but at least two of them were killed. What concerned Winifred was the news that the Germans, incensed by what they claimed was the killing of men who were tied up and helpless, were now shackling Allied prisoners of war with chains in retaliation. She had no way of knowing, of course, whether this included Henry.

Letters were occasionally still arriving from Henry, but all predated the closure of the camp at Warburg, meaning his whereabouts were still unknown. By the first week of October 1942, Winifred had sent 12 letters to his old camp without receiving any response whatsoever. She wrote, 'My God! I don't know where Henry is since they were moved – the latest news I have of him is 24 August…'

She continued to write to Henry at Warburg and at another camp that she thought he might have been sent to. She also despatched parcels in the hope that they would somehow reach him. A rumour reached her in early November 1942 that another officer who was a prisoner of war had told his family in passing that Henry was all right and was being held at Oflag VII-B at Eichstätt, near Munich. This was only a rumour, of course, and what Winifred sought was concrete evidence of just where her son now was. And firm evidence seemed very hard to come by in the autumn of 1942.

Over the Wire

It had been in October 1941 that the newly established Escape Committee at Warburg had begun evaluating ideas about how an escape from the camp could be effected. In January 1942, Major McLeod of the King's Own Scottish Borderers had the idea of staging an escape bid by climbing over the wire fence under cover of darkness after the camp perimeter lights had somehow been extinguished. At first the idea was rejected as being impracticable and the focus remained on the almost mandatory method of getting out of the camp by going under, rather than over, the wire. As camp inmate Major Albert Arkwright noted, there were usually three ways to get out of a camp: you could go under, over or through the barbed wire. Tunnelling was the prevalent mode of escape but Warburg had seen several failed projects using that method and an alternative means of escape would be very welcome.

That was not the end of the matter and it came to the fore again in April, when the possibility was examined in greater detail and produced some interesting results. It was Kenneth Searle, who had been captured while serving in the Royal Electrical and Mechanical Engineers, who gave the embryonic plan the boost it needed. While Searle was walking around the internal perimeter of the camp for exercise purposes, his mind had drifted to matters that interested him on a professional level and he began to mentally note the layout and character of the various electrical circuits in the camp. As he had suspected, the telephone handsets in the numerous sentry boxes shared a single telephone wire that was fed back into the main guardroom. The telephone wire was carried on the same poles as the cable that powered the camp boundary lights, as well as the guards' sentry-post searchlights, with a pole being positioned about every 25 yards along the perimeter fence. Power to the camp huts for domestic lighting purposes was provided by another cable. There were two barbed-wire fences around the perimeter of the camp, with a gap of several feet between them. Even if a prisoner were somehow to scale

103

the inner barbed-wire fence, once clear of that he would be confronted by another fence that would almost certainly delay him until the camp guards arrived.

While most of this detail was of minor professional interest to Searle, what he also observed was quite astonishing in the context of a prisoner-of-war camp. A major and unfused spur line had been taken from the cable that powered the camp perimeter floodlights and fed into a small hut within the camp that housed a workshop where cobbling, tailoring and barbering work was carried out by prisoners of a lower rank who had volunteered to work as orderlies for the captive officers. As Searle realised, the electrical arrangement made it possible for the prisoners to interfere with the power supply to the camp from within the workshop. Even better, access to the workshop hut meant that prisoners would be able to perform their meddling out of sight of the camp guards. With two electrical cables entering the hut to power the machinery, it would be possible to cut the electrical power to the camp perimeter lights by simply short-circuiting them.

At first, the camp Escape Committee struggled to accept that the perimeter lights could be so easily short-circuited. It was agreed that while the Committee gave some thought to what future use could be made of this discovery, a demonstration should first be arranged. To that end, the German guard who normally controlled access to the workshop was momentarily distracted so that a wax impression of its key could be taken. An identical key was cut by a prisoner who was an amateur locksmith. Access to the hut was then possible whenever it might be required by a camp inmate.

Searle and a comrade subsequently entered the hut under the cover of darkness using the illicit key, and took measurements to determine the kind of apparatus they would need to put the short-circuiting plan into effect. They decided on a pair of 'arcing horns', two Y-shaped implements that could be attached to the incoming cables to produce a short circuit. Other bits and pieces that were essential to the plan (copper wire and aluminium rods, in particular) had already been purloined by prisoners over several months, mainly in pursuit of escape-tunnelling activities, and so were readily to hand.

To prove the effectiveness of the idea, it was decided that a five-minute interruption of the power supply to the camp perimeter lights would be sufficient. It was important to show the Escape Committee that this could be done, but it also needed to be done in a manner that did not damage anything in the hut or arouse the suspicions of the camp guards. The demonstration went off without a hitch in May 1942. Kenneth Searle recorded that the hut was easily entered and everything went to plan. The perimeter lights were extinguished, as were the lights to the German guardroom, causing much confusion to the sentries.

Even when the short-circuiting apparatus was quickly and stealthily removed from the cables in the hut (happily without any damage being caused), it was noted that the lights in the camp didn't come back on for a further 30 minutes, presumably while the camp guards fumbled around in the darkness, trying to replace fuses in the camp's main electrical control panel. All evidence of the presence of Searle and his helper, Ronnie Moulson, having been in the hut was carefully removed and the cables they had touched even had specially brought-in dust sprinkled over them, to give the appearance that they had not been interfered with. The demonstration had been a resounding success and the Escape Committee immediately accelerated the planning for a breakout utilising this new-found ability to interrupt the camp power supply at any chosen minute. The escape plan was given the codename 'Olympia' and the target date for the operation was set for early September 1942, when the position of the moon would be conducive to a night-time escape attempt.

The plan that was devised to get over the wire involved making a number of ladders, each with an accompanying duckboard. A ladder could be placed against the inside fence of the camp and its duckboard could then be placed across the gap between the inner and outer wire fences. Once a man was up the ladder, he could cross the duckboard and jump down on the outside of the camp's defences. While the Germans were routinely repairing the wooden ceiling of the dining hall, the requisite lengths of wood were quietly ferreted away by prisoners and hidden in the roof voids of various huts within the camp. Initially, a single ladder and duckboard device was assembled in secrecy and tested in the music room, which had enough height for the purpose. The test proved successful and the ladder was dismantled and hidden around the music room while work commenced on the additional ladders and duckboards that would be needed for a large-scale breakout. Amazingly, the Germans routinely searched the music room but failed to appreciate the true purpose of the various wooden items that they came across.

Having reviewed the prospects for success of the rapidly developing Operation Olympia, the Escape Committee thought that it might be possible to get as many as 250 men over the wire on the selected night. Indeed, ten officers from each of the camp's five 'battalions' were chosen as team leaders for that purpose, before common sense prevailed. Realising that an escape involving 250 men was probably over-optimistic and might actually prejudice the success of the entire operation, it was sensibly decided to scale things back. The initial 50 officers who had been chosen as team leaders simply became the actual contingent who would make the escape attempt. Ultimately, the number was reduced to 40, with one team of 11 (including Henry Coombe-Tennant), two of 10 and one of 9 men.

Over time, the camp perimeter fencing was subjected to careful examination by various prisoners, who appeared to the camp guards to be simply stretching their legs. The perimeter fence ran to almost a mile in length and it became apparent that the best prospect of success seemed to be on the north side of the camp. The wire fences were about ten feet high, with a gap between them of several feet. There was an elevated sentry box in the north-west corner and then a run of about 300 yards of wire to another sentry box. The gap between the sentry-boxes was patrolled by one guard during the day but by three at night, with each of the night-guards walking a beat of 100 yards. Dogs sometimes accompanied the patrolling soldiers. Each elevated sentry box contained a guard and a mounted, hand-operated searchlight. Clearly, the timing of the escape attempt would have to take account of the anticipated positions of the sentries as they went about their duties.

In mid-August 1942 rumours reached the camp that the entire company of prisoners was soon to be transferred to other prisoner-of-war camps, an action that would scupper any hopes of a September escape. The rumours were confirmed towards the end of August when preliminary orders for a move were indeed issued by the camp authorities, necessitating a swift change of plan as regards the date of the escape attempt. A new date of 30 August was set, with the operation starting at 9.45 p.m. to make the best use of the rising moon.

Kenneth Searle had been busy fine-tuning the process of short-circuiting the perimeter lights and had made two significant changes to the procedure. Firstly, since timing would be of the essence in the operation, he needed to be sure that he extinguished the lights at the precise moment when the night-sentries were at the furthest end of their respective beats. This would provide a good length of perimeter wire that would be essentially unobserved for a short time and could be tackled by the escape parties under the cover of the manufactured darkness. The simple expedient of a concealed lookout observing the guards and signalling with a torch to those inside the hut containing the electrics made the job of knowing exactly when to short the electrical circuit that much easier. Secondly, the earlier test-run had increased Searle's confidence in the apparatus he had devised and he had modified it by connecting it to a long piece of string, a very simple addition that gave Searle the benefit of being able to leave the hut while the perimeter lights were out, while still being able to later disconnect the shorting apparatus by merely tugging on the string from the outside. Leaving the hut quickly while the sentries were – hopefully – still in a state of confusion would reduce the risk of being shot by a nervous and trigger-happy guard.

To increase the hoped-for confusion amongst the German sentries, diversionary tactics were also to be deployed on the night of the escape. It was planned that a small number of dummy ladders would be placed against other parts of the fence, well away from the stretch the escape parties would aim to climb. German-speaking prisoners would bark out orders in the darkness to the effect that any German sentries near to the dummy ladders should remain on alert and where they were. This would help pin sentries to unimportant points on the perimeter fence while the real action took place elsewhere. Additionally, two grappling hooks attached to long ropes were to be flung into the perimeter wire and then pulled hard through the windows of two huts. This might have little practical effect, but by producing a great deal of noise, it would hopefully draw sentries away from the actual escape area.

Henry was to be part of Team 1, with four teams in all. In Team 1 were twelve officers, in six pairs of two men each. Once over the wire, each two-man team was to make for a slightly different compass point so as to avoid any unintentional 'bunching', while at the same time forcing the Germans to spread out more thinly in any pursuit. In early August 1942, Henry's planned partner decided that his recurring attacks of rheumatism meant that he did not think himself fit enough to endure what would be a gruelling escape attempt through hostile territory. He therefore withdrew from the operation and Henry – left without a partner – was added to the two-man team that consisted of Major Albert S B Arkwright of the Royal

Scots Fusiliers and Captain Rupert J Fuller of the Royal Sussex Regiment, making it a trio. Arkwright had been captured near St Eloi in Belgium on 28 May 1940, while Fuller had been bagged by the Germans during the afternoon of 29 May near Poperinghe, also in Belgium.

A great amount of thought had already been put into the type of clothing and supplies of all kinds that would be required by an escaping prisoner. After weighing up the pros and cons of having civilian clothing prepared by those prisoners who had pre-war experience of tailoring, it was decided instead that escapees would simply wear British Army battledress. That was, of course, ready to hand, needed no alteration and it was thought that, on a psychological level, escapers would be much more cautious – and thus less prone to detection – if they were compelled to hide during the daylight hours so as to avoid being spotted in uniform.

Major Albert Arkwright stated that great care was taken in deciding what food could be taken on the journey, should the escape be successful. It was thought prudent to carry enough dry rations to sustain the party for, at most, 20 days. It was hoped that potatoes and fruit could be found along the way, though cooking would probably be an issue. That said, the value of an occasional hot meal in poor weather conditions was recognised as being very important and good for morale. Risks might have to be taken if spirits were to be kept up.

In the event, each man carried about 12lb of foodstuffs for his personal use, including biscuits, cheese, chocolate, porridge, sugar, Marmite, Horlicks malted-milk tablets and tinned fish. It was hoped that it might also be possible to cook a hot meal of scrounged vegetables over a concealed fire every other day. Non-food items included a communal razor and shaving brush, a bar of soap, a comb, a toothbrush and a towel each. Vaseline, plasters, cigarettes and matches added to the burden, but had been found by the past experience of other escapees to be much valued while on the run. In relation to finding one's way around in enemy territory, an astonishing number of maps of Germany had been smuggled into the camp in seemingly innocent parcels and letters, and Rupert Fuller had made a quite accurate compass for direction-finding, though the observation of the stars on cloudless nights would also play a part. Finally, camp-made kitbags provided the means to transport the foodstuffs and other items in a lightweight and reasonably dry environment.

Much of the planning for their escape attempt had been done by Arkwright and Fuller before Henry had joined their team. Although Henry did not therefore take part in much training with his new teammates, he had already undertaken much the same sort of exercises himself. To improve stamina before the escape attempt, potential escapees were walking around 15 miles a day within the camp confines, while also running for almost a mile. The camp was situated about four miles from the small town of Warburg, which was about 40 miles north-west of Kassel. There were no houses or buildings adjacent to the perimeter fence, with the nearest settlement being the village of Dössel, half a mile away.

Consideration was also given to where to head if the escape attempt proved successful, an outcome that was by no means certain. Escapees would, of course, be in the middle of hostile territory and every person encountered along the way would be very likely to help effect their recapture. Three possibilities presented themselves to Henry, Arkwright and Fuller as possible escape destinations. The first option was neutral Switzerland, though that had a border that was well guarded by both the Germans and the Swiss and would involve a lot of travelling on foot, which would potentially increase the risk of discovery as well as physical debilitation along the way. Weighing heavily on the minds of the would-be escapees was the knowledge that two tough-as-teak Royal Air Force officers had earlier attempted such a route. They had marched on foot for 16 days but had still been several days' march from the

Swiss border when they were apprehended. It was known that when recaptured, both men had been mentally and physically exhausted by their exertions. On balance, Switzerland was most definitely not a preferred option. The second possibility involved a trek to a point on the German coast from which a boat trip to neutral Sweden could be made. This had the significant disadvantage that arranging a sea-crossing would unavoidably involve dealing with German officials and civilians, a prospect that did not inspire confidence.

Discounting these two options left only one plan as a prime contender: a journey out of hostile Germany and into the only slightly less dangerous terrain of an occupied country. Holland seemed to be the best option, as it would take the escapees through sparsely populated countryside with few large towns. Once the difficult job of getting safely off German soil had been achieved, it was hoped that the population of an occupied country would, in the main, be friendly towards the escapees, so even if practical help were not offered, with any luck nothing would be done to hinder the men on their journey. With the preferred initial destination established, all that could sensibly be prepared for had been done. How thorough and effective the preparations had been would only be revealed when the escape attempt was actually made.

In the run-up to the planned escape date of 30 August 1942, there was a major hitch. The prisoners already knew that the camp was to be vacated in the very near future and on 27 August the Germans posted the first list of men who were to be taken by train to a different camp. Several would-be escapees were down to move camps on the day of the escape and the list included Rupert Fuller. Training a replacement for Fuller was impossible in the few days remaining before the escape attempt so it was decided that another officer would pretend to be Fuller and would move to the new camp in his stead.

At 2 a.m. on the morning of 30 August, prisoners who were to be transferred from Warburg started passing through a wicket-gate into the German quarters. Several German officers sat at a table under a powerful arc lamp and checked each prisoner who presented himself against the photograph in his file. One substitute was immediately identified as not being who he said he was – due to the absence of an appendicitis scar – and was promptly marched off to the guard-room for questioning. Rupert Fuller's behaviour in the camp had hitherto been so unremarkable that he was not as well known to the Germans as a troublemaker would have been, and fortunately his substitute closely resembled him. The ruse worked perfectly and the fake Fuller soon disappeared into the darkness with the other transferred prisoners, while the real Fuller remained hidden in the camp, awaiting the hour of the escape attempt.

After breakfast, the four escape teams set to work, secretly assembling their ladders and duckboards in readiness for the breakout. A close watch was kept on the patrolling German guards and work was halted temporarily on several occasions due to the uncomfortably close proximity of a sentry, but by around 4 p.m. Henry and his team had completed their apparatus and were ready to go. There was still time for one more alarm that, while tragic in nature, did not derail the escape plan.

Even hours before those involved in Operation Olympia were due to go over the wire, other efforts were still being made to go under it, and an escape tunnel was being dug so as to be ready for use before the camp was emptied of its captives by the German authorities. Lieutenant John Bourlon De Pree of the Seaforth Highlanders had been working at the head of the tunnel when he accidentally came into contact with a live electricity cable that was being used to power the tunnel lights. He received a powerful shock and, though alive when brought out of the tunnel, he died shortly afterwards without regaining consciousness. This tragic event naturally caused great sadness and consternation in the camp and some senior Allied officers questioned whether it was fitting and proper for the planned escape attempt to continue as planned, following the death of a fellow officer. The would-be escapees argued strongly that, as a committed escapee himself, it was very likely that Lieutenant De Pree would not want Operation Olympia to be abandoned on his account. After some discussion, it was agreed that the escape plan would proceed as scheduled.

The evening roll call came and went, and once that was out of the way, life in the camp appeared to the sentries to be continuing in its usual humdrum way. This display of seemingly routine activity disguised the fact that the escapees were busily packing kitbags and making last-minute preparations for the breakout. With those tasks completed, a final meal was taken – some struggling to eat it due to nervous tension, despite all knowing that it might be the last hearty meal that some of them would get for a considerable time. Indeed, if the escape plan failed disastrously, it might be the last meal that some of them would ever eat.

At around 9 p.m. Henry's team entered the hut where the escape apparatus was concealed and moved the equipment – while the perimeter sentry was patrolling some distance away – to the hut from which the escape attempt would be made. Leaving nothing to chance, they smeared dripping along the duckboard runner that would bridge the gap between the two perimeter fences so as to ensure it could be deployed smoothly. With the planned zero-hour of 9.45 p.m. now approaching, the tension rose as men waited anxiously for the escape controller to signal that the sentries were temporarily out of the way and the attempt could be launched. The 11 members of Team 1 (including Henry, Arkwright and Fuller) had already donned dark gloves and balaclavas, or smeared coal dust onto their exposed skin to help conceal themselves in the darkness.

The verbal command of "Go!" seems not to have reached Henry's hut, but the sudden extinguishing of the perimeter fence lights and the energetic emergence of another escape team from an adjoining hut meant that it must be now or never. Kenneth Searle and Ronnie Moulson had completed their work of short-circuiting the electrical system and the duo quietly left and locked the hut as pandemonium broke out. They became aware of confused shouts (some of them helpfully provided by German-speaking prisoners), a few gunshots and a 'remarkably curious clattery sort of noise from further afield, which we reckoned must surely represent the planned diversionary activities.' This was undoubtedly the grappling hooks being applied to the fence and sharply pulled. As the noise eventually subsided, Searle and Moulson carefully retraced their steps to the hut in the darkness and, from the outside, tugged on the string they had attached to the shorting apparatus, an action that cleared the cause of the short circuit but still left much of the camp in darkness. Other prisoners were treated to the amusing sight of several camp guards peering closely at various camp lights by torchlight, in a vain attempt to locate the cause of the problem. But what of Henry and the other escapees?

Once it became obvious that the escape attempt was under way, the members of Henry's Team 1 burst out of the hut and, carrying their escape ladder and duckboard, headed for the perimeter wire only 15 yards away. The leading men lifted the ladder so that it rested against the internal perimeter fence before Arkwright climbed upwards holding the duckboard. As he hurriedly deployed the bridging device, he snagged it in the electricity wires that were strung along the fence, but managed to rapidly disengage it and reposition it correctly. He quickly crawled onto the duckboard and scuttled across it before dropping down outside the camp, where he heard a gunshot. Ignoring that unwelcome distraction, he ran through a field of sugar beet and promptly fell over a German tripwire, of which he had previously been unaware. Picking himself up, he was cheered to see that Henry and Rupert Fuller were alongside him. For the moment at least, they were free.

CHAPTER NINE

On the Run

THOUGH HENRY AND his two comrades were unaware of it, 30 men (including themselves) had got over the wire and into the countryside surrounding the Warburg camp. Two members of Henry's 11-man team had failed to clear the wire, while the 9-man Team 2 and 10-man Team 3 had all successfully made their exits from the camp. Disaster had struck Team 4 when the deployment of the duckboard had gone awry and seriously delayed proceedings. The result was that only two of that ten-man team had been able to clear the wire.

Now that they were outside of the camp, the first potential problem for the escape team of Albert Arkwright, Rupert Fuller and Henry Coombe-Tennant was to determine whether the German sentry party that routinely patrolled outside the camp perimeter was nearby. That unit would have been alerted by the commotion that emanated from the camp and would undoubtedly have headed towards the nearest stretch of camp perimeter fence to see what was happening. Luckily, there was no sign of the patrol, so the trio made off in a north-westerly direction through a beet-field and into some corn. Stooping low so that the crop would conceal them as much as possible, they ran and then walked to a road that they carefully crossed once they were certain it was not under enemy observation.

Exercising great caution, the escapees traversed a railway line and skirted a wood until, at about 4.30 a.m. on 31 August, shelter was taken in another wood near the villages of Nörde and Willebadessen. The escapees were, of course, dressed in British battledress and a key element of the plan was that they should remain hidden during the day. Water was obtained from a spring and some potatoes were scrounged before they settled down for what sleep they could manage. The arrival of daylight revealed that the position they had chosen was far from ideal, being a little too close to the edge of the wood. They decided to stay put, however and awaited the arrival of darkness and the next leg of their dangerous journey.

At 8 p.m. on 31 August, Henry and his comrades set off northwards through the woods and continued walking for rather longer than they would have liked, due to the fact that water proved hard to come by and they had to take the risk of being seen if a supply was to be found. They stopped at around 5.30 a.m., again hiding in a wood and getting water from a drainage spout in a railway embankment. The three men tried to quickly establish a routine that would help them during the dangerous and arduous journey that confronted them if they could evade recapture. After choosing a hiding place at the end of each night, they planned to sleep for two hours to partly recover their strength and then, on waking, to eat before going to sleep again in readiness for an evening departure on the next stage of their journey. On the evening of 1 September, they gained entry to a hut that adjoined a disused quarry and decided to use it as a shelter until setting off again some hours later. Things did not quite go to plan as they became aware of a German soldier strolling along with two women. If he did catch sight of the escapees, he made no enquiries and, once he and his lady friends had moved out of sight, the relieved trio left the hut and scrambled up a hill into a dense thicket of fir trees, a much safer hiding place.

On the night of 1 September, Henry and his comrades walked on the sleepers of a railway line towards Altenbeken, but had to hurriedly leave the tracks after a challenge from a signalman. Though nothing came of the incident, it did slow down their progress as they continued carefully onward by a hopefully safer route. They spent the following day (2 September) in woods to the east of Altenbeken. Resuming the journey in the evening, they passed cautiously through a village without being challenged and reached a wooded area to the south of Berlebeck on 3 September. Matters became more fraught early in the morning of 4 September when the group found themselves in a German military training area, though fortunately there was nobody to be seen.

They were again desperate to find a water supply and were forced to move by daylight in search of it. As night drew in, they passed through another village and were dismayed to find it packed with German soldiers. In the darkness their by now unkempt battledress and home-made caps luckily attracted little attention. As they were leaving the village, there was a moment of panic when someone shone a torch at them, but that person took no further action, possibly mistaking them for forced labourers. They still weren't out of the military training area, and at one point found themselves at the gates of a German barracks. Again, fortune was on their side and no one challenged them as they hastily retraced their steps before proceeding by an alternative route.

In the early hours of 5 September, they were approaching the town of Paderborn and decided to lay up in a wood for the day before once again setting off as darkness fell. 6 September was a Sunday and they were disturbed by parties of children who were picnicking in the woods. One group of youngsters did see the escapees, but no consequences flowed from that nerve-jangling incident. On moving off, they approached the village of Bielefeld to find the streets thronged with people, though as it was a very dark night, no-one paid much attention to them. Some confusion arose in this area as they seemed to be in a suburb that was not shown on their maps but, in due course, they neared the village of Dissen and decided to lie up and rest for 48 hours.

They set off again on the afternoon of 10 September and the following morning reached the village of Lengerich, where they rested during the day before walking along a canal tow path. By the evening of 12 September they were still following the canal, though the next day – another Sunday – the canal path was busy with people taking recreational strolls, forcing Henry and his pals to remain hidden. They left by night and moved through an area that contained a number of searchlights and anti-aircraft guns, as well as an airfield from which German night-fighter aircraft could be seen taking off. They were now close to the Dutch border.

On the night of 14 September the trio crossed from Germany into Holland, though they saw no obvious sign marking the border. They had crossed near Denekamp and planned to make for Vaassen, where it was understood that the local priest might be able to offer some assistance. They were dirty, hungry, cold and almost exhausted. As the trio later noted regarding 15 September:

> We spent the day in sparse cover. It was raining, and we were very uncomfortable. We were seen by a child during the day, and our presence was reported to a farmer who came to see us at dusk. He thought at first we were French escapers, of whom about 60 a week crossed the frontier in that district, and he seemed rather taken aback when we said we were English. The farmer and a friend talked to us in German, and we asked for food and a place to sleep in. The farmer took us to his farm and put us into a hayloft, bringing us hot milk and bread and butter. We dug ourselves into the hay and slept comfortably for the night.

Conversation the following morning was difficult due to the language barrier and the farmer, Mr J H Eppink, who had fought as a member of the Dutch Army before its surrender in 1940, was naturally wary of his new acquaintances. To be caught helping the enemies of the German occupation forces carried very heavy penalties. Despite his worries, he let the men remain in his barn, where they were amply fed and medicine provided for Arkwright, who was temporarily unwell. A number of visitors came to see the escapees and listen to their hopes of getting back to Britain, though no-one ventured to provide any practical help in what would clearly be a risk-laden enterprise. Things perked up dramatically after a couple of days holed up in the barn, when a visitor arrived who spoke English and said he was able to connect them to an escape organisation. He was a vet and the fugitives soon began referring to him as 'the doctor'. He returned a day later with three suits for the trio.

A little later it became apparent that 'the doctor' had been in touch with members of a clandestine escape organisation who, before making contact themselves, wished to be assured of the mysterious trio's *bona fides*. This proved a little problematic as the men – understandably – had little in their possession to prove exactly who they were. The difficulty was overcome, however, when Fuller was able to produce a photograph of his wife and child that was stamped with the address of the firm that had processed it back in England. Similarly, Arkwright was able to display a label on his windcheater bearing the name and address of an English company. These issues having been dealt with, the men had little to do other than to rest in the hayloft and enjoy the hospitality offered until their hosts were ready to move them on.

Every morning at around 7 a.m. Henry and the others were awoken by a soft "Hello" from one of the farmer's two young daughters. They brought with them a breakfast which, as time went on, might typically include bread and butter, bacon, eggs, cheese or honey. Arkwright and Fuller were married men, while Henry was a confirmed bachelor and appeared awkward and ill at ease when talking to the girls. His comrades gleefully appointed him as their unofficial liaison officer and watched with amusement as he became tongue-tied and embarrassed while attempting to engage in conversation with the breakfast-bearers.

As they had to remain in hiding, there was little else for the men to do following breakfast but to perhaps wash and shave and then await the arrival of dinner, which usually consisted of meat, a giant pot of potatoes and another type of vegetable, all of which was produced on the farm. For pudding there would be stewed pears, fruit or rhubarb. The evening meal followed a similar pattern to breakfast, leaving the fugitives quite replete and, during the time they remained at the farm, their gaunt faces filled out as they gradually put back on the weight they had lost during their strenuous journey.

On the fourth day of their stay at the farm a man named Jan arrived. A Dutchman in his thirties, he spoke fluent English and immediately impressed the escapees with his apparent disregard for his personal safety. He told them that he could certainly help them to reach the border between Holland and Belgium where they could be passed over to 'friends' in that country, though things might move rather more slowly than he would have liked due his currently being under occasional surveillance by the Germans. He would take no undue risks for the moment and, once his covert watchers had become bored with him, he would get the trio to a house he owned which was located in a quiet, rural area. He told them that they were the first British soldiers he had helped – French military personnel on the run were commonplace, while British men were quite a novelty. After several days of very welcome relaxation, the vet made ready to take them to Jan's house by car. His rural practice meant that he had access to petrol to allow him to perform his important duties and his journeys to often remote farms raised no suspicion with the German authorities. Much of the local livestock was in any event destined for the German Army and it was seen by the occupying forces as being important that those involved with animal welfare should not be unduly interfered with.

They changed into the suits that had previously been supplied and all of their personal belongings were carefully examined and items that had marks or labels that indicated that the item was of British origin were either discarded or the incriminating tag or label removed and destroyed. They were then driven – occasionally at an alarming speed – down narrow country lanes and past fields, woods and heathland until they reached what they hoped was the safety of Jan's house. The house contained – in addition to Jan – his Swedish wife, their young daughter and a tough-looking local who worked nearby and also helped around the house and garden. They received a warm welcome with plenty of food and enjoyed the chance to get some fresh air in the garden, though it was necessary to keep a sharp lookout for strangers. Henry was invited to play on the family's piano and did so with his usual skill, although it was customary to remain silent in one's room should any visitors arrive at the house.

It soon became apparent that Jan was having some difficulty in making contact with his friends in Belgium. After a week or so, two French fugitives arrived at the house seeking assistance. After some deliberation, Jan decided also to provide them with shelter and later take them with his three British guests towards the frontier with Belgium. After all, a couple of Frenchmen might be handy to have on the journey, their knowledge of the French language and local customs being beneficial once the group reached France.

Another week passed with no change in the situation of the five fugitives. Jan worked as a factory inspector and was able to use the travel opportunities presented by that role to pursue contacts in the south of Belgium. After a three-day trip, he finally returned with some cheering news. He had been given the address of a house just over the Belgian border where he had arranged to meet a helper known as 'The Blue One' (*Den Blauen*). They would first have to cross the Dutch-Belgian border on foot and at a precise place indicated by Jan's new Belgian friends. But beyond that scant information, there was little else of substance.

Though it would not have been clear to Henry and his comrades at that time, they were soon to be entrusted to the care of the 'Comet Line', a group of people who clandestinely sought to remove Allied soldiers, sailors and airmen (and the occasional woman) into a safe country, away from the clutches of the Germans. They did this despite the enormous personal risks it involved.

After what had been a restful time at Jan's, the group enjoyed a farewell drink before setting off the following morning for the border crossing-point shown on a map-tracing. They said their farewells to Jan's family and, with a three-day supply of sandwiches, set out on a cold, dark morning towards the local railway station, a distance of about three miles. As they neared the station, they came into contact with civilians also intent on taking the train but, muffled up against the cold, the five fugitives and their escorts avoided all conversation with strangers. It was more difficult to remain aloof in the station waiting room as easy access to the platform was blocked by the crush of people waiting in the doorway. The group almost instinctively decided to lounge around in different parts of the waiting room and feign sleep. To the British trio, the two Frenchman looked completely at ease with their situation while the British themselves felt that every action they took only highlighted their nervousness. They needn't have worried: if any of the locals harboured any suspicions about shifty-looking new commuters, they kept them strictly to themselves. The tension was partly broken by the welcome reappearance of Jan, who surreptitiously handed each man his train ticket. They then boarded the train.

After about three fraught hours, the journey ended at Utrecht and the group and their guides dismounted from the train. There was a need to change trains that involved an unwelcome, though unavoidable, wait of one hour. Though there was no obvious German presence in the station, a Dutch collaborator was seen strutting up and down the platform, apparently quite happy to bask in what he saw as the prestige and power attached to his traitor's uniform. He did not interfere with Henry or his friends, however, and the group settled down on a bench and began to eat some of their sandwiches. Jan and his assistant hovered in the background and kept a watchful eye on their charges though, to casual onlookers, displaying no obvious connection to them.

At last, the train arrived and the party was able to completely fill a compartment so that no strangers were able to enter. The mood relaxed and the men were able to talk and celebrate the success – so far – of their plan. The Dutch ticket inspector entered the compartment and eyed each man carefully while punching their tickets. He made no comment but left the compartment with a knowing wink, having probably guessed what they were up to. They later got off the train and eventually reached the village of Weert, a place that Jan was unfamiliar with, so he had to make enquiries with the locals as to which road they required. They soon set off again and passed several uninterested Dutch officials, who simply ignored them. As they finally reached the correct path, Jan stopped and let the five men pass by him, giving and receiving smiles and a whispered expression of thanks from each of them. They were now close to the Belgian border and, for the next part of the journey, they were on their own.

They had their rough maps and Rupert Fuller's compass to help guide them and, after following a bridle path for some distance, they stopped in the cover of a wooded area and rested. There were about two hours of daylight left and they estimated that they might be only 300 yards from the Belgian border and possibly three miles from the Blue One's house. They decided to try and locate the Blue One's village and then to lie up in cover until it got dark. The darkness could then be used to hide the movement of one of the Frenchmen, who would be sent into the village to try and find the right house. The maps were proving to be inaccurate in parts and the actual

123

border was not marked in any obvious way on the ground so determining whether they had actually crossed it was difficult. The confusion was resolved by the simple expedient of one of the Frenchmen asking a fisherman that they came across how the fish were biting. The fish weren't biting, apparently, but aspects of the deliberately brief conversation convinced them that they were now on Belgian soil.

They continued cautiously towards the Blue One's village and were surprised to see a ploughman in an adjacent field beckoning to them. They decided to send one of the Frenchmen over to see what he wanted, and on his return the Frenchman told the party that the farmworker had warned him that the road ahead was often used by German military vehicles. He had added that he could put them into contact with people who would be able to help them on their way. This was an unexpected and surprising offer but one that had to be viewed with caution. To accept, however, would mean that a potentially hazardous trip into the Blue One's village could be avoided. They decided that the man seemed trustworthy and that they should accept his help. The ploughman told them to remain in cover and await his return, which they did, while keeping a close watch for any approaching Germans. The ploughman's workmate continued to toil in the field and the fugitives were amused to hear him whistling the French national anthem.

The ploughman eventually returned and assured the men that they would soon be on their way to safety. He was then somewhat alarmed to see two women approaching from the direction of the main road. These were the mother and daughter that he had contacted by telephone, though he was dismayed that they had arrived in broad daylight in an area that saw a lot of passing traffic both on foot and by car. The ladies were Tita Ada Bemelmans and her daughter, Solange Groenen. Their obvious pleasure at seeing the men that they had come to help soon disarmed the ploughman and Henry and his comrades had the opportunity to look at the badges that earlier escapees had presented to the duo as a mark of thanks for their help. They spoke good English and provided the welcome news that the party would, with a little luck, be in England within a week! The ploughman and the women left, telling the men to remain in hiding until they were collected after dark.

When it was dark, the ploughman returned and led the men to his home. They were once again given the sort of hospitality that they were becoming used to while on the run. The table was laid out with bread, cheese, ham, butter and fruit, with beer and milk to wash it down. After an enjoyable meal, they were led out into the darkness – it was now 25 September 1942 – and taken by the ploughman and his brother to the house of Tita Ada Bemelmans and her husband, Doctor Michel Groenen.

The Groenen family lived in Kloesheuvel, an imposing property near the village of Tongerlo. Tita immediately produced a bottle of wine and several glasses before explaining that while her husband (who was asleep upstairs) did not mind her helping Allied fugitives by concealing them in farm buildings, he did object to her bringing them into the house, where their discovery could have fatal consequences for the family. For that reason, they would need to keep out of his way at all times and, after finishing their wine, they were taken to a disused coach-house, told to show no light and to remain in hiding until instructed otherwise. As well as having to conceal them from her husband, she mentioned that there was also a local who seemed a little too friendly towards the occupying forces. Having absorbed the warnings, the men settled down for a welcome sleep among the hay.

Major Arkwright had settled so deeply into the comfort and warmth of his hay bed that, in the darkness of the following morning, when Mme Bemelmans visited the trio, she stepped on his head. She explained that she was unhappy at the thought of them having to hide in the coach-house and that she had decided to conceal them in the more comfortable attic in her house. Eventually Mme Bemelmans confessed all to her husband, and, thankfully, he took it in his stride.

The two Frenchmen went their own way at this time for some reason, and news was later received that both had been recaptured – though with no adverse consequences for the escape line. In the evening, three young men arrived at the house. They were the next link in the escape chain and would take the men – by bicycle – to a house about five miles away. Grateful farewells were made to the Groenen family before they cycled to Maesecyk and the house of Catherine Salle-Coolen and her husband, a couple who were obviously accustomed to receiving strange guests at odd times. One of the young guides handed a revolver to the lady of the house and explained to the escapees that had any troublesome Germans been encountered during the journey, they would have shot them without hesitation. It had been a 'kill or be killed' situation.

The next morning, breakfast was served and newspapers and playing cards provided. The trio was told that they would be moved that evening – again by bike – and to help pass the time, Catherine Salle-Coolen somewhat surprisingly offered to read their fortunes, using a well-thumbed pack of cards. As Major Arkwright remembered, they were told that they were all lady-killers who would find good luck in the future; and they would be home in three weeks.

In the evening, a young woman and an older man arrived, in the company of two of the men who had earlier brought the trio of fugitives to the house they were currently staying in. With the next phase of the journey about to begin, the usual farewells were made and sincere thanks for the help provided were proffered. Such was Madame's lack of concern for her own safety that she breezily gave Henry and the others her calling card, an action that would land her in potentially deadly trouble with the Germans should the escapees be recaptured. Needless to say, once they were out of her sight, the cards were destroyed – even without them, they would never forget her and the support she had so willingly provided.

The party set off in the dark with their guides and made for a farmhouse located just off a main road. It was the home of the young lady – Gertrude Moors – who had accompanied them and they spent the night there before rising to a 5 a.m. breakfast of bread and a quite palatable ersatz honey, washed down with hot coffee. With Gertrude Moors, they boarded the train for Liège, a journey of about 20 miles. After completing part of the journey, it was necessary to change trains, involving a wait on the platform of about half an hour. The platform was quite busy and Belgian police could be seen stopping and questioning various would-be passengers. It is likely that they were looking for black marketeers but inevitably, Henry, Arkwright and Fuller feared it was themselves that were being sought. The entire party felt anxious, but the Belgian police did not bother any of them and they got on the train and resumed their journey to Liège.

In Liège, they followed Gertrude Moors, passing numerous German soldiers, until she eventually led them into a café and left them in the care of the owner. He confidently advised them that the worst part of their trial was now over; they would be moved to another location in Liège in a few days' time, before commencing the next stage of their journey. After lunch, the café owner's wife revealed the worrying news that the house of a friend of her husband had been raided by the Germans and his wife and child had been taken away for questioning. As that man also helped escapees, there was a worry about what his wife might reveal and also what incriminating evidence might be found in his home. There was a risk that the café might be raided, news that led Henry and the others to offer to leave at once – without any guides – rather than see their hosts in danger should the fugitive trio be found on the premises. That offer was refused and they were told to sit in the public bar of the café, sipping a beer and trying to appear nonchalant.

The café owner was in the process of arranging their removal and, should the Germans arrive in the meantime, they would probably not pay much attention to people who merely seemed to be enjoying a drink.

Henry and his companions sat in anxious silence, trying not to attract the attention of any of the other café customers, as Madame nervously pottered about the bar area with one eye fixed on the door. As time went on, the men were moved to the rear of the premises and, at last, a man and a woman arrived by the back door. More hurried farewells were made and good luck wished before they left the café and followed the latest set of guides into the busy streets of Liège and potentially more danger. Reassuringly, the busy thoroughfares soon gave way to a series of quieter, residential streets with few pedestrians and even fewer vehicles. Another café was the destination and, on arrival, it was once again necessary to pose as customers as there were members of the public present. One of the guides bought everyone a drink before, as the café quietened down, the group moved into the rear kitchen.

Time passed slowly before, much to Henry and his comrades' astonishment, the next guides turned up in the shape of two middle-aged ladies, each of whom was dressed in sombre black. The first impression was that they must be nuns; the second impression was that though they were not actually nuns, their appearance almost guaranteed that they would raise no suspicion with the authorities as they went about their business, whatever it might be. Their business that day was helping Allied soldiers reach safety and they led the escapees to a small, semi-detached house. The group was visited there by the first café owner with the friend whose house had been raided. The friend, though very worried, had decided that there was little he could do to help his detained wife and child. If no evidence was brought against them, they might simply be released. In the meantime, he intended to keep well clear of the Germans while continuing to help the escape line.

Cadoxton Lodge, near Neath, where Henry was born in 1913.

WGAS – D/D T3707

Winifred Coombe Tennant.
Public domain

Charles Coombe Tennant.
WGAS – D/D T4715

Gerald Balfour.
Public domain

Charles, Winifred, Alexander (standing) and Henry.
Coombe-Tennant family

Alexander, David Lloyd George and Henry, in the garden at Cadoxton Lodge in 1923.
WGAS – D/D T4166

Henry at Eton College.
Coombe-Tennant family

Henry (right) on a skiing holiday in the 1930s.
WGAS – D/D T5150

Henry (second from left, front row) at the Fifth Biennial Conference of the Institute of Pacific Relations, Banff, 1933.
WGAS – D/D T5147

The Welsh Guards in Paris, 1939.
WGAS – D/D T5162

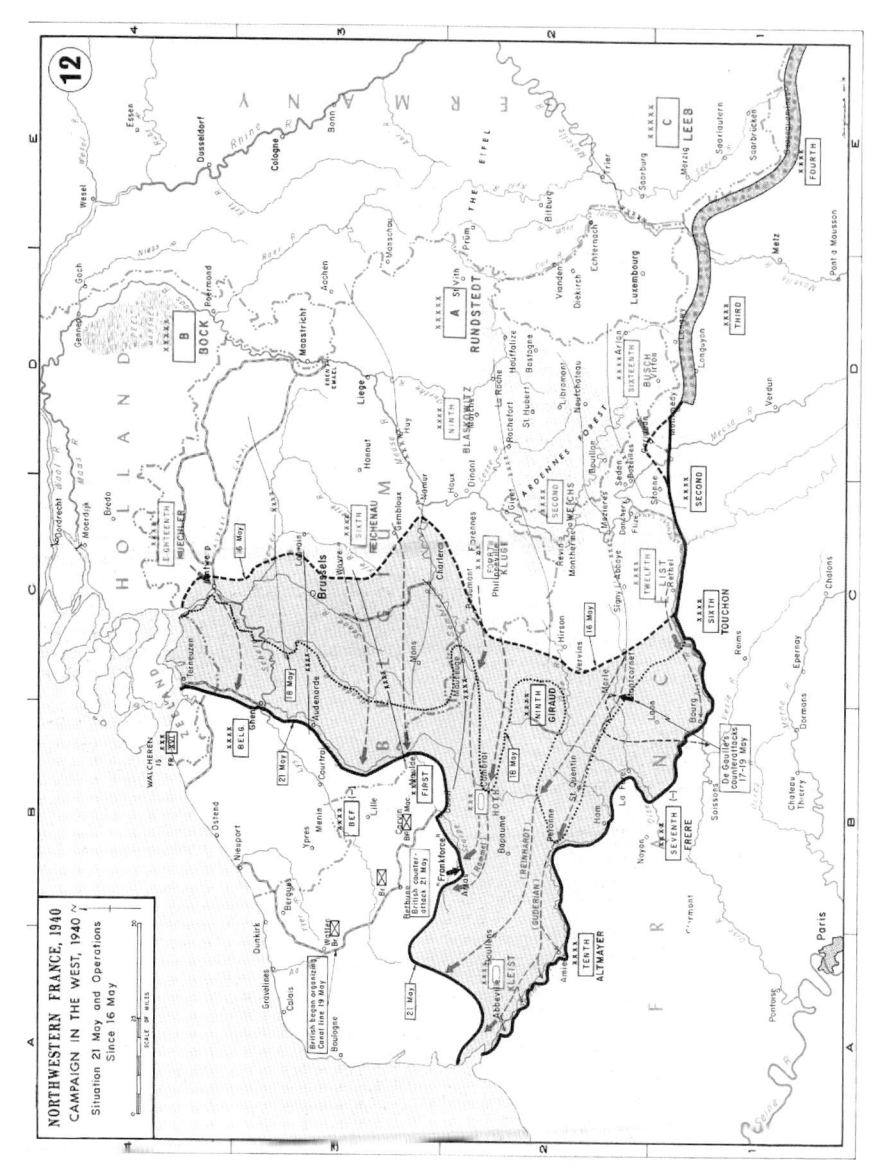

The German advance in France and Belgium, May 1940.
Public domain

Henry and his dog.
Coombe-Tennant family

Alexander (Sammy) Stanier. He fought the Germans in both World Wars.
Sir Beville Stanier, Bt.

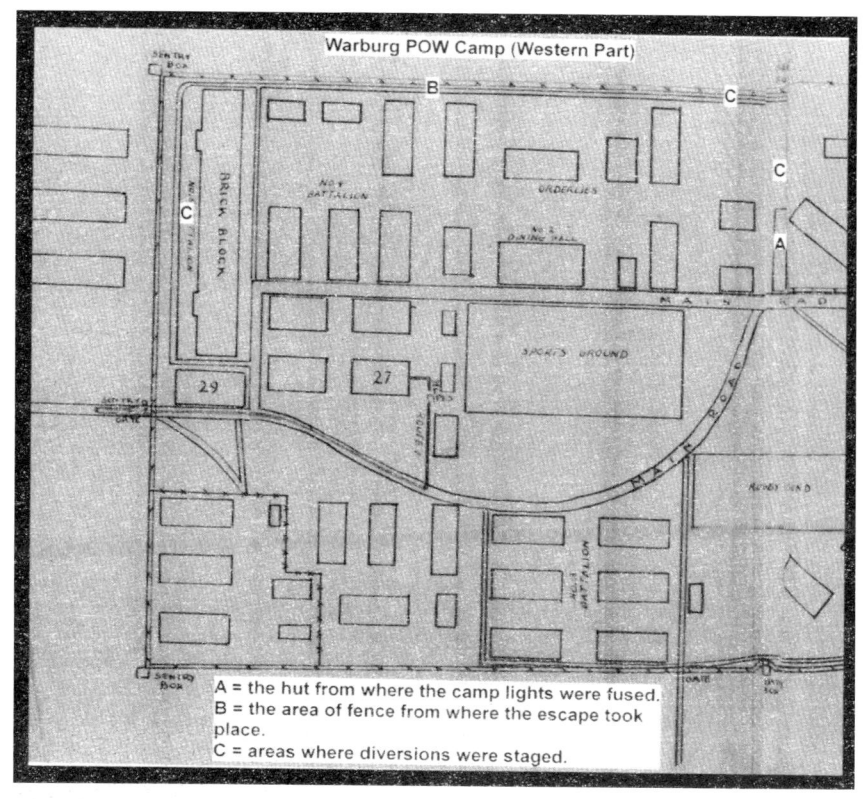

A = the hut from where the camp lights were fused.
B = the area of fence from where the escape took place.
C = areas where diversions were staged.

Sketch plan of Warburg Prisoner of War camp.
National Archives WO/208/3290 (public domain), with author's annotation

After the escape: a ladder and duckboard over the camp perimeter fences.
Public domain

Henry (centre) with fellow Warburg escapees Rupert Fuller (left) and Albert Arkwright (right).
Public domain

Andrée de Jongh, who created the Comet Line.
Public domain

Edouard d'Oultremont. As well as guiding Henry after his escape from Warburg POW camp, he later joined him on Jedburgh Team Andrew.
Brigitte d'Oultremont

Henry in an image used for a forged identity card while an escapee.
Brigitte d'Oultremont

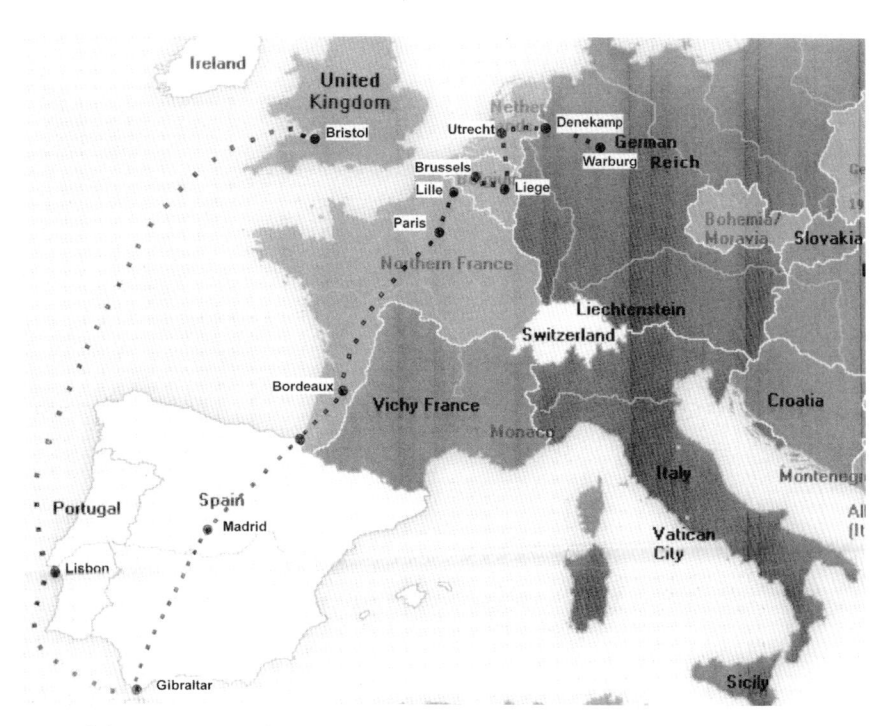

Map of the escape route followed by Henry and his two comrades, with help from the Comet Line. It covers around 1,000 miles.
Author modification of map by San Jose (public domain)

A Jedburgh training session, 1944: high-level climbing practice.
Public domain

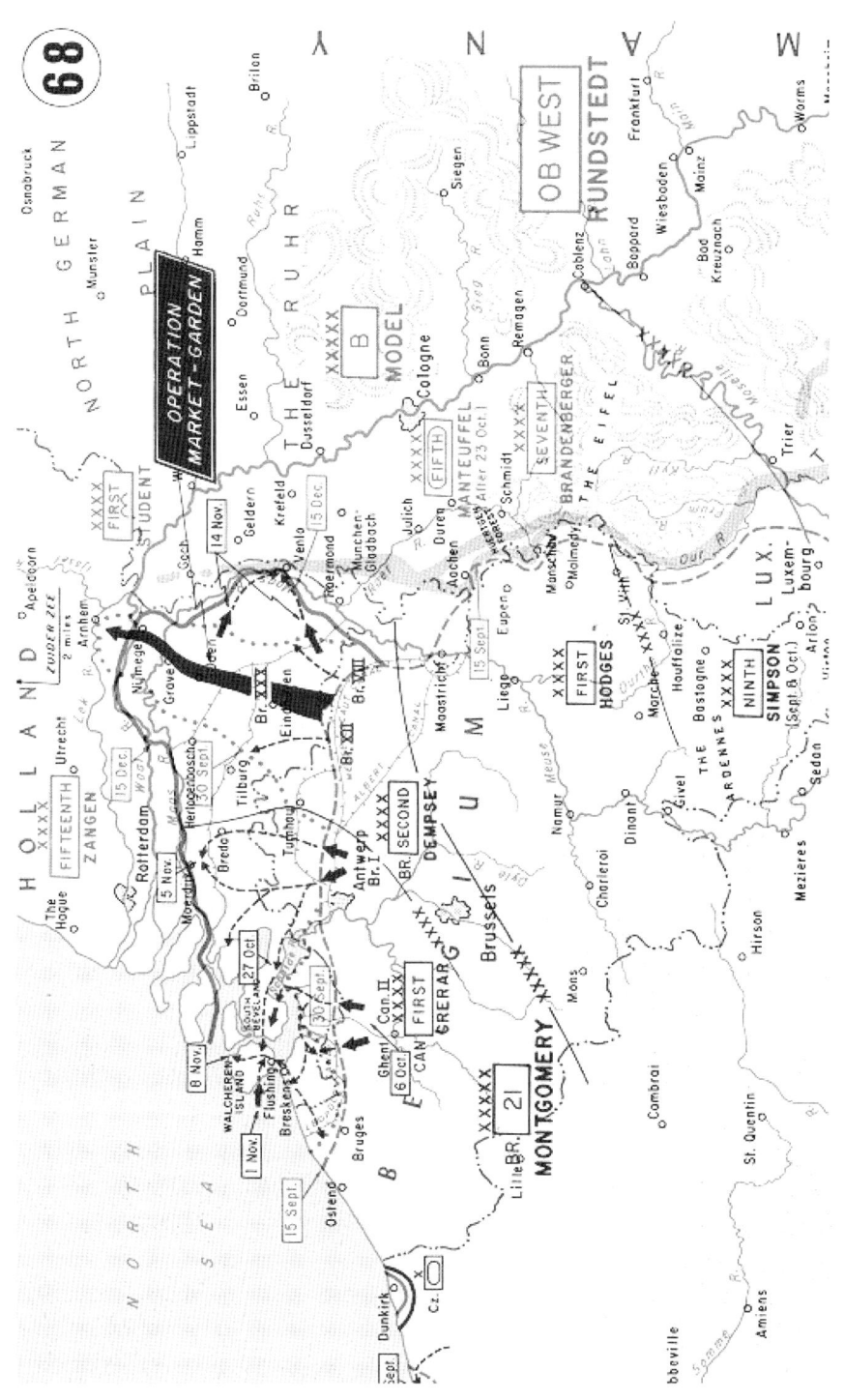

Operation Market Garden, September 1944.
Public domain

Henry and the Groenens in 1944. Left to right: Dr Michel Groenen, Mérèse Groenen, Henry, Solange Groenen, Paule Groenen.

Anita Teuwen and Angelo da Silva Cosme

British troops advance during Operation Veritable, February 1945.

Imperial War Museum – BU1749 (public domain)

The battered town of Nijmegen, September 1944.

Public domain

Map of Palestine in 1947.
United Nations, Map no. 3067, Rev.1 (public domain)

Jebel Rum. Henry became the first non-Bedouin to climb it, in 1947.
WGAS – D/D T5136

Henry Coombe-Tennant in his Welsh Guards uniform.
Coombe-Tennant family

Winifred Coombe Tennant.
Public domain

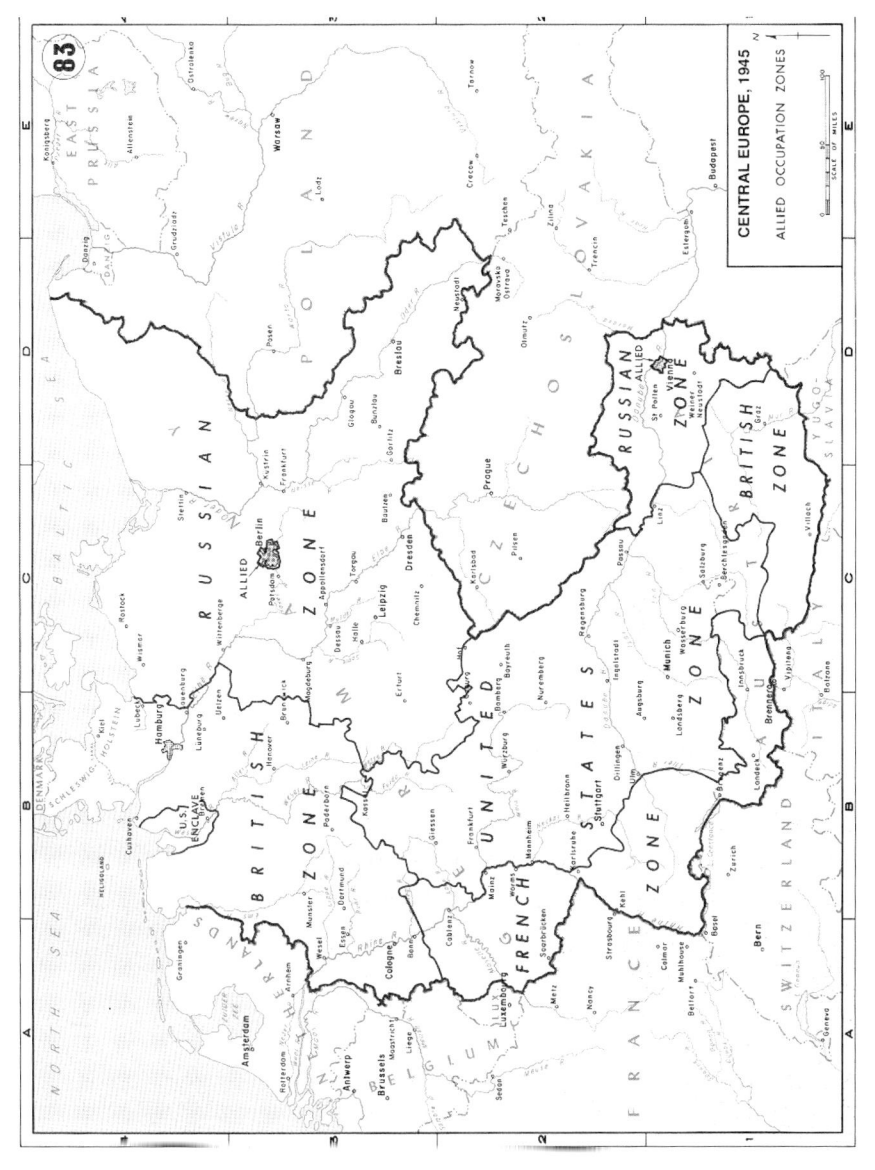

The post-war Allied occupation zones in Germany and Austria.
Public domain

Downside Abbey, Stratton on the Fosse.
Author's own photo

Henry (left) after entering Downside Abbey in 1960. He is pictured with Dom Ralph Russell, the Novice Master.
Downside Abbey archives

Henry Coombe-Tennant in later life – studying a problem on his travel chess set.
Coombe-Tennant family

As part of the preparation for the next stage of their journey, Henry and the others had their photographs taken so that counterfeit identity cards and travel documents could be obtained. The next day, the fake documents arrived and were gleefully received by the men. Each document had the correct stamps and signatures, all painstakingly forged to a high degree of apparent authenticity. They had all been given false names and addresses, with each being described as an artisan and living near to the Belgium-France border. The hope was that if they needed to speak any French on the remainder of the journey, while they would obviously not fool a local, they might pass unnoticed by a German who was largely unfamiliar with the language.

The stay at the Liège safe house was cut short by bad news. A man claiming to be a Belgian airman wishing to reach Great Britain who had previously been helped there had been revealed as a Nazi agent. He had provided his German comrades with information on some parts of the escape line, so the house would have to be quickly abandoned, at least for the time being. Henry, Arkwright and Fuller were to be taken by the two ladies – Jeanne and Mathilde Ritschdorff – to the railway station as a matter of urgency. It was now 10 October 1942, and they took a tram to a station further down the line so that the crowds at the busier main railway station could be avoided. The party boarded the Brussels train and, once again, feigned sleep so as not to be drawn into conversation by other passengers. Fuller could not avoid sitting near a German soldier, though nothing untoward came of the situation, while Arkwright observed two Belgians clearly discussing him, though nothing resulted from that unwelcome attention, either.

The three men and the two lady guides arrived in Brussels in the midst of an air-raid blackout and, though the ladies were initially unsure of the way, a block of flats on the Rue de la Vallée in Ixelles proved to be their destination. Arriving at the apartment, they were greeted by Doctor Antoine Goethals and his wife, who were surprised to see them as they had been unaware that their departure from Liège had been unexpectedly brought forward. The guides soon took their leave, never to be seen by Henry again.

After a night's sleep, the escapees were taken in the early morning light to a Roman Catholic church, where a service was in progress. Eventually they observed a man at a side door who indicated that they should follow him out into the street. He guided them to a residential part of Brussels where they were taken into a house on Rue Vanderhoeven occupied by Elisabeth Liégeois and Elisabeth Feraille-Warnon. After lunch, they were provided with large jugs of water with which to wash and shave before an elderly gentleman and a young girl arrived to assist them on the next leg of their journey. This couple brought with them a number of suitcases which proved to be an Aladdin's Cave, containing suits, greatcoats, shirts, ties, hats, socks and shoes, all of which appeared to be brand new and worth a great deal on the black market. The trio of fugitives were encouraged to pick whatever items took their fancy before each was also handed a pair of blue serge trousers and a matching shirt. The young girl took their identity cards and returned sometime later with newly forged permits that would allow them entry into France on account of having 'urgent business of a private nature' to attend to. In a final flourish, they were each given French francs as spending money. The serious business having been dealt with, Henry was invited to play the piano, which he did with his usual aplomb.

They would no longer need to stumble over poorly marked borders under the cover of darkness. They were now, on the surface at least, *bona fide* travellers with the appropriate documents. That did not mean that all danger had vanished, of course, but they would be able to move more easily in crowded locations with the added security of identity and travel papers that should satisfy any not-too-inquisitive officials that they might encounter along the way. Following the normal pattern of movement, they were escorted to the local railway station in the morning by the two Elisabeths and there were covertly handed over to the care of three gentlemen, having first been told to ignore all other group members during this stage of the journey. These three gentlemen were Belgian cousins George and Edouard d'Oultremont and Jean Greindl, all members of the Comet Escape Line organisation.

Their next destination was to be Lille in France. For security reasons, it was agreed that they would act as if they were all separate individual travellers and, in the event that one of the group should be apprehended by the authorities, the others would simply sit it out and try to avoid also being uncovered as escapees or guides. It was understood by all that there was no place for futile heroics in the hope of freeing an arrested comrade.

On boarding the train, the party sat separately. While Arkwright and Fuller happened to be opposite each other, alongside strangers, Henry was further down the carriage and out of sight of the first two. The three guides took seats elsewhere and kept a close but secretive eye on their charges. As the train approached the French border, nervous tension within the group rose as a German official was seen coming down the carriage, examining the papers of other travellers and asking questions in broken French. Given his aptitude for the language at school, Henry was quite confident in French and Arkwright could get by. However, Fuller could only really parrot what he had learned by rote. Anything beyond that level would see him floundering. The group's hearts sank as the German stopped and started questioning the hapless Fuller in rudimentary French.

Fuller was asked why he needed to visit France and his response was understandably curt and unforthcoming, such was his unfamiliarity with the language. He was unable to elaborate on his business affairs and slumped into a sullen silence, to be told he would be questioned further once the

French frontier was reached. This was an extremely worrying development as it was possible that the suspicions raised by Fuller's unavoidably evasive answers might mean that the papers of other travellers would be subjected to more detailed scrutiny, with unpredictable results. For the moment, however, all involved could only feign an attitude of unconcerned nonchalance and hope for the best. After leaving Fuller to worry about his fate, the German official moved on to question Henry, who had no problem in understanding and answering enquiries in fluent French.

At the French border it was necessary for passengers to alight from the train and pass through a customs barrier, reboarding the train after checks of their paperwork. Henry and the others shuffled nervously up the queue, praying that the worryingly inquisitive German official might have forgotten all about Fuller. Their hopes were soon dashed. Fuller was stopped by his German interrogator and taken away for further questioning. The train would wait until that had been concluded, meaning that, should Fuller's cover be blown, the others might also come under suspicion and be subjected to more rigorous questioning.

Rupert Fuller knew that his inadequacy in French meant that he had no hope of satisfying his questioners in the normal way. As ideas raced through his mind, he quickly settled on a risky strategy that he thought might just enable him to bluff his way out of trouble. If he could not answer the Germans' questions satisfactorily, he would try not to answer them at all. As he recorded later:

> I was then taken into a room and shouted at by a German officer. I had already played 'the idiot boy' and now pretended to be even more stupid. The German gave me a cigarette and questioned me about my passport. I answered in a rambling manner. The Frenchman then asked if I suffered from nerves and if I felt ill, and I pretended to collapse at the table. When I was asked for my address, I did not answer directly, but wandered round the room

looking at the notices and occasionally repeating the address to myself... I was then asked whether I was married and what my wife's name was. When I answered the latter question correctly, I made a profound impression, and apparently the German officer and the French official came to the conclusion that I was feeble minded. They returned my papers and put me on the train.

On the train, meanwhile, Henry and the others had been nervously watching the carriage doors, expecting a squad of rifle-wielding German soldiers to enter and stride purposefully towards them at any moment. Instead they were treated to the astonishing and unexpected sight of Rupert Fuller entering the carriage alone, winding down the window and theatrically waving a handkerchief at someone on the platform as the train drew away from the station. As Fuller later told his comrades, he thought he had got away with it but wanted to be perfectly certain that neither of his interrogators had joined the train by another door, with a view to keeping him under covert surveillance. With the train setting off again, an exhausted Rupert Fuller promptly fell asleep.

They reached Lille without further incident, though the next stage of their travels would involve yet another nerve-wracking trip – this time to Paris. As it happened, although there were numerous German soldiers and officials on the Paris train, the journey proved happily uneventful. After leaving the train, the men were guided to an apartment block in the city where two of the flats were being used by the Comet Line. The three escapees and their three guides were treated to a huge meal, much of which appeared to have originated on the black market. There were a number of people in the flat, including a Belgian man (who had met the party at the railway station in Paris) and his daughter, who was in her mid-twenties. Henry and the others were now at the very centre of the Comet Line organisation. They could have been excused for thinking that the father was the driving force behind the escape line, with his daughter acting as a fetcher and carrier under his direction. Actually the roles were reversed and it was the young lady – Andrée de Jongh – who was the beating heart of the Comet Line, with her father subordinate to her.

Andrée de Jongh had been born in Schaerbeek in Belgium in 1916. Schaerbeek was the town where British nurse Edith Cavell had been executed by the Germans during the Great War for helping British soldiers get out of German-occupied Belgium, and it seems that this story had inspired the young de Jongh. While working as a volunteer nurse with the Red Cross in German-occupied Brussels in 1940, de Jongh became aware of a number of Allied soldiers who were being hidden in safe houses in the city. She decided to follow the example of her heroine and try to assist them in reaching Allied territory, regardless of the risks involved.

With the assistance of her father, Frédéric, she established links with those hiding the Allied soldiers in Brussels and also made contact with sympathetic parties in occupied France, as well as in the part of France controlled by the Vichy Government of Marshal Pétain. The plan was that fugitives would be escorted out of Belgium, through France to the Spanish border – a journey of around 700 miles, much of which would be completed by train. The first attempt failed and de Jongh decided to escort the next escape group herself, while also restricting it to a smaller number of fugitives.

In August 1941, she surprised the British Consul at Bilbao by arriving unannounced in the company of a British soldier and two Belgians, men she had successfully guided through Paris and Bayonne before undertaking a gruelling journey on foot over the Pyrenees and into neutral Spain. Having proven the viability of the escape line, she requested assistance from the British to help facilitate further escapes. Though they were at first suspicious that she might be in the pay of the Germans, she convinced the British of her integrity and was given the support of MI9, which specialised in aiding escape and evasion in occupied countries.

Until now, Henry, Arkwright and Fuller had been travelling by train with a cover story that they needed to visit France on urgent business of a personal nature. Now that they were in Paris, with further travels in France still to come, it made sense for them to be issued with new identity papers that proclaimed that they were French. Once he had a photograph of each man, Frédéric de Jongh forged the papers himself, using a range of apparently official stamps and expertly forging signatures where necessary. With the paperwork attended to, the three escapees, together with Andrée and Frédéric de Jongh, set off for the railway station and yet another tension-filled stage of their odyssey.

At the railway station, Frédéric took his leave of the group, which was then joined by another guide and a surprise addition to the expedition in the form of a Russian airman named Piotr Pinchuko, whose aircraft had been shot down while on a bombing mission against Berlin. He had very little language in common with the others, but proved happy to answer to the nickname of 'Stalin'. This meant that the party now numbered six, just the number required to fill a compartment in the train and minimise the risks posed by unnecessary contact with strangers. The train headed south towards Bordeaux and it was noticeable that every village, bridge or railway station had one or more German sentries in evidence. The train rumbled onwards until it reached the sleepy little town of St Jean de Luz, tantalisingly close to the Spanish border, where they disembarked. The journey from Warburg had so far seen the three escapees travel around 1,000 miles.

A small and discreet welcoming committee met them as they alighted from the train. It consisted of a woman of not quite middle age and a swarthy, powerful-looking man who could have been from the Basque country. Security was paramount, as usual, and the party left the station in small groups, one of which made a slight detour to enjoy a view of the sea. In the distance they could see a range of hills, which one of the guides explained to them was actually in Spain. Freedom and safety were now very close indeed, though reaching them would involve a risk-filled trek of about 20 miles, punctuated by several hard climbs and the crossing of some very rough terrain. Again, the party retired to a safe house and enjoyed lunch. In the evening, they tried on shoes which would cope better with the topography they would encounter while crossing the Pyrenees. The 20-mile march over the mountains was to be undertaken the following evening, wearing the blue serge shirts and trousers – staples for men of the local area – that had been given to them in Brussels.

Andrée de Jongh and her assistant led the men to a farmhouse about three miles from St Jean de Luz, where supper was awaiting their arrival. The man who would guide them over the mountains arrived under cover of darkness. Jean-François Nothomb was a 'grizzled, wiry-looking Basque peasant who looked more like a poacher than anything [that] had been seen for a long time and indeed from a chance remark he made later on it was clear that one part of his annual income was made by taking salmon by illicit means out of the rivers of the Pyrenees.' Also making the crossing as a guide was Albert Johnson, an Englishman who went by the name of 'B'. He had had the misfortune to be in Belgium as a civilian when the Germans invaded and had found himself unable to flee the country. In the end he decided to stay rather than trying to escape, and devote himself to guiding fugitives over the Pyrenees.

It became clear that Jean-François made a living by the keenness of his wits and had at least one more noticeable strength: his body odour was so potent that he left a discernible trail in his wake. While he would not have any time to filch any salmon on their trip over the mountains, he had thoughtfully brought along several cartons of saccharine, which he knew would command a good price in Spain. No commercial opportunity was to be spurned by Jean-François as he combined outwitting the Nazis and pursuing his own business interests.

On the Run

They set off in the dark on the night of 24–25 October 1942. After climbing almost 1,000 feet, they breasted a plateau before clambering down towards a river that marked the boundary between France and Spain. Their gasping breaths showed up in the frosty air as they slithered and stumbled over loose stones, trying to minimise any noise. Several flocks of mountain sheep were surprised and scattered before the party finally reached the banks of the river. Jean-François then paused and listened carefully for any sound of the border guards but, when nothing was heard, he promptly plunged into the shallow but strongly flowing river, with the others following in single file in his wake. Henry and Rupert Fuller had some difficulty in maintaining their balance in the swirling water, not making best use of the stout sticks they carried with them, but all soon reached the other bank safely.

Once they were all on dry land, there was no time for rest and the group followed Jean-François over a railway line and up a sloping bank towards a road. They were now well inside Spain and moving away from the river that marked the border. Though German border guards were no longer a cause for concern, there was still a risk that they might meet unsympathetic Spanish sentries. If arrested, there was little doubt that the men would eventually be repatriated to Britain from neutral (though Axis-leaning) Spain, but a spell in a Spanish prison after the trials and hardships endured in a German prisoner-of-war camp and the subsequent two-month journey across Europe was not an attractive prospect.

The party continued the journey overland, passing the town of Hendaye and arriving at a small village near San Sebastián, and a house where they received a friendly welcome. The by then tattered and torn blue serge clothing was discarded and the smart suits that had been given to them in Brussels were donned. Once again, the hospitality of their helpers was fulsome and a hearty breakfast – including wine – was consumed before a car arrived and the driver conveyed Henry, Arkwright, Fuller

137

and 'Stalin' to his home in San Sebastian. During the next couple of days, a visitor from the British Consulate in Bilboa arrived and told the group that arrangements were being made for their conveyance in a diplomatic car to the British Embassy in Madrid, a ploy that would give them a degree of diplomatic immunity from inquisitive Spanish officials. They were subsequently driven a short distance out of town before being handed over to British officials who had arrived in a Sunbeam Talbot motor car, on the bonnet of which proudly stood a small Union Jack.

They reached the British Embassy in Madrid after a journey of some 300 miles, to discover that they were not the only fugitives to find refuge there. In fact, there were around 20 others utilising it as a temporary safe haven, including several Frenchmen who had arrived from unoccupied France, two Canadian pilots who had been shot down over France, a French-Canadian who was so keen to have a crack at the Germans that he had deserted from the French Foreign Legion and intended to enlist in the Allied forces, a number of seamen whose ships had fallen prey to German U-boats and several Poles who had somehow turned up in Madrid after all sorts of adventures. All were confined to the safety of the Embassy and Henry in particular enjoyed several hours each day engrossed in a poker school, though the level of his success or failure was not recorded.

After almost a week, the foursome (and a number of others) were at last provided with false travel documents declaring them British subjects who had been properly authorised to leave Madrid by train for Gibraltar. After arriving at the La Linea railway station, they were briskly greeted by two members of the British garrison of Gibraltar before being bundled into a bus which took them to a Spanish police station. Each man provided the false information about their supposed identities before reboarding the bus and having the pleasure of seeing the barrier between Spain and Gibraltar being slowly lifted to allow their entry to 'The Rock'. They were back on British territory at last. And, after all they had been through since their escape from Warburg, they were finally free and out of immediate danger.

To put this achievement in context, of the 30 men who succeeded in escaping over Oflag VI-B's perimeter fences in the 'Warburg Wire Job' on 30 August 1942, Henry, Fuller and Arkwright were the only three to make it back to British soil. All of the others were recaptured.

On 7 November 1942, Henry's mother wrote in her notebook:

> At 9.40 was called to the telephone – it was HENRY speaking from LONDON. The child of so many prayers.

Winifred Coombe Tennant's lengthy period of intense worry over the fate of her son was, for now, at an end. Though, as it transpired, Henry's war was far from over.

CHAPTER TEN

Special Forces

SAFELY BACK IN Great Britain, Henry soon rejoined his regiment and, early in 1943, spent ten days training with it under active service conditions. During that time, the Welsh Guards travelled around the countryside, with Henry and his comrades suffering the sort of hardships that they could expect to experience in the field – although, happily, no-one was firing live bullets at them. Henry found himself sleeping in barns or sheds and, occasionally, in wet and muddy ditches – all part of the Army's hardening-up process for its soldiers, many of whom had not yet taken part in combat. He took his dog, Queenie, along with him and she proved to be a very useful canine hot water bottle, sleeping on her master's feet or chest in harsh weather conditions. He also spent six days on attachment to the American 175th Infantry Regiment, a duty that he had anticipated with some trepidation, not being sure what to expect from a raw American unit that had only arrived in Britain at the end of 1942. His concerns proved unfounded, as his mother later recorded:

> He had enjoyed it thoroughly and said he had come away 100% pro American – He was struck by their keenness – their immense kindness – and their modesty. They said to him that they knew that the British had had much experience and taken hard knocks – that they were green and would have to take hard knocks too before they became seasoned troops.

Special Forces

In early March 1943, Henry temporarily left the Welsh Guards' training programme to travel to London to receive the Military Cross awarded to him for his escape exploits. He met his mother and Alexander at a London club for dinner, though the occasion was cut short due to the fact that he had been up most of the previous night on a training exercise. The morning of 9 March 1943 dawned with bright sunshine. Henry collected his mother and brother and the trio walked through Green Park on their way to Buckingham Palace. Winifred recalled him 'looking like a giant', wearing his Army overcoat against the early-spring chill, as well as a blue cap adorned with a leek, the emblem of the Welsh Guards. Outside the palace they were joined by Henry's fellow escapees, Albert Arkwright and Rupert Fuller, who were also to be awarded Military Crosses.

On entering the palace, Henry was led off and his mother and brother took their seats close to the dais on which His Majesty the King was to stand as he presented the various decorations. Winifred recorded her thoughts as she patiently awaited the arrival of the King with her usual directness:

> After a wait, during which the most trivial trumpery music was played by a very indifferent band – reminiscent of the worst sort of Cinema stuff – an official came out from the room at the back of the dais and surveyed the scene – told us to stand when the King entered, to resume our seats when he desired us so to do, and not to talk out loud during the ceremony – and that in the event of an air-raid we should be taken to a place of safety.
>
> Presently the doors at the back of the dais opened and the King came in to the strains of God Save the King – on his left was an equerry who handed him the decorations – to the left again was Lord Clarendon, the Lord Chamberlain, looking like an old crab.

A procession of recipients passed by Winifred on their way to proudly receive an award before Henry came into view, close to the back of the line and preceded by Arkwright and Fuller. The King's attention was drawn to the fact that Henry had escaped from a prisoner-of-war camp and he posed several questions regarding the escape after first pinning the award to his chest. After several minutes of conversation, with Henry standing rigidly to attention, the King shook his hand as they parted and the next award recipient took his place at the dais. It was a very proud moment for both mother and son and the day was rounded off with lunch at the Guards' Club, before Henry departed to dash back to his battalion in a military vehicle.

By 1944 it was becoming clear that the defeat of Germany by the Allied powers was only a matter of time. Hitler's decision to attack Russia in the summer of 1941 had proved to be a major miscalculation as the Soviet forces gradually recovered from their catastrophic losses of the first six months of the campaign. The crushing German defeat at Stalingrad in the winter of 1942–43 meant that Germany no longer had the strength to win its war in the east; the subsequent failure of its major offensive at Kursk in the summer of 1943 meant that it would most definitely lose it. Hitler's decision to declare war on the United States of America in December 1941, in support of his ally, Japan, had also tilted the ultimate balance of power very much in favour of the Allies.

As the summer of 1944 approached, German forces in Russia waited nervously for the beginning of the long-anticipated Russian offensive. A little earlier, the Allied powers in the West had entrusted the task of invading German-occupied France to Major General Dwight D Eisenhower, the American officer who had already planned and commanded the successful Allied invasions of French North Africa and Sicily. Eisenhower knew that a seaborne invasion in northern France would be an enterprise of enormous danger and difficulty for the men under his command. He would, of course, have a vast array of forces to deploy in the attack, including American, British, Canadian and French units, amongst others. The Allied Supreme Commander knew that he would need to utilise every possible resource if the invasion was to succeed. As well as the conventional forces under his command, he gave thought to how best to marshal other, less conventional forces in aid of the common cause.

By the spring of 1944, it was estimated that the French Resistance could call upon over 100,000 combatants, a potential force that – if organised and commanded effectively – could wreak mayhem behind the German lines. Though General de Gaulle, the French leader in London, saw himself almost as the living embodiment of a free France, the American President Franklin D Roosevelt was not quite so convinced that the confident – but unelected – Frenchman had the full support of his countrymen.

His doubts led him to defer recognition of de Gaulle as *de facto* French leader until the invasion was imminent, a delay that did little to help the planning of how best to use Resistance fighters once the landings had started. Roosevelt was primarily concerned with defeating the German Armies in the field, while de Gaulle also had one eye firmly fixed on future political control of France – something he saw himself playing a very prominent role in, even if he had not yet faced an election. The French Resistance consisted of several quite separate factions and it was the chance to bring together all of those components under the authority of de Gaulle that eventually left Roosevelt little option but to reluctantly accept him as French leader and bring him and his senior officers into the upper reaches of the Allied high command.

With that issue settled, Eisenhower considered how best the Resistance forces could be controlled and directed so as to provide the right sort of action against the enemy in the right place and at the right time. He felt there needed to be experienced men with the Resistance fighters to coordinate their efforts. The matter had already been discussed in other quarters, such as in 1942 when a British Brigadier, Colin Gubbins, had outlined the possible role of the Special Operations Executive in operations in north-west Europe.

The Special Operations Executive (SOE) had been formed in July 1940 at the request of British Prime Minister Winston Churchill, who had sought the creation of a unit that could fight behind enemy lines and thus take the war to Germany in the various countries that had already fallen under its control. Churchill, a man who was never short of a quotable phrase, had famously told Hugh Dalton, the newly appointed political head of the organisation, 'And now go and set Europe ablaze.' After the previous incumbent had been dismissed over a political squabble, Colin Gubbins was appointed to the role of military head of the SOE and his task was to coordinate the use of sabotage and subversion activities against the enemy on foreign soil. He was also directed to establish training centres for prospective agents and to develop efficient operating procedures that met with the approval of the naval and air force commanders on whom his agents would usually depend for deployment and supply. A close working relationship would need to be established with the higher echelons of the Allied command structure so that his plans and operations could neatly dovetail into high-level offensive planning.

Looking ahead to the expected Allied invasion of Nazi-held northern France, it was agreed by Gubbins and the Chiefs of Staff that the role of SOE during the initial assault would be: 'by the organisation and arming of patriot forces, [to] take action generally against the enemy's rail and signal communications, air personnel, etc.', while after the landings it would: 'provide guides for British troops... enrol personnel for use as guards of vital points and labour parties and will also organise raiding parties capable of penetrating behind the German lines.' In fact, SOE was already active in helping organise the various resistance groups in France, Belgium and Holland, though the paper that Gubbins presented for discussion also contained the kernel of an idea that evolved into what became known as 'Operation Jedburgh', a mission that Henry Coombe-Tennant would eventually participate in during 1944. Gubbins' paper envisaged the dropping of small teams of men who would make contact with friendly organisations on the ground and facilitate the supply of any required arms and equipment.

The idea involved each three-man team normally including a 'guide' (an officer from the country that the team was deployed into), a 'British officer' (who could actually be British or American), and the vital wireless operator (who would be an appropriately trained non-commissioned officer). The plan was to parachute the first men into enemy territory as part of Operation Jedburgh at the time of the invasion of France, with further teams being dropped as the Allied advance developed.

The men in the embryonic teams began to be referred to as 'Jedburghs' or 'Jeds', and it is hard to imagine a role for which Henry Coombe-Tennant was better suited at the time than Jedburgh team leader. He was, after all, an experienced soldier who had seen action in both Holland and France, even if the results had been less than ideal. He had also proved that he had the requisite strength and mental resilience by coping with over two years of frustrating captivity in a prisoner-of-war camp. His positive attitude had not been blunted by captivity and he had jumped at the chance of escaping from the camp, despite the dangers involved. With Arkwright and Fuller, he had avoided recapture while on the run in Germany and occupied Holland, Belgium and France. To cap it all, he was a fluent French speaker, an ideal quality for a man who would be required to impress on strong-willed and potentially volatile French Resistance fighters the need to accept orders and advice from Jedburgh team members, who were strangers to them. It is likely that by late 1943 Henry was already working for SOE at its headquarters in Baker Street, London, a desk-based role that he soon abandoned in order to become a Jedburgh agent.

The Jedburgh concept was tested in March 1943, when 11 Jedburgh teams were included in an exercise codenamed 'Spartan', also involving regular Army units. Every Jedburgh team managed to link up with the parties in the field acting as

Resistance groups for the purposes of the exercise. A number of tasks were attempted, such as carrying out or preventing the demolition of bridges, attacking 'enemy' headquarters, cutting lines of communication and performing general guerrilla warfare in the field. A number of important lessons were learned from the Spartan exercise. For example, it did indeed become obvious that one of the officers in the three-man team needed to be from the country in which the team was to operate. This would require the recruitment of suitable French, Belgian or Dutch personnel. The aim was, as well as bringing local knowledge to the team, to ease relations with newly encountered Resistance groups in the field.

While operating behind enemy lines, the Jedburgh teams would usually wear military uniform. This would make them easy for the enemy to identify if discovered, but it was felt that the sight of a friendly soldier in uniform was likely to have a galvanising effect on the morale of Resistance groups, who would see that they were no longer alone. Clearly, the tasks allotted to a Jedburgh team needed to be within its capabilities. Given the lead-in time required to select a three-man team, organise air transport and the requisite supplies of equipment, arms and ammunition, it was impractical to expect such teams to be dropped in without at least 72 hours' notice.

The Jedburgh team's activity was to revolve around guerrilla operations away from the main fighting rather than urgent tactical missions close to the front line. In the field, a wireless transmitter would be essential for requesting supply drops to Resistance groups, while the Jeds would also be able to show Resistance fighters how specialised arms and equipment worked and how to use them effectively. Where a local Resistance group lacked effective leadership, a Jedburgh team was to step in and provide it. Jedburghs would act as a post-D-Day reserve, available to be called in by regular Army commanders for sabotage missions behind enemy lines wherever the need arose.

Special Forces

With the Jedburgh team concept looking so promising, consideration moved on to the composition and training of the teams. It was agreed that 300 men (mainly British, American, French, Dutch and Belgians) would be recruited and trained, and Milton Hall, Peterborough – the grand home of the Fitzwilliam family – was requisitioned for the training.

To be selected as a Jedburgh officer, as Henry Coombe-Tennant eventually was, you needed to be a certain type of man. Typically, he would be:

> An Officer able to adjust himself to conditions of clandestine warfare for a period, if necessary, and acquainted with the potentialities of the clandestine Resistance forces, but also an Officer accustomed to commanding men in action, of some administrative ability, and able to organise and lead, if necessary, a military operation involving a small number of men and designed to attack a specific objective or harass enemy troop movements within a specified area.

He would need a good knowledge of the Resistance forces in the target country and how they could best be deployed against the enemy. He would be well-grounded in military training and tactics and the deployment of groups of men up to the size of a company, which was true of Henry Coombe-Tennant as he had already gained experience in commanding men in the Welsh Guards. A knowledge of military weapons of several types was a clear necessity, as well as some familiarity with explosives and their use in demolitions. How to work a wireless set and the use of secret code and cyphers was required, as was a working knowledge of French. The man would also have to have a high level of physical fitness, be able to withstand possibly extreme weather conditions and be tough enough to survive in harsh terrain in enemy-occupied areas – another sphere that Henry had already proved himself in, after his escape from Warburg.

The training of Jedburgh recruits in Great Britain began in earnest in January 1944 at three training schools, each school being responsible for the tuition of about 60 officers, while the wireless operators were trained elsewhere. The initial stage of training lasted for six to eight weeks and, during this time, the move was made to Milton Hall, where all the Operation Jedburgh recruits were gathered by the second week of February 1944.

Almost every recruit would need to be parachuted into his target country, so expertise in deployment by parachute in all weather conditions was essential. The Jedburgh's life would, after all, depend on a successful drop. All candidates therefore went through training at Dunham House near Altrincham, close to RAF Ringway, where each man undertook a number of jumps from both high-level training apparatus on the ground and from aircraft. This training took place early in the programme since, if a man proved incapable of parachuting safely or suffered a serious injury during drop training, he could realistically proceed no further on the course.

One of the key instructors at Ringway was John Kilkenny, a keen cricketer. He was also an athletics coach, swimming instructor, life-saver, first-aider and qualified football referee. At the outbreak of war, Kilkenny had volunteered for service with the Royal Air Force but had soon migrated to parachute work. He eventually made over 100 jumps while also training a great many SOE agents to successfully deploy a parachute. The risks can be seen in the fact that even the expert Kilkenny shattered an ankle during one jump, a fact that he shrugged off as just being a part of the job. He continued in his role despite the injury never properly healing.

Once on the ground following a drop, a Jedburgh agent needed to quickly rejoin his comrades and make sure that his first encounter was with a friendly Resistance (known as the 'Maquis' in the case of France) reception committee, rather than a squad of heavily armed Germans who had located the drop-zone. In the latter event, he would have several weapons to hand, including a commando knife for use in very close combat, as well as an American-made rifle which had a folding stock so as to minimise the space required for storage or concealment. An American Colt .45 revolver was also carried – a weapon that Jedburgh agent Stanley Cannicott thought could probably stop an elephant. Every man was well versed in the use of the various weapons and would be able to demonstrate to Maquis units how to use them effectively.

One of the main ways in which a Jedburgh team could make itself a nuisance to the enemy was with explosives. These could be used against bridges, roads and railway lines frequented by the enemy, in an effort to prevent or delay the movement and deployment of their forces. Explosive or incendiary charges could also be used to attack physical infrastructure such as electricity generators or other heavy equipment, hampering the enemy war effort.

Close-combat training was based on the methods advocated by William Fairbairn, a former soldier who had joined the Shanghai Police in 1907 and, during a 30-year-career, had been involved in over 600 recorded fights with criminal gang members there. He had also created, organised and trained a special anti-riot squad in crime-ridden Shanghai. Fairbairn had studied several Oriental martial arts and had distilled the techniques into a series of blows, throws and holds that he termed 'gutter fighting'. He was brought back to Britain by the SOE in 1940, to act as an instructor in fighting techniques for commando-type soldiers. He cautioned against any misplaced 'gentlemanly principles' when fighting the enemy:

> In war, your attack can have only two possible objects: either to kill your opponent or to capture him alive. You must realize that he will be fighting for his life or to prevent capture, and that it will be a very difficult matter for you to apply a 'hold', etc., without first having made him receptive by striking him… with your hand, foot, or knee, etc., thus disabling him or rendering him semi-conscious, after which you will have no difficulty in disposing of him by one of the methods shown.

The 'methods shown' included chin jabs, the bronco kick, use of the knee, the Japanese strangle, the hip throw and the back break. Fairbairn, assisted by his equally deadly associate, Eric A Sykes (not the noted comedian!), often ended demonstrations of painful blows and unbreakable holds with the practical advice, 'and then kick him in the testicles!'

Instruction was given in map reading, though this was often merely a refresher course as – like Henry – most Jedburgh officer recruits were already proficient in the subject. The application of tactics in small-scale operations was also discussed, such as when an enemy headquarters was to be raided or a surprise attack launched on an enemy position. Since it was likely that much of a Jedburgh's time would be spent in the field, advice on how best to survive in the wild was also proffered. This included information on the best places to hide, how to use the tracks of animals to find a village or water source, how to detect the unseen presence of other humans by observing the behaviour of animals such as cows or sheep, and the use of woods, disused quarries or old lime kilns as temporary living places. It was stressed that food could be obtained in the wild by setting snares to trap birds or rabbits, while fish could often be caught with a simple hook and line and a variety of birds' eggs could be collected at particular times from rushes, woods and hedgerows. These items could usually be cooked in simple field ovens based on a large metal tin, or on a basic campfire, over which a rudimentary spit could be positioned.

By the end of February 1944, more advanced training commenced and the volunteers began to work in teams of three. It had been decided that teams should be allowed to develop naturally and this typically involved two officers agreeing to team up, having discovered that they got on and that their differing character traits complemented each other. This proved to be a straightforward task for Henry as he had been surprised to meet at Milton Hall Edouard d'Oultremont, one of the Belgian Comet Line members who had helped

Special Forces

guide him through France and on to neutral Spain. Edouard had been in the railway carriage when Rupert Fuller had been closely examined by the suspicious Nazi official. Shortly after Henry's escape from occupied Europe, the Comet Line had been betrayed and over 100 of its members were subsequently arrested. Edouard had managed to escape to Britain in December 1942 and it was there that he had volunteered for service with the Jedburghs. The third member of Henry's team was Sergeant Frank Harrison, the radio operator. The name allocated to the team was to be 'Andrew'. Henry would be the commanding officer of the team and he was given the codename 'Rupel'.

The teams' advanced training included the use of enemy arms and ammunition – since many Maquis units were partly armed with captured weapons – and personal anti-tank weapons such as the British PIAT (Projector, Infantry, Anti-Tank) and the American bazooka. Once a Jedburgh team had been safely parachuted into enemy territory, one of its first objectives would be to determine just what sort of arms and other supplies were needed to make the local Maquis group an effective guerrilla force. They would then be supplied by parachute drops.

To help build cohesion within the newly formed Jedburgh three-man teams, a number of exercises were staged in the first half of 1944, at Peterborough, Uppingham in north west Leicestershire and Alconbury Airfield, near Huntingdon in Cambridgeshire. At Alconbury, experience was gained in reception committee work at drop-zones, while at the other places simulations of cooperating with resistance groups and planning and carrying out guerrilla operations were undertaken. The use of reconnaissance techniques to establish an alternative safe camp for the Resistance group in the midst of enemy activity was also studied, as were the difficulties inherent in simultaneously controlling and communicating with several separate resistance groups.

A report said that the exercises gave the Jedburgh officers:

...the opportunity of handling a number of men, from a small group to a Company, during operations, such as *coups de main* attacks, ambushes and reception committees. The Schemes and exercises usually lasted from one week to ten days and everything was done to simulate conditions in the field as realistically as possible, by using the Home Guard as the 'enemy' and making the Jedburghs live on such resources as they had with them. Also, owing to distances involved, a great many forced marches by day and night were included, such as might result from counter-measures by German troops.

At the end of the training period, 300 suitably toughened Jedburgh agents were ready for deployment. In the first four days following the D-Day invasion of Normandy on 6 June 1944, an initial wave of seven Jedburgh teams was despatched to France. Henry's Team Andrew was not a part of this first echelon and it would be August 1944 before Henry and his two comrades were deployed. They were put on alert on 8 August and travelled on 10 August to a specially appointed briefing house at Devonshire Close in London. It was not ideal, as the number of teams present in the house at any one time was greater than the space available to quietly study maps and receive verbal updates. It is not clear just how badly this affected Henry and his team members, but whatever the administrative shortcomings at the briefing house, they were not sufficiently grave to prevent Jedburgh Team Andrew being tasked with a 15 August 1944 deployment into the French Ardennes. The training and waiting were finally over: after his unhappy experiences at The Hook of Holland and Boulogne with his Welsh Guards battalion, Henry was about to face the enemy once again.

CHAPTER ELEVEN

Behind Enemy Lines

Major Henry Coombe-Tennant and his Jedburgh Team Andrew comrades, Belgian Lieutenant Edouard d'Oultremont and British Sergeant Frank Harrison, were to be parachuted into the French Ardennes near to the Belgian border on the night of 15–16 August 1944. The team's task was to contact the head of an inter-Allied military mission that had earlier been dropped into enemy-held territory in that region. The inter-Allied mission was codenamed *'Citronelle'* ('lemongrass') and its commanding officer was Colonel Jacques Pâris de Bollardière, a French career soldier.

De Bollardière had served in a French infantry regiment before joining the French Foreign Legion in 1935, subsequently completing tours of duty in Algeria and Morocco. Following the outbreak of the Second World War, de Bollardière had returned to France and had seen action as a company commander in Narvik during the ill-fated Allied military expedition to Norway. He had been stationed at Brest during the Battle of France in May and June 1940 and, on seeing the eventual hopelessness of the French military situation, had boarded a ship and made his way to Britain, where he was one of the very first Frenchmen to respond to General de Gaulle's rallying call to his fellow countrymen. He had then served with the French forces commanded from London and seen action in April 1941 in East Africa, where he received a gallantry award for his part in the capture of an Italian-held fort. By September 1941 he was in North Africa, and he was wounded during the battle of El Alamein in October 1942.

After recovering from his wounds, de Bollardière had volunteered for Special Forces training with a view to being parachuted into occupied France, which was achieved in April 1944 when he was dropped in the Ardennes region. As the head of the *Citronelle* operation, he was given the codename of *'Prisme'* ('prism') and his job was to help create a Maquis force in the region, drawn from patriotic French men and women. De Bollardière had largely achieved his aim by June, by which time he had around 200 armed Maquis under his command. His work inevitably attracted the attention of the German Army and, on 12 June, his forest camp was attacked by enemy forces and just over 100 of the group were killed or captured.

Saddened but undaunted, de Bollardière began to rebuild his force of enthusiastic amateurs. In the difficult circumstances in which he found himself, Allied leaders in London thought that some additional professional assistance would be useful, which is where Henry Coombe-Tennant and his Jedburgh Team Andrew comrades came in. Henry's orders were to make contact with de Bollardière and to offer assistance and training that would make the *Citronelle* group more effective. Henry's team member, Sergeant Harrison, was a wireless transmitter expert and his expertise would open up another channel of communication with London for the *Citronelle* group. Progress could then be reported upon, orders received and Jedburgh Team Andrew could help decide what weapons and equipment should be requested from London via airdrops to supply the Maquis in the Ardennes.

Before leaving for France, Henry and his two Jedburgh comrades were given a briefing in London by a representative of the French Forces of the Interior (FFI) command, a body that sought to coordinate the actions of the various Resistance forces that had sprung up in France. As Henry and his team would be jumping into the unknown, given that circumstances on the ground could change in the time it took for a truckload of German infantry to reach a newly detected landing site, he was keen to know what awaited him as regards friendly forces, in the event of any difficulty. The answer from his Special Forces superiors seemed to him to be frustratingly complacent. He was told that the team would be met by a friendly reception committee on the drop-zone. While that sounded fine, Henry wanted to know what would happen in an emergency. What if, perhaps, the reception committee's arrival was disrupted by enemy activity? Or bad weather resulted in the drop-zone being missed, with the team landing in the wrong location? He enquired about the existence of a safe house and a password that could be used in such circumstances, to be informed that neither existed – there would simply be a reception committee. All would be fine, he was told. Henry remained unconvinced by the arrangements but had no other option than to simply carry on and hope for the best.

On 15 August 1944, Henry and his comrades made their final preparations for their flight into occupied France. Assisted by a despatcher, they received their personal weapons, each man checking his rifle carefully and making sure that the ammunition magazines were loaded correctly and there was no risk of them jamming in the presence of the enemy. They were given a compass, a map, a vial of morphine, a field bandage, first aid dressings and a pair of binoculars. Water bottles and field ration packs were also handed over, as was a sum of money that included American dollars and forged French francs. Cash was always useful in the field as it allowed an agent to buy items locally, as well to offer bribes in suitable circumstances.

Among the final items were a parachute smock and a helmet – the helmet being vital as hurried parachute landings, especially at night, were fraught with difficulty and the risk of injury – or even death – was high. One American Jedburgh had gone through this process in other postings and was surprised to find that he was not required to sign for the equipment. He slowly realised the stark reality of his situation was that the despatcher (and the Special Forces Headquarters staff) didn't really expect to ever see the equipment – or the Operation Jedburgh agent – again, such was the danger attached to a typical mission. The final item of 'equipment' that the despatcher handed over was the most difficult to explain to a keyed-up Jedburgh agent. Henry and his teammates would have already been issued with amphetamines that would enable them to remain awake for up to 72 hours in a crisis. They were now each handed an ampoule of potassium cyanide. In the event of capture, faced with the prospect of being tortured by the enemy in the pursuit of information, this ampoule could be bitten into, resulting in a very quick death.

Jedburgh Team Andrew, led by Henry, would not be jumping alone. Also on the aeroplane would be two French officers going by the codenames of 'Jean' and 'Robert' – codenames being used so that in the event of capture, their family members in France would not be at risk of German reprisals. Their role was to take up command positions under de Bollardière in his Maquis group. Additionally, a party of nine Belgian Special Air Service (SAS) soldiers was to be dropped into the Ardennes, with the mission of contacting the Belgian Resistance just across the border. Henry and his team were specifically forbidden to meddle in the affairs of the Belgian Resistance – the *Citronelle* group in France was to be their only focus. The Belgian SAS contingent were to be dropped from the aircraft first, followed by Henry and his Jedburgh team, the two French officers and the equipment for all parties.

At 10 p.m. Henry's flight into unknown territory began. He and his comrades were flown out in a Stirling aircraft of 620 Squadron, from a Royal Air Force base at Tempsford, near Sandy in Bedfordshire. A great deal of enemy anti-aircraft fire was encountered on the journey, though no damage was sustained to the aeroplane. It was a rough ride due to high winds and everyone on the aircraft suffered from airsickness before they reached the drop-zone at around 1 a.m. After the aeroplane had circled the target several times, the Belgian SAS team leapt out into the darkness. Henry and his team, plus the two French officers, then approached the 'Joe Hole' – the exit hatch from the aircraft – and waited there for fully 20 minutes while the pilot tried to manoeuvre into the correct position for another drop.

Finally, a sequence of lights in the aircraft bay indicated that the moment to leave the plane had at last arrived and Henry dropped through the exit hatch. At the time of his jump, he had seen no obvious sign of any lights on the ground indicating the position of the expected reception committee. His parachute soon opened and as he fell, he thought he might have glimpsed bonfires that possibly indicated the welcome presence of friendly forces.

The lights soon vanished from view, however, and Henry found he was uncomfortably close to the tops of some trees, though they soon dropped out of his sight and he realised he was descending from one side of a sloping, tree-clad valley to the other. He drifted into the trees and inevitably his parachute snagged on some branches, though his landing was quite soft in the difficult circumstances. He found himself alone in the darkness and surrounded by what seemed to be almost total silence, except for the sound of the breeze passing through the trees. The silence was broken by a softly whistled letter 'V' in Morse code. Henry answered in the same manner, assuming the whistler to be a member of the reception committee. He was disappointed to find that it was only his comrade Edouard d'Oultremont. The duo managed to find the French officers a short distance away, though of Sergeant Harrison and the reception committee there was no sign. After a quick discussion, it was decided that to split up and look for Harrison in the darkness and unfamiliar terrain would risk the group members losing contact with each other. As it was now around

2.30 a.m., they bedded down for what was left of the night, leaving one man on sentry duty.

An uncomfortable night did not improve with heavy rain at dawn, though they were then able to see that they had landed halfway up the side of a heavily wooded valley. They cut down the remains of their parachutes from the trees prior to burying them, so as not to alert any German patrols to their arrival. Though the terrain was dotted with paths, it proved impossible to match their location to the features shown on the maps they had of the drop area. They were lost in hostile territory and only had with them their personal weapons and emergency ration packs that would sustain them for just 24 hours. After further discussion, Henry – as the senior officer in command – decided that the best option was to strike out and try and find a farm, in the hope that the occupants would be friendly.

Sometime after setting off, they came across some of the parachutes that had carried down vital panniers of equipment and decided that, rather than trying to hide them in daylight, it would be safer to return after dusk. They could then also search for other panniers that were still missing, having probably become detached from their parachutes after hitting the treeline. After walking for two hours or so they had found no obvious signs of any farms and therefore retraced their steps. As they rested for a moment, they became aware of tapping noises in the distance and Jean went off to cautiously find out what the source of the noise was. He came back with the very welcome news that he had found two local lads trying to open a pannier of equipment and that they seemed to be friendly. They offered to guide Henry's party to their parents' farm. The group took some time recovering and burying parachutes and located several panniers of equipment, though of the vital wireless transmitter, and its operator, there was still no trace.

They reached the farm at about 10 p.m. and its occupants provided a warm welcome for their unexpected guests. Even better was the discovery that Sergeant Harrison had found the farm some time earlier, though the whereabouts of his radio set remained unknown. The farmer and his wife provided a supper of omelettes, bread and butter and warm milk before it was agreed that to minimise any risk to them, the men would spend the night in the woods. The farmer told Henry that he would be able to advise the local Maquis Colonel of the team's arrival. Henry was convinced that 'the Colonel' must be none other than Jacques de Bollardière, the man they wanted to find. The following night a member of the Maquis arrived and confirmed that he had indeed been sent by de Bollardière to guide the party to the Maquis camp. The bad news was that the men had landed some 10 miles from the planned drop-zone and an even more disheartening 20 miles from the camp. There was no option but to march the 20 miles under cover of darkness. Shouldering their heavy loads of equipment and other items, they set off on a gruelling trek, stopping after just over two hours for food at a farm that Henry described as being optimistically referred to by the guide as "Halfway House". After a very trying and tiring journey, the challenge barked out by a Bren gun-wielding Maquis sentry indicated their arrival at Colonel de Bollardière's camp.

The camp had been established in a clearing in the almost continuous forest that cloaked the area and was one of several such camps dotted around a circle about 20 miles in diameter. The aim of having several camps was to enable the Maquis force to rotate its presence and present the Germans with a harder-to-hit moving target for their anti-guerrilla operations. Colonel de Bollardière now commanded around 120 men, split into three platoons, plus a company headquarters. Bren guns were in evidence, as were Sten guns, carbines and pistols. The Maquis group contained several French officers, most of whom had either been regular soldiers or had been trained in Britain before being parachuted into France to assist Colonel de Bollardière. The men they commanded were a mix of ages and trades, though the majority were young men of around 20 years old. Apart from the officers, most of whom wore battledress or even pre-war French Army uniforms, the clothing worn by the Maquis was at best rudimentary: 'the majority of the youngsters had nothing but a pair of civilian shorts or trousers, a pork pie hat (very popular), and a ragged coat to keep the rain out. Boots were often in bad repair. Some comforts had been received – pullovers, scarves, leather jerkins. Every man had a weapon and something to put in it, and morale seemed to be good.' Food seemed to be plentiful and local doctors and priests were always ready to attend at the camp when required.

Since forming the group in April 1944, Colonel de Bollardière had followed the preferred tactics of his London-based commanders in avoiding direct conflict with German forces in the Ardennes area if at all possible. London wanted groups such as *Citronelle* to 'stand ready' for the time being and only to act on receipt of direct orders, which would only be issued when the time was right to prevent or delay the deployment of German units against the post-D-Day Allied invading forces. Despite this instruction, it proved impossible for the *Citronelle* group to evade combat when German forces actively sought a confrontation and on a couple of occasions pitched battles had been unavoidable. The fighting of 12 June 1944 had resulted in heavy losses of both men and equipment for the *Citronelle* group, a situation exacerbated by subsequent resupply problems.

When forming the group in April 1944, sufficient supplies of equipment, weapons and ammunition had been airdropped from Britain. However, after D-Day, Maquis units in regions of France nearer to the battlefront were prioritised for airdrops. Though Colonel de Bollardière was in daily contact with London via his unit's wireless transmitter, his regular requests for resupply after the 12 June losses had not yet been met.

The first meeting between Henry and his Jedburgh Team Andrew comrades and Colonel de Bollardière did not go as well as they might have hoped. It was immediately apparent that communications had somehow become garbled between the *Citronelle* group and London. After the preliminary introductions had been dealt with, Colonel de Bollardière stated that he was happy to place his group at Henry's disposal, just as Henry was about to offer to place his team at the Colonel's disposal. When Henry explained that the Jedburgh team would provide another link between *Citronelle* and London and might improve supply issues, the Colonel assumed that this also meant that Henry and his team had arrived with a supply of arms and equipment for the group. This left Henry having to politely disabuse him of that hope, as the supplies dropped had only been for the equipping of the Jedburgh team, the two French officers and the Belgian SAS unit.

Colonel de Bollardière told Henry that, on the night of the Jedburghs' arrival, he had actually been expecting a long-awaited supply drop. He had been at the drop-zone in person and kept it in darkness as a fairly strong wind was blowing that was likely to extinguish any torches that were prematurely lit. It seems that his group lacked the newfangled S-Phone or Eureka devices that helped guide aircraft to a drop-zone. After hearing the aircraft circling over the site, he had given the order to quickly light the torches and had then looked skyward, expecting to see the two French officers, Jean and Robert, whom he was expecting, together with a large quantity of supplies exiting the aircraft. He was surprised to instead see nine parachutes descending (the Belgian SAS team, who they were not expecting) with no obvious supply panniers. To make matters worse, the Belgians had landed "all over the place" and, on being rounded up by members of de Bollardière's Maquis group, they had jabbered away in broken English to their finders. They had been ordered to speak English – whatever their level of fluency – when in enemy territory, so as to conceal their identity and minimise the risk of reprisals against their families in occupied Belgium should they be captured by the Germans. Maquis suspicions that they might actually be Germans who had been parachuted in to draw out the Resistance fighters were happily dispelled before any of them were shot as enemy infiltrators.

The Colonel's confusion was added to when, after being told of the unexpected arrival of the nine Allied soldiers, he was also informed that another five men were about to be dropped. He waited patiently on the drop-zone but to no avail since, as he scanned the heavens, Henry, his Jedburgh comrades and the two French officers were actually being launched out of the aircraft some ten miles away from their target. After waiting in the dark for over an hour, Colonel de Bollardière finally gave up and went back to the camp, assuming the second drop had been aborted. He was later astonished to hear that there were another five Allied soldiers some miles away who were very keen to meet him. He told Henry that while he had been expecting Jean and Robert, he had never heard of the Jedburghs or Team Andrew. It seemed to him that his requests for resupply had once again been ignored in London and, as a very poor substitute, he now had an unexpected Jedburgh team that he did not know what to do with.

The atmosphere of disappointment was lifted a little when Henry's Belgian comrade, Edouard d'Oultremont, suggested that the Jedburgh Team could still be useful by at least opening up another channel of communication with London, provided the team could occasionally utilise the Colonel's wireless transmitter. This was immediately agreed to and a message requesting resupply drops at various locations was carefully encoded and sent off to London by Sergeant Harrison, using the Colonel's wireless set. Several days of silence ensued before a reply arrived from London. It was a disappointing response. The message had been deemed 'indecipherable' by the French team in London. It soon became apparent that the French had been attempting to decode a Jedburgh radio message rather than referring it to the Jedburgh section in London, who had access to the Jedburgh codes. With increasing exasperation, the Colonel repeated that the message was from Jedburgh Team Andrew and should be urgently passed to the correct team for deciphering. This was then done, though valuable time had been lost.

A full ten days passed by before a reply was finally received from London. Once again, it was a huge anti-climax. The Colonel was asked to kindly advise Team Andrew that the message had now been received and understood by London – and that was the sum of the reply. No other comment was made by London, no other messages were sent to the team and the team's request for resupply drops was not acted upon. Though there were a large number of potential recruits to the existing *Citronelle* group, it was obvious that they could not be mobilised if there were no weapons to arm them with. The Colonel had no option other than to make do with what he had, and his plans for expanding the group would have to be shelved unless the inexplicable impasse with London could be unblocked. Henry's later view of the situation was delivered with his usual bluntness. The mission of Jedburgh Team Andrew had been a failure due to circumstances that were beyond the team's control. He commented:

> Therefore, there was nothing left for us to do but to attach ourselves to [the Colonel's] H.Q. and make ourselves as useful as possible about the place. Harrison was completely spare without his set. d'Oultremont could have done excellent work as liaison officer between the Belgian and French Maquis groups if this had not been specifically interdicted. I was perhaps of some use as a clothes peg for British uniform; several of the French officers were kind enough to say that my presence showed the solidarity of Anglo-French relations and on the whole they seemed genuinely pleased to have us with them.

Henry and his Jedburgh comrades therefore settled into the daily routine of camp life and awaited developments. Typically, a breakfast of bread and butter or honey was followed by weapons training before a lunch of meat and vegetables. Training continued throughout the afternoon and ran to about 7 p.m., when a meal was provided along similar lines to lunch. The military backbone of the *Citronelle* mission was provided by the Colonel, assisted by an American officer and a British RAF officer. Radio communications for the group were handled by a rather remarkable Frenchman, who was almost inevitably codenamed 'Pierre'. Henry understood that Pierre had been captured by the Gestapo on two previous undercover missions but had amazingly managed to escape on both occasions. Conscious that he was a marked man but still keen to help liberate his homeland, he had even undergone a facelift to alter his features before joining the *Citronelle* mission.

The camp set-up was quite simple with very few tents, though most men had blankets and a covering of sorts to keep off the worst of the rain, while a salvaged parachute did service as the cookhouse tent. It was in no way a comfortable lifestyle and Henry noted that effective sanitary arrangements were largely neglected though he was more alarmed by the scant attention given by the Maquis to keeping their weapons clean. The defence of the camp had been well thought-out, however, with sentries posted on key paths within the wood, and several rough but important tracks were to be strongly defended in the event of an enemy attack.

Henry's original mission orders had included an instruction not to cross the border into Belgium or have any liaison with the Belgian Resistance. Events conspired to undermine that, however. At about 2 p.m. on 25 August, a young lad arrived at the *Citronelle* camp with a request from the local Belgian Resistance group for urgent assistance. The Belgians had ambushed a German unit on the road near Nafraiture, just across the border with France. The Belgian commander had been wounded and his men pinned down by an unexpectedly robust German response, and they needed urgent assistance.

The Colonel resolved to take about half of his men with him to try and assist his Belgian allies and Henry decided to go along too, despite his orders not to cross onto Belgian soil.

Hurriedly setting off, the *Citronelle* force cautiously emerged from the woods near the site of the ambush. Frustratingly, there was no sign of the Belgians they had come to help, though a German vehicle was parked on a nearby bridge and several enemy soldiers could be seen standing around. The Colonel decided that he would attack the Germans, hoping that the element of surprise would enable his forces to quickly rout them and then disable the truck before beating a hasty retreat to safer pastures. Before the plan could be put into action, a complicating factor arose. Henry spotted what he took to be German nurses near the truck and drew the Colonel's attention to this. It seemed possible that the truck contained wounded German soldiers under the care of the nurses, and to attack in such circumstances would contravene the accepted norms of warfare. As the Colonel pondered his options, the decision was taken out of his hands when an unauthorised burst of fire from a member of the *Citronelle* force scattered the nurses and peppered the truck with bullets.

A French officer then sought to drive home the attack by advancing onto the bridge, but he and two of his comrades were cut down by fire from a concealed enemy position. The group eventually reached the truck and found several dead German soldiers inside, though luckily all of the nurses seemed to have escaped injury. The *Citronelle* force left the scene and moved back into the shelter of the woods. On the way, they captured two German soldiers who had fled the attack, having thrown away their weapons during their flight. They claimed to be line of communication troops who had been proceeding from Paris to Brussels when they got lost. They were subsequently used for menial tasks in the Maquis camps before being handed over to the American Army when the area was liberated in September 1944.

After the skirmish on Belgian soil, there was no doubt that the Germans would urgently turn their attention to the troublesome Resistance groups on both sides of the Belgium-France border in the Ardennes region. Colonel de Bollardière decided that it would be prudent to switch campsites as soon as possible, banking on 24 hours' grace before the enemy could organise an attacking force and locate the current camp. 24 hours proved to be optimistic, however, and as Henry and his comrades enjoyed their lunch on the day following the incident, a single shot rang out. Single shots often occurred when careless Maquis members cleaned their weapons, but the Colonel thought it best to place everyone on alert for a potentially speedy departure from the camp.

The *Citronelle* group had no interest in holding territory when attacked. Instead the strategy was to thin out the group utilising multiple escape routes, while taking every opportunity to inflict loss on an enemy working in unfamiliar terrain. The group could then reform at a pre-arranged location some miles away. With everyone in the camp on edge following the gunshot, the process of packing up equipment ready for a march began, but was interrupted by the distinctive noise of a German sub-machine gun in the distance, quickly answered by the tat-tat-tat of a British-made Bren gun.

The Maquis in the camp immediately deployed to the camp perimeter, while de Bollardière and several close aides held a position in the centre of the camp to deal with any Germans who might fight their way through. Henry now saw himself as merely a private soldier, albeit an experienced and professional one, and took his place on the fringe of the camp to await developments. He did not have to wait long, as a number of Maquis soldiers came rushing back from the furthest sentry outposts shouting that a retreat was necessary. Colonel de Bollardière was having none of that and ordered that anyone falling back should rally around him. He would not countenance fleeing headlong and was prepared to stand his ground for now, before staging a phased, fighting retreat to a safer position. Henry observed a number of German infantrymen milling about in the woods firing wildly, creating an almighty din that was augmented by loud shouting on both sides. Though he had a narrow field of fire, he managed to target three German soldiers and, at fairly short range, he was able to hit each of them in turn with well-aimed shots.

As the skirmish continued, Colonel de Bollardière's second in command, an elderly and long-retired French officer, insisted on showing his disdain for the Germans by marching around the firing line, dressed in his best tweed suit and loudly encouraging his men before he was felled by a burst of German machine-gun fire. The shouted orders and insults of the enemy were now joined by the groans and screams of the wounded as the German advance slowly petered out and the situation stabilised, with neither side trying to actively gain ground. This lull proved to be short-lived and Henry's ears pricked up as he heard the distinctive 'pop' of a German mortar-bomb launcher being fired. He and his comrades had an uncomfortable five minutes as mortar shells landed all around the command post where he was now positioned, and Colonel de Bollardière, d'Oultremont and several French officers were wounded by the explosions. It seemed to be a good a time to vacate the camp and the Maquis began to fall back in stages, still firing bursts into the dense foliage so as to discourage any Germans trying to follow them.

With the Maquis fighters having scattered inside the wood prior to making their way to safer locations, Henry found himself in a column of between 20 and 30 men, including Colonel de Bollardière, who was hobbling from a leg wound and soon had to be practically carried along. Several other wounded men were being helped, meaning it took an hour to travel only one mile. On the way, the French officer Robert, who had been parachuted in with Henry, sadly died of his wounds. Fears that the Germans might be able to cut the column off from safety proved to be unfounded and eventually they reached the agreed rendezvous position. Already there were a number of men who had arrived by different routes and they greeted Henry and his party with some very welcome bread, butter, eggs and milk.

The group's numbers had now swelled back to about 70 men, though there were still about 30 others missing, a large portion of whom were feared dead. Though they were helpless to do anything about it, there was great sadness over the likely fate of any Maquis who had been captured by the enemy. Atrocities had previously been committed in the treatment of prisoners of war, and it was best to try not to think of such things.

On the following day, Henry took a well-armed patrol back to the site of the recently vacated camp. He was astonished to see that the Germans had withdrawn without obviously interfering with the camp in any way. Food, equipment and even weapons were found where they had been abandoned during the hurried evacuation. The area stank of death and around a dozen or so of the fallen Maquis were speedily buried, the bodies almost unrecognisable after only 24 hours of humid, thundery weather. Of the German dead, there was no sign. Outside the camp perimeter, they were shocked and upset to discover the body of a child. Henry guessed that the lad had been forced to lead the Germans to the camp and had then been callously killed by a single shot to the head.

Henry summed up the situation for the Maquis unit:

> [Our losses] were nevertheless such as to reduce very considerably our utility as a fighting force. Three officers killed, the Colonel a stretcher case, appreciable losses in men and equipment, and a considerable expenditure of ammunition that could not be replaced until we had another delivery by air. As repeated demands over a period of three months had produced no results, we could not count on further supplies of ammunition arriving in time for our period of active operations, when we should receive orders from London to start guerrilla activity.

The new camp was located to the east of the Croix Scaille, a plateau of the forested *massif* in the Ardennes. It rose to a height of over 500 metres and stood on the Franco-Belgian border. The area was a hotbed of Resistance activity and near the new camp was a previously abandoned Belgian one. The derelict Belgian camp impressed Henry as it had log cabins, lavatories and even a chapel, facilities which stood in stark contrast to the spartan conditions of the camps that Henry was experiencing with his French allies. If the French Maquis camps lacked amenities, camp discipline also fell short of Henry's demanding military standards. Multiple campfires spewed smoke into the sky, while no task could be undertaken without much laughing and shouting, accompanied by the noise of the tools. German fighter aircraft frequently flew over the new camp, probably using the prominent features of the Croix Scaille as a navigational aid – though, happily, they did not seek to launch an attack from the air.

Around this time, a German convoy travelled close to the camp. It seemed prudent to Henry and the Colonel not to undertake another offensive action so soon after the last one so, as an alternative, a couple of *Citronelle* Maquis members were ordered to pose as workmen and cautiously approach the enemy. It transpired that the column was actually lost so an offer of assistance was gratefully accepted by the German commander and he was given directions by the Maquis members. Not the correct directions, as it happened, but by the time they realised that they had been misled, it would be too late for any effective retaliatory action.

At last, the *Citronelle* group heard the coded message broadcast on BBC radio that indicated that the time for it to commence harrying operations against the Germans had arrived. The group began to make preparations for offensive operations and hoped for the long-awaited resupply drop. However, it seems that Henry's team did not have the up-to-date communication aids needed to guide an incoming aircraft to a drop-zone. If Henry had dropped into the Ardennes with such equipment, it had obviously been lost or damaged in the process, so frantic torch-waving would have to suffice. As he noted later, he was in command of signalling on the night of the expected drop, flashing his light in the direction of aircraft he could hear but not see. After a couple of hours, with no obvious results, the enterprise was abandoned.

Despite the obvious disappointment of being let down by London yet again, there was little that the Colonel, Henry and the rest of the group could do, other than try and make effective use of what they did have. They did not need orders from London to decide on their next task. By 1 September 1944, the Germans in France were in retreat and on that day a messenger entered the *Citronelle* camp. He explained that the town of Nouzonville, about 12 miles away, had been hurriedly evacuated by the Germans, leaving a bridge over the River Meuse intact. If the bridge could be secured by the Maquis, it would greatly assist the advancing Allied forces in crossing the river.

De Bollardière decided at once that he would proceed to the town by car to see what could be done to hold the bridge, and asked Henry to accompany him. The Colonel donned his best battledress and, still suffering from his leg wound, hobbled painfully to the vehicle. Henry suggested that the vehicle should avoid using main roads as there were numerous groups of retreating German soldiers heading along them towards Germany, but his advice was politely ignored. The Colonel did pointedly cock his revolver and hold it at the ready as he took his seat in the rear of the car. He was prepared for anything. Henry piled in alongside him while in the front passenger seat, another member of their group pointed a Sten gun out of a wound-down window.

The driver, a jocular, red-faced Frenchman, seemed to know how to drive only in two ways: fast, or very fast. The vehicle sped off and careered along the road at around 60 mph, often seeming (to Henry, at least) to take corners on two wheels. The party entered the town at breakneck speed before screeching to a halt as the driver slammed on the brakes close to the house of Max, a local Resistance chief. The passengers got out of the car, which immediately left the town at high speed. If the Colonel had envisaged being greeted by the townsfolk as a liberating hero, he was to be sadly disappointed, as Henry noted:

> Max greeted us with mingled joy and consternation. Did we not know that the Germans had come back, about 30 of them, that there was a section post only just down the street, and here was the Colonel and an English officer, both in full uniform! We went to the window to look out, and saw a motorcycle combination drive past from the direction we had come in, with two fat Germans.

A hastily convened council of war was held in the house and Henry was alarmed to hear that Max was in favour of attacking the German forces in the town, with a view to driving them out before defending the all-important bridge against demolition. The Colonel thankfully took a more measured view of the situation, pointing out that even 30 well-armed Germans, who could probably call on mortar and artillery support, could easily defeat 100 semi-trained irregulars, many of whom had never fired a shot in anger and had no access to heavy weapons. Even if the enemy was initially routed, given the importance of the bridge to retreating German units, a counter-attack was inevitable and would in all probability succeed. Once the Germans were back in control of the town, there would undoubtedly be enemy reprisals against innocent civilians and their property and, viewed dispassionately, to attack the Germans now would be an act of folly. The idea was abandoned and it was agreed that Henry and the Colonel would leave town immediately, though runners would carry updates to the *Citronelle* group on the evolving situation.

On rejoining the main body of the *Citronelle* group, Henry was surprised to see that many of the men now had military uniforms of a sort, having broken into a German clothing store.

He noticed that unit morale had experienced an immediate uplift simply due to its members looking slightly more professional in appearance. With regard to the situation at the time, it was known that the Germans were grouping their forces around Nouzonville, but that much of the rest of the district was devoid of enemy troops. The Colonel decided that a show of strength would help cheer up the local population and he proudly led his men through the main street of Hautes-Rivières, where they were greeted with loud cheers by the residents – with many people openly weeping – as it seemed that liberation was finally at hand. The group then moved back into a nearby forest to set up a temporary camp. Later in the afternoon, it proved necessary to move further into the wood as several German armoured cars came down the nearby road, each one sending a burst of machine-gun fire into the woods on the off-chance that unseen Maquis members might be massing for an ambush. No casualties were sustained and the enemy vehicles were allowed to go on their way.

An unexpected message from the headquarters of the French forces in London arrived at this time, sadly doing nothing to improve the Colonel's blood pressure. London apologised for the supply failures but – astonishingly – stated that several more Jedburgh teams were to be sent to the *Citronelle* mission, though still no supplies. After this disappointing news, the Colonel relocated the group to some high ground in the middle of the Bois des Hazelles and made preparations for what limited guerrilla activity was actually possible, given the dearth of arms and ammunition. The most practical plan seemed to be to send ambush parties in various directions so that they could harass small parties of retreating Germans. It was known that American units were approaching and, indeed, the rumble of their guns could be clearly heard in the distance. Precise information was proving hard to come by, however, as the remaining German units were enforcing strict curfews in many of the local towns and villages, thus reducing the flow of intelligence to the Resistance. It was understood that the bridge at Nouzonville had finally been blown up by the enemy, so as to prevent the Americans using it.

Henry's original orders for Jedburgh Team Andrew had included the instruction to try and make contact with any advancing Allied forces, once they were within ten miles or so of his position. On that basis, around a dozen men were given notes that contained the best information that Henry and the Colonel had on German positions and were told to try and pass through the thinly held German front line and get the information to the advancing Americans. Henry subsequently heard that some of the messengers had managed this, though he did not know whether any use was made of the information by the advancing forces. Colonel de Bollardière, in the meantime, had realised that as well as apparently having scant concern for his supply problems, London also had no real understanding of the position on the ground in his area. Rather than wait for the arrival of a set of probably muddled orders from the French Headquarters in London, he decided to make his own plans for engaging with the enemy.

His first tactic was to ambush any German column found retreating along the road that ran to the north of Nouzonville. Once again, Henry regarded the plan as being rather half-baked, though his advice seemed to produce no significant changes in the Colonel's intentions. Though the strategy envisaged almost the entire *Citronelle* group being deployed in two groups, there was no attempt to devise a coordinated fire plan – with the resultant risk that, in the heat of battle, the irregular soldiers might well end up shooting each other as well as the enemy. There was also to be no attempt to block the road and no variation to the plan if the enemy column consisted of armoured cars as opposed to less dangerous vehicles. *Citronelle* did have two anti-tank weapons (American bazookas) though they had not yet been used in action by group members. Despite Henry's concerns, ambush positions were taken up as directed by the

Colonel, even though that meant a safe retreat would be almost impossible. Henry, having nothing better to do, found himself a spot at the side of the road with a number of other riflemen and awaited developments.

He did not have to wait very long as two German armoured cars with a saloon car sandwiched in between soon came into view. This was an ideal opportunity for the bazookas to be brought into play and both were fired at the enemy column. It appeared that the leading armoured car was struck by a projectile but, very disappointingly, with little obvious effect. The convoy immediately increased its speed and, in response to the blizzard of small-arms fire directed at it by Henry and his comrades, both armoured cars randomly machine-gunned the foliage on either side of the road and were soon out of harm's way. The bazooka teams were left to stare forlornly at their seemingly ineffective newfangled weapons, and mourn the lost opportunity to destroy some German light-armour.

The Colonel did not let that frustrating encounter diminish his enthusiasm for further action against the enemy. He promptly planned two new missions for 3 September, the first of which was another attempt at an ambush. This time it was a road near Nouzonville which was selected as the ambush point, as that road had seen a lot of traffic as the Germans pulled back. On this occasion, the luck of the *Citronelle* group changed for the better, which was bad news for the enemy. After a lengthy and uncomfortable wait concealed some 50 yards from the road, German infantrymen were observed to be approaching in a hot and sweaty column, three men wide. It was an ideal target with minimal protection and the *Citronelle* men opened fire with devastating effect as the column drew near. Despite suffering heavy losses, the Germans quickly recovered their discipline and brought a mortar into play – though by the time that had started pinging bombs in the direction of the ambushers, most of the *Citronelle* men had simply drifted away into deeper cover.

Henry did not take part in this ambush, instead going to help attack an 88mm artillery-piece, a powerful weapon that the Germans had deployed near Ferme du Loup. His mission was anti-climactic as, by the time they reached the location, it was American soldiers in scout cars rather than German artillerymen that they encountered, the gun and its crew having vanished. Hearty greetings were exchanged, an American officer was despatched to pay his respects to Colonel de Bollardière at the Maquis camp and Henry's French comrades sat around, happily sampling the freely offered American K-Rations.

Nouzonville was now completely free of the enemy and the Colonel resolved that the time was right for a ceremonial march by himself and his men into the town. This took place on the following day as Henry recorded: 'By the time [the Maquis] reached it, all semblance of military order had vanished and everyone was decked in flowers, and straggling all over the street and laughing and joking with the girls. Nevertheless, the entry into liberated Nouzonville was a moving event. Allied flags were flying everywhere and crowds of people were standing about, some laughing, some weeping, many just dazed with the shock of liberation after four years under the Nazi heel.' Two days were spent eating and drinking to excess, while all thought of chasing any remaining German troops out of the area was put on hold. It was clear to Henry that his role with the Jedburghs, frustrating as it had been, was now drawing to a close.

He and his two Jedburgh Team Andrew comrades had only been one part of a far larger effort, of course. In all, 101 Jedburgh teams had been despatched to the field following the D-Day invasion, a total force of around 300 highly trained operatives. The outcomes were a mix of successes and failures that saw 17 Jedburgh agents killed in action and a further 21 captured. Henry's team had experienced a frustrating time with the lack of requested supply drops clearly hampering its work with the Resistance.

Though Colonel de Bollardière requested that he remain with the *Citronelle* group, it was obvious to Henry that most of his key French allies were now shifting their attention away from military matters and towards the cut-throat business of French parochial politics. As that activity held no attraction for him, on 8 September Henry cadged a lift to Paris from an obliging American GI, determined to rejoin his regiment at the earliest opportunity. His war was not yet over.

CHAPTER TWELVE

Advancing on Germany

On 12 September 1944, Henry Coombe-Tennant joined the Prince of Wales Company, 1st Battalion of the Welsh Guards with the rank of Acting Major. In September 1944, the 1st Battalion was advancing in the vicinity of Helchteren in Belgium, having crossed the Albert Canal at Beringen on 6 September. In the advance towards Beringen, the battalion had been met only by cheering civilians. Once they reached the town, though, they encountered machine-gun fire and discovered that the bridge over the canal had been partially destroyed by the enemy. The Germans were soon observed retreating, however, and the Welsh Guards were able to carefully cross the surviving parts of the bridge in single file in pursuit of the enemy.

By 7 September Helchteren had largely been secured, though it was still susceptible to German counter-attack. The nearby hamlet of Hechtel was stubbornly defended by the enemy and the first British tank to approach it was destroyed by an anti-tank gun, with German machine-gun positions stopping the advance of other units. Over the next few days, attacks by the guardsmen failed to capture Hechtel and, on the morning of 12 September (the day that Henry rejoined the battalion), it was decided to send in two battalions to finally dislodge the enemy. While mortars, machine guns and six-pounder field guns provided support for the attackers, the Royal Northumberland Fusiliers also assisted by firing 900 mortar bombs and over 40,000 machine-gun rounds at the enemy.

The four companies of Welsh Guardsmen who carried out the attack were also supported by two squadrons of tanks from the 2nd Battalion of the Welsh Guards. The tanks advanced steadily, firing into any house from which resistance was encountered, with the infantrymen following. By noon on 12 September the central crossroads had been secured and an hour later the entire hamlet was under British control. German dead were counted at 150 and over 700 were taken prisoner, figures that caused the Corps Commander General Sir R N O'Connor to remark, "It is one thing to gain ground, but it is quite another to destroy a complete enemy battalion."

On 17 September, the battalion had orders to continue its advance as part of Operation Market Garden. The objective was to reach the town of Arnhem and relieve the Allied paratroopers who had been dropped behind enemy lines to secure bridges. However, tough German resistance was encountered, slowing the advance. At 7.30 a.m. on 18 September the 1st Battalion, the Welsh Guards set off towards Valkenswaard, south of Eindhoven. Henry and his Prince of Wales Company comrades achieved a minor success at this time by overrunning a German anti-tank team. The advance was slow and was hampered by the unnerving habit of the enemy of first evacuating and later reoccupying local hamlets and villages after Allied troops had moved on.

By 19 September, the battalion had advanced through Eindhoven, which was full of enthusiastic citizens, and then Veghel, which only seemed to contain American paratroopers engaged in clearing out the elusive remnants of enemy resistance. The Welsh Guards then reached Grave, on the banks of the River Maas (the Meuse in French), where it was detailed for guard duty. Henry Coombe-Tennant and his company were posted in the centre of Grave, while other companies held a number of nearby bridges. The battalion headquarters was based in an asylum that had previously been devoted to the care of what the Welsh Guards war diary referred to as 'lunatics', no doubt giving rise to comments from the other ranks on the eminent suitability of such accommodation for their officers.

The advance ground on slowly. On 21 September they reached Nijmegen, where the battalion raided an abandoned Hitler Youth headquarters and a German Army canteen, with pleasing results for the Orderly Room and Officers' Mess pantries. That evening, Henry's company sent out a patrol which succeeded in linking up with American airborne troops at Elst. An attack was made towards Bemmel on 23 September, with the Prince of Wales Company, including Henry, leading the attack. German small-arms fire caused a number of casualties and the advance soon foundered. A captured German soldier revealed that the enemy force was in well-prepared positions and almost 50 strong, with the benefit of six light machine guns, which represented a formidable amount of firepower. It was left to another unit to complete the attack and nullify the enemy position. On 24 September, it became clear that Market Garden had failed and that as many paratroopers as possible needed to be evacuated.

On reaching the village of Aam, the 1st Welsh Guards battalion headquarters was initially set up in an abandoned jam factory, a building sardonically described in the Welsh Guards war diary as 'about the most obvious artillery target this side of the Eiffel Tower'. The vulnerability of such an exposed position was soon realised and the very conspicuous factory was promptly abandoned in favour of safer and less obvious quarters. The month was rounded off by the Germans blowing a large hole in a bridge, leading the war diary writer to lament that 'the mobile bath unit have inconsiderately established themselves on the far side of the bridge', preventing the Welsh Guardsmen from having a well-earned clean-up.

Early October 1944 was fairly quiet for the 1st Battalion, the Welsh Guards, though on 7 October Henry Coombe-Tennant assumed command of its Prince of Wales Company. The battalion was now in a rest area near to Huis Oosterhout.

In the second week of the month the war diary recorded that 'Short leave to BRUSSELS for officers has been going on for the past few days, where over and above the joys of wine and women are added the delights of Sunday horse-racing.' To detract from the enjoyment, the weather began to deteriorate – though it did not prevent a rugby match between men of the 1st and 2nd Battalions in the stadium at Nijmegen.

Temporarily relieved of front-line duty, on 13 October Henry took the opportunity to revisit the Groenen family at Tongerlo. The village lay in an area that had by then been cleared of German troops and no doubt he was keen to check on the safety of the family and to thank them once again for their invaluable and courageous help while he had been on the run in Belgium two years earlier. He received a hearty welcome and was updated on the family's fortunes after they had helped him on his way. Doctor Michel Groenen and his wife Tita Ada Bemelmans had both been arrested after their assistance of Allied soldiers and airmen had been discovered. Tita had eventually been freed without any charges and Doctor Groenen had subsequently been released from the prison at the Beverlo cavalry camp near Leopoldsburg, but there had still been concerns regarding the Germans' attitude towards him. He had taken the precaution of secretly staying with one of his patients until the Allied advance reached him. His caution had been justified: several other men who had been released with him were later rearrested and executed by the occupying forces. One of Dr Groenen's daughters, Eliane, barely in her teens at the time, had been rescued from a threatening situation by a sympathetic German soldier. Having ushered her to safety, he presented her with a swastika badge as a token by which to remember him.

At the end of October, the 1st Welsh Guards were responsible for the security of the Nijmegen road and rail bridges. The trials of defending key positions against enemy incursions, attending various training courses on defusing enemy booby

Advancing on Germany

traps and map reading, amongst other subjects – as well as coping with the frequently inclement weather – were partly offset by the Army's ability to feed the men well whilst on campaign. Rations included savoury puddings, stews or meat and vegetables as well as essentials such as tea, sugar, milk and the inevitable cigarettes. Depending on their location, it was often also possible to obtain bread, poultry, eggs, fruit and vegetables from local sources.

As November 1944 arrived, the battalion was still engaged in guarding important bridges in and around Nijmegen. Enemy artillery shells were a constant threat and there were several near misses. On 3 November, the news arrived that the 1st Welsh Guards were to relieve a King's Shropshire Light Infantry battalion at Veulen. The battalion reached its destination the following evening, finding it to consist of one very muddy main street which had been heavily shelled and mortared by the enemy. The Germans were very close by and regularly sent out patrols towards Veulen and the surrounding area. As it transpired, despite the Welsh Guards battalion remaining in a state of high alert, the night passed peacefully.

At around this time – though Henry would have been unaware of it until later – a request from General Kœnig, commander of the French Forces of the Interior, had been received in London. It requested permission to award Henry the Croix de Guerre with Palm for his work with the *Citronelle* group. The Allied Supreme Commander, Dwight D Eisenhower, duly endorsed the request.

Several patrols were sent out in November 1944 by the Welsh Guards, a number of which had encounters with the enemy, on a small but still potentially deadly scale. On 7 November, Henry and some of his Prince of Wales Company were involved in a raid on a house known to be occupied by the Germans. The plan was to expel them by force of arms and then booby trap the premises in case they returned. The raid was led by Lieutenant D Bruce and consisted of 15 men and, though it was a success, that was only achieved at some cost. Lance Sergeant L A R Webb had reached a position close to the target house, but Bruce was severely wounded as he tried to join him. Webb carefully made his way to his fallen comrade and dressed his wounds, but two stretcher-bearers were hit as they tried to reach the two men.

Undaunted, Webb dragged Bruce back to relative safety, though the duo still remained in No Man's Land and some way short of friendly positions. With the aid of another guardsman, Webb returned to help fetch in the wounded stretcher-bearers before leading his men to the house and holding it until the booby traps had been set. With that task completed, Webb led the patrol (seven of whom had been wounded) back towards the safety of his own lines, taking 40 minutes to cover 120 yards while under constant fire from the enemy. As they finally neared friendly positions, others ran to help bring in the wounded. It seems that Henry Coombe-Tennant was wounded in the hand at this point, necessitating his subsequent evacuation – against his will – for treatment. He returned to his company the following day.

Though Henry was temporarily absent, the completion of the raid was not the last excitement of the day for his comrades. During the evening, a German shell struck the building that was being used as a cookhouse and set it alight. A petrol tank exploded and, with a number of trucks laden with ammunition and other flammable materials parked nearby, the conflagration spread rapidly and in minutes the entire area was ablaze. Efforts to tow vehicles out of the danger area were hampered as ammunition exploded in the heat. Luckily, only two men were wounded, though seven fifteen-hundredweight trucks and their entire contents were lost.

The battalion remained in Veulen as the roads in the surrounding area slowly turned to mud and became almost impassable without the benefit of a tracked vehicle. Even tracked personnel carriers often got bogged down and had to be towed free. The casualty list continued to creep upwards as men fell ill or were killed or wounded by the enemy. On 8 November, for example, two guardsmen jumped into a ditch to escape German artillery shells only to trigger an enemy mine, resulting in both their deaths. Lance Sergeant Millward went missing and was known to have been wounded. Attempts to find him were unsuccessful and it was assumed that he had been captured by the Germans – sadly, he had been killed in action. Henry and his Prince of Wales Company comrades had an unsettling time on the morning of 10 November as the enemy repeatedly fired mortar bombs at their position. The mood was lightened at the unusual sight of Regimental Sergeant Major Baker 'flying' across the main street of Veulen while trying to visit the company, hotly pursued by a string of falling mortar bombs. Despite the gallows humour contained in the war diary entry about the incident, Baker happily came to no harm. During its time at Veulen, the battalion had lost almost 40 men to combat, accident or sickness. All ranks were glad to eventually see the back of the place.

On 11 November, the 1st Battalion, the Welsh Guards left the town – with some difficulty due to the swampy nature of the terrain – and set off for Deurne, where it rested for one night. Just before midnight on 12 November the battalion reached Sittard, where it went into temporary billets before taking over from an American light-tank battalion. Sittard was only two miles from the German lines but surprisingly the town had been largely undisturbed by war and a number of its inhabitants still lived there, not having fled in fear of their homes becoming part of a battleground.

It seemed to the Welsh Guards that the Americans had adopted a 'live and let live' attitude to the enemy, minimising contact with them and leaving them alone as long as that privilege was reciprocated. On that basis, it was hoped that – for a while at least – the posting at Sittard would be far more agreeable than the horrors experienced at Veulen. Henry and his company were actually positioned just inside the German border, where the villages contained mainly old people, women and young children, men of military age having been conscripted. The one downside was that it appeared that the Americans had been quite liberal in their placement of booby traps in the surrounding countryside, without keeping a record of just where the deadly devices had been set. It was expected that the Royal Engineers would have a happy time of it in finding and deactivating the dangerous gadgets.

The second half of November saw the recommencement of patrol activity by elements of Henry's battalion, during which great care had to be exercised to avoid the attentions of the enemy, as well as the American booby traps. The battalion headquarters received a direct hit from an enemy shell but, happily, the only casualties were a number of drinks glasses. More serious was the death of a guardsman as he was setting trip hazards to hinder any enemy forays in front of the Welsh Guards positions. A patrol that went out on 20 November advanced further toward the German lines than any previous effort and had the effect of alarming the enemy so much that they seemingly fired off every weapon that they had, though to no great effect. Another patrol carefully approached a wood that was thought to contain enemy soldiers. A flurry of German stick-grenades aimed at the patrol confirmed that it was indeed still held by the enemy.

The enemy was active, too. A concealed German self-propelled gun spent some time lobbing shells at Prince of Wales Company positions before being heard rumbling away, to the great relief of Henry and his men. An enemy shell struck the house opposite that in which the battalion commanding officer was billeted, breaking the window and showering his room with shell splinters and fragments of glass as he sat up in bed with an early morning cup of tea. In another billet, two Welsh Guardsmen were nonchalantly cooking chips when they became aware of other soldiers entering the room. On turning

Advancing on Germany

around, they were shocked to see not hungry comrades but three heavily armed Germans. The guardsmen were being bundled down the stairs as captives when Guardsman Lloyd managed to trip his man and then punch him. Guardsman Brookes did much the same to his adversary and the duo made a run for safety, though not without Brookes being wounded by enemy gunfire.

Mother Nature also proved a capable enemy and in November, with rain an almost ever-present feature of each day, the slit-trenches dug by the men were starting to collapse. The waterlogged conditions led to 13 men coming down with trench foot, all of them needing to spend some time in an improvised sick bay. December saw the usual mix of bad weather and patrolling. On 4 December, an enemy shell landed alongside the position held by Henry and his company, though fortunately the only damage done was to their dinner, which was being prepared nearby.

At this time, the Allied high command was anxious to identify the enemy units that were engaging with the Welsh Guards battalion and several unsuccessful attempts were made to capture a German soldier. On 7 December, the 1st Welsh Guards were relieved by a battalion of the Devonshire Regiment and Henry and his company moved to the area of Geleen, where they were billeted several men to a house.

For the first time in weeks, the guardsmen had a good night's sleep and were not roused from their slumbers until the luxurious hour of 9 a.m., with breakfast served at 10 a.m. The leisurely pace of life away from the front line was soon interrupted, however, firstly by a demonstration of dogs specially trained to detect mines and then by an illustration of the deadly efficacy of the flamethrower. Every company held a parade of some sort before a much more enjoyable interlude arrived. Two Welsh Guardsmen were selected to play in a rugby match between a team representing the Guards Armoured Division and a Royal Air Force side, and the officers of the battalion felt it necessary to despatch a contingent of guardsmen to support the duo during the match, which was to be played in Brussels. In the event, it proved possible to send an astonishing 200 guardsmen to watch the game, as well as later allowing them to enjoy some free time in the Belgian capital. As the battalion war diary gleefully noted, 'it seems to be an all-Welsh racket which might be worked again.'

The battalion was moved to the area of Gangelt to relieve a motorised unit and Henry and his company found themselves in the village of Kreuzrath, where a quiet night was only briefly interrupted by the passage overhead of a V1 rocket bound for Antwerp or England. An inspection of the new positions revealed that the men were spread out far too thinly, though a lack of further manpower meant that nothing could be done to improve the situation but to dig in further and fortify the ground held. The usual patrols were sent out over the following days, though the sector remained largely quiet. Henry and his Prince of Wales Company, however, found themselves the target of unwelcome attention from some German mortar teams. An agreement was quickly stitched together with the commanding officer of a couple of British artillery batteries and, on receipt of the codeword 'CAMEO', all guns fired on the suspected enemy mortar position, with the result that the irritation soon ceased.

17 December saw the 1st Welsh Guards cross the River Maas and pass through Bree in order to reach Veldhoven. This new area was not especially suitable for billeting a large number of soldiers, with the result that the men were spread far and wide, with remote cottages providing the base for clusters of guardsmen. One platoon of X Company found that the best billet available to it was actually a barge moored on a canal, with the added advantage of a nearby café complete with a piano and accordion both played via concealed mechanisms.

On 16 December, the Germans had launched a major attack in the heavily forested Ardennes region of Belgium, France and Luxembourg, with the objective of stopping the Allies from using the Belgian port of Antwerp as well as potentially allowing them to encircle and destroy four Allied armies. If those ambitious aims could be realised, Hitler hoped to force the Western Allies to the negotiating table, with the possibility of a separate peace treaty being concluded that would allow him to concentrate his forces to try and stem the Russian advance from the east. By 19 December, the alarming news of initial German successes led to 'a considerable flap' within the Allied command structure, which quickly filtered down to the 1st Welsh Guards. This threw doubt over a possible move to the area around Louvain, where it had been planned that the battalion would spend a fairly quiet Christmas.

After a troubled night of orders and counter-orders, the battalion finally set off at 10.30 a.m. on the morning of 20 December, pleased to hear that the destination was indeed to be what the Welsh Guards war diary happily referred to as 'the promised land near LOUVAIN'. The happiness proved to be short-lived as, soon after arriving at Louvain, orders were received to move again, this time to the vicinity of 'Autgaerden' [Outgaarden] near Tirlemont. This was the area where the battalion would try and enjoy Christmas, though spirits plummeted with the news that it was likely that, rather than soon returning to Britain for some well-earned leave, it would remain at the front until at least April 1945.

Any plans that Henry had harboured for a modestly pleasant Christmas were dealt a heavy blow when he and his Prince of Wales Company comrades were ordered to guard the railway bridge at Namur, a tiresome duty that would straddle the Christmas Day festivities, such as they were. Worse was to come with the news that the entire battalion was to be on the move during Christmas Day itself, with Henry and his company being required to defend a command post in Erpent. The war diary noted with disdain that all this unseasonal and very unwelcome to-ing and fro-ing took place despite the surprise enemy advance in the Ardennes being at least 25 miles away and facing strong American defences. The bad weather, which had aided the early German attacks, had now improved considerably so the battalion was pleased to observe the commencement of Allied air activity against the enemy on 'an enormous scale'. With a relief battalion arriving on the afternoon of 27 December, plans were made to move to Hoegaarden, where shooting of a different kind took place: a Welsh Guards officer shooting party bagged ten pheasants and a couple of hares for the cooking pot.

With the stress and danger of the front line finally being some distance away, the decision was taken that the battalion would enjoy a belated 'Christmas Day' on 29 December. Although still on alert to be ready to move at six hours' notice, the company cooks could only hope for the best and commence their preparations for the festive celebrations. As the war diary for 29 December recorded:

> Every Coy. had its own church service in the morning... the Commanding Officer then had involuntarily to spend the most alcoholic half hour of his life. He started off with Christmas dinners at POW Coy, which, unfortunately, were being held in 4 separate billets. He then continued to Sp [special] Coy, 4 Coy and X Coy, all of which in turn gave him a rapturous reception and far too much to drink. However, he safely reached the haven of the Officers Mess to find that the 2-in-C had had a similar alcoholic experience with HQ Coy and 3 Coy, whose dinners he had visited...

On the following day, the welcome news arrived that the battalion was unlikely to be moved from its present positions for at least two weeks, with training of various types in the meantime. As New Year's Eve approached, the weather turned decidedly cold and the roads were covered with a treacherous layer of ice, making even local movements hazardous. The dark, winter mood was lightened by the arrival of a mobile cinema unit, as well as the hosting of traditional Hogmanay celebrations by X Company, where the alcohol imbibed 'made work for them on the next day entirely out of the question.' It was now 1945 and still the war dragged on.

January 1945 saw the battalion being trained in various disciplines, as well as enjoying a concert given by the regimental band of the Coldstream Guards. The ground conditions were still unpleasant, since an otherwise welcome rise in temperatures inevitably led to widespread slush, with the result that a planned parade in Tirlemont involving Henry and his comrades had to be postponed – though they did relish snowball fights with the locals. The war diary for 11 January recorded the cancellation of a training course with the comment, 'the police who were picquetting [guarding] the route were salvaged just in time to prevent them freezing solid. It really was a bitterly cold day.' In the evening, several battalion members were revived by 'a very potent rum punch made with more skill than wisdom by Lt. KOPPEL.'

In amongst the skating on icy roads and paths and the trudging through snow and slush, time was still found for several officers to attend a dance in Tirlemont, where the entertainment included two acrobats and some songs by a female Belgian singer referred to by the war diary as 'Bitchette', noting that she seemed to be permanently attached to British forces in the area. As the month ended, orders came through for the battalion to move towards Louvain, a requirement that was only met with some difficulty, as X Company was so hemmed into its positions by snow and ice that it was necessary to tow it out. Though the battalion was on the move, its final destination still remained clouded in secrecy. Even a visit by the Corps Commander, Lieutenant General Brian Horrocks, failed to reveal a glimmer of information about any future plans.

The battalion settled into its latest location, where its headquarters was established in the Chateau de Kercom – an impressive-sounding establishment, though the reality was that 'there is no light, little heat and no water except for a considerable quantity which comes through the roof and drips down the walls.' If the battalion Headquarters Company was literally in the dark in its dilapidated chateau, it was also still in the dark over any plans for the future deployment of the unit on offensive operations. No word filtered down from the higher command on future intentions until the end of the first week of February 1945.

The next operational plan was to be Operation Veritable, part of an Allied pincer movement that would see British and Canadian units (including the 1st Welsh Guards) forming the northern arm of the pincer while the Americans, under the name Operation Grenade, formed its southern arm. The Allied objective was to clear German forces from the area between the River Maas and the Rhine, opening up the prospect of an advance into the Rhineland. The launch date had originally been set for 1 January 1945, when it had been anticipated that the ground would be frozen and thus passable by heavy vehicles. The German attack in the Ardennes on 16 December 1944 had delayed the start of Veritable/Grenade and, by the time both arms of the pincer were actually ordered to move, the frozen terrain had largely given way to mud, slush and ice, greatly hampering vehicle movements.

On 7 February, around 700 Allied aircraft and over 1,000 guns bombarded enemy positions in preparation for the attack, with the towns of Kleve and Goch being saturated with bombs. The British and Canadian attack commenced on 8 February and involved 50,000 men and 500 tanks, though Henry and his Welsh Guards comrades did not take part in this phase of the offensive. What they did was a common experience for many soldiers: they merely waited, and listened to the pandemonium up ahead. On 9 and 10 February the expected orders to move failed to materialise and the waiting went on. On 11 February an order finally arrived, but it did not herald the start of attacking operations, instead only instructing the battalion to concentrate in the Nijmegen area. The troops made their way there, passing through 's-Hertogenbosch and Malden, though it proved very difficult to find billets on arrival as the area was already swarming with troops. To add to the joy, the weather was once again deteriorating and the proposed route of the advance was found to be totally impassable to tanks and other heavy vehicles. Despite all these impediments, the battalion was still told to be ready to move at six hours' notice.

Finally, on the evening of 13 February, a message arrived informing the battalion commanding officer that 'BG [Brigade Group] will attack tomorrow afternoon.' The battalion's commanding officer, Lieutenant Colonel Heber-Percy, promptly left for a conference at brigade headquarters and was considerably delayed there. Henry and his fellow company commanders waited patiently in a makeshift office for the commanding officer's return with further information – time that was pleasantly spent, as the war diary noted that 'fortunately there was a piano in the Orderly Room and Maj. AHS. COOMBE-TENNANT, MC to play it.'

The target of the planned attack was a wood situated about two miles to the south-west of the village of Gennep. The wood was quickly captured without anyone seeing an enemy soldier, though problems were caused by concealed mines and a German self-propelled gun, which fired for a while before moving away. Casualties were light, with only three men killed and nine wounded, all victims of shellfire. Two Germans appeared and indicated that they wished to surrender, having obviously decided that they would prefer to outlive Hitler's 'Thousand Year Reich' than lose their lives in a futile attempt to stem the steady advance of the Allies. Henry's company accepted their surrender and sent them off to the prisoner of war cage.

The next target for the battalion was the German village of Hassum, and the advance began at 4 a.m. on 17 February 1945. The objective was achieved without loss, though Hassum was found to be utterly devastated. Eight German soldiers were extracted from ruined buildings and cellars and a surprising number of civilians also emerged from the rubble of their homes. If the village was a scene of destruction, at least the surrounding area proved to be rich in livestock, including geese, ducks and pigs. Lieutenant Colonel Heber-Percy made the customary commanding officer's tour of his men's positions and returned to his headquarters in a scout car so laden with livestock that it resembled a butcher's van.

Several patrols were sent out on 19 February and made some contact with the enemy. Two Germans were shot by one patrol but, as they fell close to the positions of their comrades, it was impossible to recover the bodies and identify their unit. Another patrol 'captured' several dozen eggs and reported that a number of houses in the area were well stocked with foodstuffs and abandoned German military equipment. Also captured was an unwary German Panzer-Grenadier, who was caught while enjoying his regular teatime meal with a local farmer. Henry busied himself with helping prepare a plan to capture a nearby bridge. The bridge, near Terporten, was captured and crossed on 27 February, though it is not clear if Henry's plan was followed.

St David's Day on 1 March was a dreary sort of day. The war diary noted that the men had been so well fed of late that it proved impossible to indulge them in a 'special' meal, worthy of the national day of Wales. On the plus side, some Dutch beer was rustled up from somewhere and provided about a pint per man. The day, poor as it was, took a downward turn in the early afternoon when orders arrived to move the battalion on the next day to the vicinity of Siebengewald, an area known to have been badly knocked about by Allied weaponry. A reconnaissance patrol quickly confirmed this depressing fact.

The 1st Welsh Guards marched to Siebengewald on 2 March, pondering the value of the exercise as the area seemed to be already well protected by other Allied units. The Welsh Guards companies took over a number of abandoned houses that had been converted into strongpoints, the ground being too sodden for the digging of slit-trenches. Henry and his company went off to help guard a nearby bridge but returned in the evening. He later let his superiors know that, in his opinion, all the last few weeks' to-ing and fro-ing with little obvious coordinated direction from above meant that the entire battalion – and the Prince of Wales Company in particular – had been operating in a tactical vacuum.

On 4 March, orders came through that a night-time advance was to take place, a prospect that filled the officers of the battalion with dismay. A move by night, over roads already choked with vehicles of every description, seemed a very unwise decision. And so it proved. Shortly after the battalion set off at 2 a.m. on 5 March, the bridge that allowed the passage of tanks and other vehicles collapsed under the weight of traffic, imposing an unavoidable delay on operations. Once the bridge had been patched up, the route followed was Goch – Weeze – Kevelaer, the latter being reached at 7 a.m.

The battalion's next objective was a wood near Kapellen, and the attacking force – including Henry's company – was to be supported by a troop of self-propelled guns. Breakfast was served to the men at the ungodly hour of 4 a.m., after which they began moving off, over heavily congested roads, at 5.30 a.m. As the advance neared the wood, German machine-gun fire proved very heavy, especially around the Prince of Wales and No. 4 Companies. It was left to a number of armoured vehicles to silence the enemy guns, and they noted that many of the enemy appeared to be paratroopers of a somewhat fanatical disposition. With the wood eventually secured, a second attack was made on Bönninghardt, beginning at 5.15 p.m. on 6 March. Despite some enemy shelling, the objective was captured as early as 6 p.m. After a night's rest, the village was searched and around 50 German soldiers dug out of various cellars and taken into captivity. One German aroused the curiosity of Regimental Sergeant Major Baker when seen to be laughing to himself. When challenged, the German captive told Baker he was laughing because 'I have finished with the war, which is more than you have.' Baker had no suitable answer to the unkind retort.

There was still uncertainty regarding the future role in operations of the battalion and its brother units, though the situation around Kapellen soon quietened down considerably. Orders were received for the battalion leave for a dispersal point near Malden, setting off at 2.30 a.m. on 12 March and arriving at 6.30 a.m. The rest of the day was spent in settling into billets which had been left filthy by their previous occupants. Good news was for once not slow in arriving: the 1st Battalion of the Welsh Guards had 'done its bit' and would finally be going back to Great Britain. The cleaning of weapons, equipment and kit commenced, though numerous items of clothing were simply condemned as unfit for further use and discarded. The men would be going home with only their uniforms and rifles; almost all other materials and equipment were to be left behind for the unfortunates taking their place. A church service was held on 18 March as the likely date of departure for home drew slowly nearer.

The 1st Welsh Guards staged a parade at the Nijmegen Stadium on 19 March for the benefit of the divisional commanding officer, Major General Allan Adair, CB, DSO, MC. Adair addressed the men and congratulated them on their exploits before the battalion paraded past him, the pipes and drums of the 2nd Scots Guards contributing the background music. Lunch was provided after the parade and in the evening all officers of the battalion were invited to a cocktail party hosted by the staff officers of the 32nd Guards Armoured Brigade. Detailed instructions for the journey home proved to be slow in arriving and even a jaunt to Brussels by a 200-strong contingent did little to relieve the men's frustration. The war diary bemoaned the fact that the numerous curfew restrictions in Brussels were – somewhat unreasonably, in the writer's opinion – actually being enforced by the military police and therefore the opportunities for unrestrained enjoyment had been very much curtailed.

At last, at 7.45 a.m. on 23 March, the 1st Welsh Guards headed for the safety of home. Once again, the pipes and drums of the 2nd Scots Guards were on hand to give the men a happy send-off as they embarked on the train that would convey them to Ostend. The carriages were soon packed to the brim with men, heralding the likelihood of an uncomfortable journey. Indeed, the battalion war diary dryly noted that 'The carriages, incidentally, had been acquired by the Belgian State Railways as reparations from the Germans after the last war and their loss cannot have been a very heavy sacrifice to the German State Railways.' A stop was made for tea and sandwiches before reaching Ostend at 7.30 p.m. The night was spent in a 'beautifully run' transit camp, which even had a club for officers.

The morning of 24 March saw the men of the Prince of Wales Company jostling each other as they boarded the *Ulster Monarch* with comrades from the No. 4 and Headquarters Companies. Though the records are silent on exactly who embarked for home, it must be assumed that Henry was among them, being a key member of the Prince of Wales Company. That being the case then, unlike his evacuation mishap at Boulogne in 1940, this was one ship that Henry Coombe-Tennant did not intend missing. It set sail for England at around 10 a.m., having the comfort of a destroyer escort for the journey. Docking in Tilbury, the battalion boarded a train for St Pancras and at 10 p.m. the men were able to settle down for a very welcome meal at the Chelsea Barracks in London. Matters had been arranged so that once home, there was little immediate work for the men to do other than the inevitable cleaning and polishing of equipment and kit. Every man was granted a 14-day period of disembarkation leave so that they could be re-united with their much-missed loved ones. By 27 March, there was almost no trace remaining at the Chelsea Barracks of the 1st Welsh Guards Battalion.

Though the date cannot be established with any degree of certainty, it is very likely that Henry used a portion of his 1945 disembarkation leave for a motoring trip around Norfolk. The trip was not without incident as, at one point, Henry's car broke down and he found himself stranded at the roadside. Luckily, a passing vehicle of the Auxiliary Territorial Service (ATS) stopped and picked him up. Though the circumstances are not entirely clear, it seems that Her Royal Highness, the Princess Elizabeth was a passenger in the ATS vehicle, having joined the service some time earlier. Henry was taken to Sandringham, where he enjoyed tea with her illustrious parents, their majesties the King and Queen. Her father, the King, would probably have remembered Henry from the Buckingham Palace ceremony of 1943 when he had presented the Military Cross to Henry. Henry Coombe-Tennant seemed to have a knack of meeting interesting people on his adventures.

With the 1st Battalion, the Welsh Guards at least temporarily becalmed in Great Britain after its service at the front in north-west Europe, Henry seemed anxious that his undoubted military skills and experience were still utilised. To that end, as early as 28 March, his name appeared in a report from the headquarters of the Special Allied Airborne Reconnaissance Force (SAARF), a body at that time still in the process of being set up. Henry's name was listed as being an 'officer volunteer' for the embryonic unit. As in Henry's Jedburgh days, SAARF was being established to undertake high-risk missions with agents operating behind enemy lines in three-man teams. Once again, Henry showed no concern at confronting the enemy, voluntarily placing himself at risk.

As early as 1943, with the course of the war gradually changing in favour of the Allies, some thought had been given to the fate of Allied prisoners of war, who might be at risk following a collapse of German military resistance and a breakdown in

Advancing on Germany

its civilian administration. It was perceived that there was a danger that, just before or immediately following a German collapse, Allied prisoners of war might be in danger from their guards, rogue elements of the German military or even local civilians. By March 1945, the problem had assumed greater urgency and the Supreme Headquarters Allied Expeditionary Force (SHAEF) suggested the formation of a force of 120 men who could be parachuted into Germany in three-man teams in order to make contact with those running or being held within prisoner-of-war camps. It was recognised that thousands of foreign workers who had been forcibly brought to Germany to prop up its war economy might also be at risk. The operation was to be code-named 'Vicarage'.

SAARF was to have a British commander – Brigadier J S Nichols – with a high-ranking American as second in command. The 120 agents comprised British and American (32 agents each), French (40), Belgian (10) and Polish (6). The Wentworth Golf Club was chosen as the training area and proved eminently suitable. At a searing pace by Army standards, by 31 March 'practically the whole of the Camp Staff had been installed, the Force HQ established and the various offices set up and in operation; barrack furniture, welfare equipment collected, NAAFI, Officers and Sergeants Messes started and signal exchange and all telephones got into operation. Also the bulk of the Force transport had been drawn.' On 2 April, most of the operational personnel arrived and everything was ready for training to be commenced.

Immediate steps were taken to try and instil an *esprit de corps* into the fledgling SAARF agents by the early issue of uniform flashes, while squadrons were promptly established for each nationality, each under a specially selected squadron command team. Operational teams were established on the three-man Jedburgh model and training advanced at a rapid pace. Many agents required parachute training as a starting point, having no experience. To fail the parachute course would place a very large question mark against their future involvement in SAARF work. Henry, of course, was already parachute proficient and would probably only have undergone refresher training.

As well as the parachute training, there were also courses on physical and weapons training as well as familiarisation with Jeep driving and maintenance. Instruction was given in patrolling and reconnaissance, map reading and use of the compass, fieldcraft, message coding and deciphering, first-aid and how to utilise captured German vehicles and weapons. Once again, Henry was well placed to complete such courses given his experience in the front line as a soldier and behind enemy lines as an escapee or Jedburgh agent.

Given that many of the anticipated SAARF missions would be into areas where the enemy was still active or clinging to some sort of authority in a rapidly collapsing Germany, great attention was paid to conditions in the country and the enemy units that might be encountered. The uniforms of the German Army and the local police forces were studied, as were their command structures. Interpretation of air reconnaissance photographs of target areas and dissemination of knowledge of the conditions prevailing in the prisoner-of-war camps were dealt with, as were the requirements of the Geneva Convention regarding prisoners of war. Each agent was also given a German phrasebook.

With training continuing at a furious pace, time was still found for preliminary planning for the sort of operations that might need to be carried out at short notice in the event of a sudden German collapse. One possible operation involved the prisoner-of-war complex designated by the Germans as Oflag IV-C – better known as the infamous Colditz Castle, near Leipzig. This camp held several prisoners of war whom the Germans regarded as VIPs and, as such, potential bargaining chips for use in any future negotiations with the Allies. Also incarcerated there were those who had made persistent attempts at escape from other camps. Flying ace Douglas Bader was held there, as was David Stirling, founder of the SAS. The camp was regarded as being very difficult to escape from, though, over time, around 30 men did actually manage to defeat the walls and the guards, with just over a dozen subsequently making it back to safe territory.

Patrick Leigh Fermor (universally known as 'Paddy') was a Special Operations Executive (SOE) agent who had worked on the island of Crete for two years while it was under German occupation. In April 1944, Paddy had led the team that audaciously kidnapped the German commander of the Crete garrison, General Heinrich Kreipe. Dressed as German military policemen, Paddy and fellow SOE agent Bill Stanley Moss had stopped the general's car for what seemed to be a routine check of identity papers. They and several Cretan partisans quickly took control of the vehicle and its two occupants before setting off for safer territory. Paddy Leigh Fermor boldly sat in the passenger seat wearing the general's cap and returned salutes at over 20 German checkpoints, whose guards were only too keen to efficiently wave through the man they thought to be their commanding officer. After an arduous trek across the Cretan mountains to the beaches of the south of the island, General Kreipe was successfully taken by boat to British-controlled Egypt for interrogation.

A year later, in March 1945, Paddy Leigh Fermor was back in Great Britain and poring over aerial photographs of Colditz Castle. He noted, 'I found myself peering at the same ones as a fellow team-commander called Henry Coombe-Tennant, a regular in the Welsh Guards and chief actor in a particularly resourceful and daring escape.' Paddy had volunteered for service with SAARF in the same way that Henry had and was busily examining the possibilities of an operation to free or safeguard the Allied captives in Colditz. The preliminary thought was that SAARF teams would need to be parachuted into the areas surrounding a number of prisoner-of war-camps in an effort to reduce the risk of the Germans removing their captives as the Allied forces approached. There was also a real fear that prisoners might be shot out of hand by a desperate enemy. For the mission against Colditz Castle, it was envisaged that there would be three teams. Leigh Fermor would lead one three-man team, Henry another and the final team would be under the command of an American officer.

Paddy Leigh Fermor thought that it might be possible to dress in tattered uniforms and join a prisoner work detail from the castle before slipping inside its walls within the group. Once inside, it should be possible to establish radio contact with the advancing Allied forces, while impressing on the castle commandant that cooperation was the only sensible option open to him. This audacious plan obviously posed great danger to the SAARF agents involved. Working inside enemy territory and then reconnoitring and even attempting to slip into a prison compound which contained a great many heavily armed enemy troops was very risky. The detailed planning was bedevilled by a lack of local information as – being located in Germany – there was no clandestine resistance movement available to collect and pass on information about Colditz for the benefit of the SAARF teams. All they had were the aerial photographs that Henry and Paddy Leigh Fermor were now studying in great detail. Soon, however, Paddy thought that he had made a breakthrough.

He learned that an old comrade of his had managed to get out of Colditz by feigning illness in such a convincing manner that the Germans had allowed him to be repatriated in a prisoner exchange. He was now recuperating at his home, where Leigh Fermor hastened to see him. Miles Reid, MC proved to have an unbroken spirit even though his physical health, after three years of captivity and the necessity of feigning illness, was less vibrant. The two old comrades happily swapped soldiers' stories until Paddy brought up the plan for infiltrating Colditz, at which point the mood changed markedly. As Paddy recorded, Reid asked him, 'Had we learnt nothing of the impregnability of the Fortress, had we no idea of the thoroughness and the rigour of checks and counter-checks of working-parties, not heard of the scrutinies and the roll-calls?' Reid insisted that it was a suicide mission with no hope of success. Indeed, so appalled was he at the prospect of brave young men being committed to such an act of folly that he promptly went to see Brigadier J S Nichols, the SAARF commanding officer, and told him the same thing. Reid and Nichols emerged from the meeting with grim faces, Reid telling Paddy on his way out that he would even raise the matter with Winston Churchill if that proved necessary. It did not prove necessary to involve Churchill: a few days later the Allied advance secured the safety of the Colditz prisoners. Henry would have to wait for another mission.

By 7 April, there were 20 SAARF teams ready for deployment and by 21 April, that number had risen to 60. Henry seems to have teamed up with Chris Maude and a Sergeant Harrison – the latter probably being the same man that he had parachuted into the French Ardennes with during August 1944. Henry later stated in a letter to Paddy Leigh Fermor that he had actually been despatched to Germany a day or so after the German surrender in north-west Europe. In May 1945, a flood of SAARF teams were deployed to France, Belgium and Germany to perform specific tasks. Several teams were placed at airfields, where they could help organise the air evacuation of prisoners of war and civilian internees. Others worked at prisoner-of-war or civilian internee camps, assessing what foods, medicines and other supplies were required to reduce the suffering of the former captives. It seems very likely that Henry was a member of one of the SAARF teams sent to Lüneburg in early May with a remit to scour the surrounding country:

> ...for any Allied Military personnel who might have been lost in outlying districts not yet occupied by the Army. The work was so well organised that by 12 May there were virtually no Military

personnel left in 2 Army Area who were not yet evacuated or ready for evacuation.

Henry himself recorded: 'I was sent to Germany a day or so after the war ended with Chris Maude + Sgt. Harrison + a Jeep. We had a good time swanning around Germany looking for agents in the D[isplaced] P[ersons] camps.' In June 1945, his mother told Lady Jean Balfour that Henry had also been attached for a while to the 1st French Army at Lake Constance, near Ravensburg, where he had assisted in the repatriation of Channel Islanders who had been taken to Germany as slave labourers.

With those post-hostilities tasks having been completed with a surprising degree of enjoyment, Henry's war came to a satisfying end. A period of post-war soldiering now confronted him and, if not quite as exciting as his war-time adventures, it would still be filled with interest, variety and occasional danger.

CHAPTER THIRTEEN
The Palestinian Mandate

ON 11 APRIL 1945, the 1st Battalion, the Welsh Guards began reassembling at Stobs Camp near Hawick in Scotland. The camp consisted of Nissan huts and was better than some of Henry's previous accommodation, though it was somewhat small for a battalion. Amidst the usual drilling, marching and polishing, each Welsh Guards company was given its own patch of garden within the camp to tend with pride, and there were also frequent ENSA and cinema shows to relieve the monotony of home-service Army life. An added bonus was the availability of a special train to transport lucky guardsmen into the not-so-bright lights of Hawick in the evenings.

The Prince of Wales Company was soon earmarked for public duties in London and, in preparation for that role, extra attention was given to drill practice, the early results of which were deemed not to be of the highest standard. That was understandable as, since arriving back in the United Kingdom, the battalion had seen a great many changes in personnel and the arrival of 300 new recruits. The participation of the regimental band of the Coldstream Guards in drill practice was instrumental, in more ways than one, in helping the battalion reach the required standard. On 28 April, the Prince of Wales Company departed from Hawick by train for London, possibly to perform guard duty at Buckingham Palace or the Tower of London. The company returned to Stobs Camp on 8 June, arriving at the rather inconvenient time of 2.30 a.m.

203

It is not clear if Henry took any part in this as the war diary noted that on 26 June 1945, he had rejoined the battalion 'from one of his periodical trips with Special Service troops', and when he had commenced those duties or what they were was not stated. Upon his return, he soon took command of the battalion's Special Company and, during July 1945, assumed temporary command of the entire battalion for several days in the absence of the commanding officer, Lieutenant Colonel C H E Heber-Percy.

By 22 July, the battalion had relocated to Selkirk (apart from the Prince of Wales Company, which had headed for Penarth) and by 4 August, it had left Scotland and was based at Kington near Hereford, where it took over huts that had previously been home to an American military hospital. It was a step up in comfort from Stobs Camp with the added benefit of a more hospitable climate than in Scotland.

Since the battalion's return to the United Kingdom, there had been uncertainty about plans for its future deployment but the war diary recorded that on 14 September the matter had finally been settled. It was to be sent to Palestine. Preparations began immediately, with packing boxes being assembled and kit being marked with serial numbers, although the date of departure proved difficult to pin down. Companies held 'mobilisation parades' on 28 September, with the parade of the Headquarters Company being wittily referred to as a 'Hello Dai parade, where people who have not emerged for years suddenly meet old friends blinking in the daylight.'

As Captain R J Southey of the Coldstream Guards noted in the *Household Brigade Magazine* for Spring 1946:

> The news of our imminent departure for the Middle East met with a mixed reception... Training in jungle warfare was dropped and in its place came training in cordoning a village and lectures on the Jewish Agency and the Arab League, on the Balfour Declaration of 1917...

The Palestinian Mandate

Before the Great War, Palestine had been part of the Ottoman Empire and had seen fighting between British and Turkish forces during the conflict, with the British eventually capturing Jerusalem on 9 December 1917. The subsequent collapse of the Ottoman Empire led to Britain being given a Mandate from the League of Nations in 1922 that allowed it to administer the territory until such time as it was able to use its newly formed institutions to run its own administration. A complicating factor had been the 1917 declaration by Arthur Balfour, at that time the United Kingdom's Foreign Secretary (and brother of Gerald, Henry's biological father), to the effect that the British Government supported the establishment of a national home for Jewish people in Palestine. Given that the Jewish population of Palestine in those days was only about 10% of the total population of over 700,000, this edict by a foreign power rankled with the Arab majority in the country.

The result was an ever-present tension between the Jews and the Arabs, with the British stuck in the middle as peacekeepers. In the 1930s, Arab paramilitary organisations harassed and killed Jewish settlers, while civilians conducted a six-month general strike. By the end of the Second World War, the British had begun to see the Mandate as the proverbial poisoned chalice, with the Jews and the Arabs having seemingly irreconcilable differences. Increased militancy in Palestine eventually resulted in around 100,000 British troops being stationed there in an effort to keep some measure of control in a fraught situation. It was into this difficult situation that Henry Coombe-Tennant was soon to be deployed, along with his 1st Welsh Guards comrades.

On 7 October 1945, Henry was aboard the SS *Volendam* as it left Liverpool for Palestine. There was much overcrowding below decks, though mercifully the calm weather meant that there was very little seasickness. The voyage saw the ship pass Gibraltar, a place that had fond memories for Henry, as well as Malta, Algiers and Bizerta, before sailing into the harbour at

Haifa on 17 October. After disembarking, as Captain Southey noted in the *Household Brigade Magazine*:

> The whole Brigade went into camp about twenty-five miles south of Haifa and five miles inland from old Caesarea (now a ruinous small village in the sand dunes called Qisariyah by the Arabs). [The camp] was well provided with NAAFIs, shops, a cinema, and football pitches, but the most popular activity for a start was swimming, until in mid-November it became too cold...

Henry's battalion was split up by companies to provide a British military presence in several locations. In early November, Henry and the Prince of Wales Company (of which he had assumed command on 1 September) were at Tiberias, where its first hostile shots since leaving mainland Europe were fired by an alert guardsman. The object of his attention was a suspicious character observed crawling about in the barbed wire that surrounded the company location, who refused to answer a challenge. He seems to have escaped without injury. Apart from this excitement, most of the battalion's work revolved around manning roadblocks and occasionally stopping and searching suspicious-looking vehicles for arms and explosives.

By 9 November, the Prince of Wales Company had relocated to Metula, right next to the Syrian border in an area that had seen Jewish fighters getting the better of an Arab Legion patrol not long before. As well as the usual manning of roadblocks, patrolling and the attempted detection of suspected illegal Jewish immigrants, training was also undertaken in cordoning off and then searching potentially hostile villages. While the training had a serious purpose, it also allowed some room for amusement. 'Exercise Ferret' commenced at the inconvenient hour of 4.30 a.m. on 29 November and saw Henry and two companies of Welsh Guardsmen gaining entry to a 'Jewish compound' peopled with other Welsh Guardsmen adopting a distinctly unfriendly attitude towards their comrades: '... buckets of water, tins, bottles and every other form of missile

[was] hurled at them... However eventually 4 and Prince of Wales Coy got into the settlement and a weird and wonderful collection of prisoners began to stream back to the cage' – the inventive disguises adopted, including women's clothing, showing that the guardsmen had entered into the exercise with some gusto!

In the real world of 1945 Palestine, the British troops were required to exercise great caution in dealing with any difficult situations, so as not to exacerbate an already tense atmosphere. Patrols were forbidden from firing unless first fired upon or attacked with sticks or other improvised weapons, while Jewish settlements were not to be entered under normal circumstances. All in all, it was a challenging deployment.

In January 1946, Henry was involved in the planning for a full-scale deployment of the battalion should hostile activity mean that a protective cordon had to be quickly thrown around any frontier settlements near Metula. In the event, the Prince of Wales Company – and Henry – moved from Metula to Tiberias at the start of February 1946, before any need to implement his plan had emerged. Over the course of the month, several houses were searched but nothing untoward was ever discovered. On one occasion, intelligence was received that a substantial arms cache was hidden in the roof of a synagogue at Safad, but the battalion was unable to act upon it as the necessary clearance for such a politically sensitive search failed to materialise.

Searches were often carried out in conjunction with the local police force, and it became obvious that the local police were either not up to the task or had insufficient interest in doing it properly. On 8 February, the commanding officer of No. 4 Company reported that they had arrived at the local police station in Safad at 6.20 a.m. ready to take part in a search with the local police force, only to find that there were no police sentries present at the station, whose doors and gates were also wide open, despite it being a potential target for militant Jews or Arabs. It had taken some time before an

207

armed man could even be found in the vicinity. It was evident that the police believed that house searches were a waste of time. A thorough search of a building for arms or explosives should have taken several hours, but the police regarded the job as being completed after sniffing around each house for no longer than 15 minutes or so. The only redeeming feature seemed to be that the process had a nuisance value for the house occupants, who were often viewed with suspicion by the Welsh Guards.

If roadblock and house-search duties proved necessary but monotonous diversions, the area was still a dangerous place to be. At the end of February, an attack was made by Jewish militants on an Arab Legion camp near Safad, and a sentry was injured. At least one of the attackers was wounded and the Welsh Guards were summoned to the scene and set off in pursuit, aided by an elderly Arab tracker and two sniffer dogs. They approached a Jewish settlement which looked more like a fort than a village, which seemed to meet with the dogs' disapproval. The inhabitants were turned out and proved to be about 25 young men, though none displayed any wounds inflicted in the last few hours. The settlement was searched in vain, though after widening the search area a little, a cache of arms and explosives was discovered, buried in an oil drum. It seemed that the settlement was a Haganah (a Jewish paramilitary organisation) training camp so the inhabitants were marched under armed escort to the Safad police station for further questioning. It was a matter of some pleasure that, at last, a search mission had produced a tangible result.

June 1946 saw several actions by Jewish resistance movements. A number of bridges linking Palestine to its neighbouring countries were blown up and railway workshops were attacked. Five British officers were abducted in Tel Aviv by the Irgun group (a Zionist paramilitary organisation), while another officer was abducted in Jerusalem. These actions prompted the British to take measures hitherto avoided in an

The Palestinian Mandate

attempt to keep tensions at a manageable level. Large-scale operations were authorised by London in an effort to end the state of near-anarchy in Palestine. It was hoped that the success of these operations would result in a reduction in the number of bombings, murders and abductions, while also encouraging the opening of channels of dialogue with what were seen as the more responsible members of the Jewish community.

The main effort was 'Operation Agatha', which took place over three days, starting on 29 June. It saw thousands of British troops manning roadblocks, flagging down trains and searching almost 30 Jewish settlements. Resistance was encountered, which resulted in several Jews being killed and almost 3,000 arrested. 15 caches of arms were discovered, containing over 300 rifles, 100 mortars and 400,000 bullets. Several offices of the Jewish Agency were raided and a large quantity of documents taken away for analysis. In a subsequent quid pro quo, the commuting of the death sentences already passed on two Irgun members to life imprisonment resulted in the release of the abducted British officers.

The 1st Welsh Guards spent two days on Operation Agatha duties, returning to the camp at Tiberias in early July to find the level of security greatly heightened in the light of ongoing events. The ongoing Jewish insurgency had already resulted in a noticeable increase in anti-Jewish sentiment within the battalion and a bomb attack on 22 July on the King David Hotel in Jerusalem made matters worse. That attack was made by members of the Irgun group in an effort to destroy potentially incriminating paperwork confiscated during Operation Agatha. It killed 91 people, including 28 British citizens.

Happily, matters soon calmed down again as far as Henry and his comrades were concerned. As August unfolded it became too hot to work in the afternoon and tasks were scheduled to be completed by 11.30 a.m. each day, with the afternoons being given over to educational activities. The standard of drill parades gradually improved and the mood was lifted by a visit from the 1st Division's entertainment troupe. The battalion left Tiberias in early October for a new camp near Azrak in Jordan. While there, Henry and his Prince of Wales Company staged a mock attack for the benefit of the visiting King Abdullah I of Jordan, the King expressing his amazement at the tremendous weight of firepower that could be called upon by a single company. It was not long before the battalion moved back to Palestine, with the Prince of Wales Company taking up a new position at Metula while other elements of the battalion were about 40 miles away.

By October, the battalion was no longer manning roadblocks every night. This was a relief to all concerned, as the gains made from such operations had been minimal on most occasions. As a result, the battalion enjoyed quite a peaceful time for the most part – though there were exceptions and, on the night of 3 November, a clash between armed Jews and Arabs near the village of Az-Zawiya resulted in five fatalities. Henry's Prince of Wales Company was rushed to the scene but, on arrival, found that all was now thankfully quiet. Nevertheless, for several weeks, a platoon was stationed near the village both day and night as a precautionary measure.

No doubt suffering from boredom brought on by what was becoming an often unexciting posting in Palestine, an ever-restless Henry managed to secure some diversionary activity. In 1946 His Majesty's Government in the United Kingdom saw some merit in providing the rulers of Saudi Arabia with a military Mission, intended to help increase the effectiveness of the Saudi Arabian armed forces. It was thought that specialised training delivered by experienced regular soldiers of the British Army would help produce a Saudi force capable of providing internal security in that country, as well as defence against external aggression from neighbouring states.

The establishment of the Mission suffered from the usual Whitehall wrangling over expense, but was finally settled as requiring a force of approximately 11 officers (one of whom

The Palestinian Mandate

would be Henry) as well as 42 other ranks, including some Indian Sunni Muslims to show the Saudis and others that British training could produce first-class soldiers, regardless of nationality. Though small in size, the Mission would be under the command of a Brigadier, an officer with the necessary authority to meet his Saudi counterparts on equal terms, as well as having some clout in the inevitable squabbles over detail and costs with the Ministry of Defence in London.

A British medical officer would be attached to the Mission since, even though the force was small in size, the remoteness of its location meant that obtaining medical aid from local resources would be very difficult. Also provided would be a contingent of British electrical and mechanical engineers, who would be needed to repair what were expected to be mainly defective and poorly maintained Saudi military vehicles. Henry would serve as the Mission's Deputy Assistant Adjutant and Quartermaster General, ensuring that all requisite supplies were available when required. It was a responsible position that covered administration and the delivery of rations, ordnance stores and all the items that were required to maintain a force in the field.

The location chosen for the Mission was the town of Ta'if, which had a population of around 15,000 and was situated some 150 miles inland from Jeddah, roughly 5,000 ft above sea level. Use of the road to Jeddah was problematic as it involved passing through Mecca, forbidden to non-Muslims. The alternative route involved rough tracks skirting Mecca and, in often very hot weather, took a tiring eight to ten hours. To avoid this logistical difficulty, it was decided that the Mission would usually be supplied by air, with one incoming aircraft every 12 days or so being sufficient to meet the needs of the force. Once an aircraft landed at the Ta'if airfield, the Mission was only a 40-minute vehicle journey away.

Advance elements of the Mission began arriving in Saudi Arabia in January 1947 and the entire force – including Henry

– had arrived by early February. The Mission headquarters was located in two houses on the outskirts of Ta'if while work proceeded, somewhat slowly, on the construction of a training camp nearby. An early niggle was related to the letters from home to those serving with the Mission. It was noted that some had gone astray, others had taken weeks to arrive and much mail had been erroneously forwarded to Aden, with multiple complaints having little discernible effect on the matter.

Henry threw himself into his new role, occasionally moving about by camel and donning Arab dress. He was learning Arabic and took the opportunity to visit several sites associated with Lawrence of Arabia, including the fortress at Qasr al-Azrak where Lawrence had based his headquarters during the winter of 1917–18. Henry's role at the Mission camp was beset with difficulties. His support team was small and included one Palestinian sergeant who assisted in making local purchases and handling the mail if it ever arrived. This man was also used by Henry as an interpreter, a role that often saw him being borrowed by the Mission's engineers and medical officer for the same purpose. Stores that arrived had to be carefully checked, as many expected items simply failed to turn up. Occasionally paperwork arrived without the items that it referred to, while at other times, the items arrived but with no sign of the paperwork, making the task of checking that all that was due had actually been received very difficult. It was, for a time, an administrative mess that took an enormous amount of time for Henry and his hard-pressed team to sort out.

The climate did not help. In April 1947, Henry had to travel from Ta'if to Jeddah by lorry in order to collect supplies for the Mission. At least Jeddah provided a cooling breeze from the sea, though the task proved problematic. There was no mechanical lifting gear available at the port so every crate (some weighing half a ton) had to be manhandled by hired Arab labourers onto the lorries. After a very welcome overnight stay in Jeddah, the journey back to Ta'if took an energy-sapping 11 hours, with the inland heat hitting the convoy 'like a sledgehammer'. The radiator of Henry's vehicle boiled over twice, meaning delay and vital drinking water being used in refilling it. It was a gruelling experience.

Maintaining morale in such an alien environment was a priority and dissatisfaction was expressed at the fact that, despite several subscriptions being taken out, magazines and books were in very short supply or simply failed to arrive. There were no facilities for relaxation and enjoyment other than those the Mission was able to provide for itself. There was a cinema show once a fortnight, and those serving had arranged, on their own initiative, cricket, football and hockey games. Tombola, darts and gramophone or radio music also helped to break up the monotony of off-duty life at the Mission. A Mission report noted: 'On Fridays the more energetic members of the Mission have been climbing the surrounding mountains.' Henry was one of those who took part in the mountaineering activities, earning an admiring mention by the respected modern-day British mountaineer Tony Howard:

> Thirty years after Lawrence [of Arabia], three members of a British Mission to Saudi Arabia travelling with the protection of Glubb Pasha passed through Wadi Rum. Inspired by the mountains, they set off to climb Jebel Rum from the vicinity of Ain Shelaali. One of the trio, Henry St John Armitage, stopped before the summit. The other two, Major Henry Coombe-Tennant, Welsh Guards and a Lance Corporal with the marvellous nickname of 'Havabash' Butler made it to the top, or more likely to the southern summit... It's a wild and complex place and anyone climbing there needs to take great care to remember the route. Many competent climbers have inadvertently spent a night on Jebel Rum! Regardless of which summit they reached, it was the first non-Bedouin ascent of any of Rum's mountains.

It is impossible to understand how Henry proved to be such a capable climber. He was familiar with the Swiss mountains, of course, due to his regular pre-war forays to the ski slopes, and had proved himself a proficient skier. But snow climbing was clearly no preparation for such a difficult climb as that posed by Jebel Rum.

The British members of the Mission had, with very few exceptions, volunteered to serve in Saudi Arabia. They had done so on the tacit understanding that, given the remoteness of the posting, oppressive climate and general lack of facilities, additional leave and financial allowances would be granted by way of compensation. This proved not to be the case and, by June 1947, morale was plummeting and a number of men had opted to leave early. The Senior Warrant Officer, a sergeant instructor, the senior engineering representative and a signaller had all already quit the Mission, while almost a dozen more had expressed their intention to leave before the end of the year. It is unclear whether Henry was one of the dissatisfied men, but there is no doubt that – while he did not need any additional financial allowance – he was bored, and probably fed up with the mind-numbing administrative difficulties experienced on a daily basis in his work. As it turned out, he would not remain in his role to the end of the year either.

Henry left Ta'if on 21 November 1947. He did so with the substantive rank of Major, as announced in the London Gazette of August 1947, having previously been promoted to that rank only temporarily. He rejoined the 1st Welsh Guards, the main body of which was at that time in the Transjordan, though initially Henry found himself in Beit Lid near Nablus in Palestine. In a letter home to his mother, he said that he was hoping to buy a second-hand car as Army transport was in very short supply and the six horses that were available to his unit were often deployed on other duties. He told his mother that while a car would allow him to do some sightseeing, it carried with it the risk of being stoned or shot at by Arabs or Jews who resented the British presence. He added, 'it is a boring life + no wonder every soldier in Palestine is hoping he will never see the place again.'

Soon a restless Henry was looking forward to post-Army days and pondering his options in another heartfelt missive to his mother. He told her that he had written to someone in the world of music seeking career advice, but had received a disappointing response. The writer (probably R O Morris, who had been a Professor at the Royal College of Music in London), advised Henry that 'The musical profession is underpaid and overworked. You may be one of the few who are predestined to it, but I should think it unlikely.' He firmly advised Henry to stick with the Army.

Henry visited Amman and then Irbid in Jordan in December, and at Irbid met Teal Ashton, a British officer serving with the Arab Legion. He found, much to his surprise, that Ashton appeared to have 'gone native', expressing a tremendous enthusiasm for the Arab cause, which Henry privately disagreed with. He noted, 'I am far too sympathetic to Zionism ever to take any part in an Arab v. Jew war + far too fond of the Arabs to ever wish to fight against them.' Teal's stance struck a chord with Henry in other ways, however, in that he had found something he could put his heart into, something Henry felt he lacked in his own life. Henry had been an agnostic since his late teens, but somewhat surprisingly he now mentioned religion in an emotional outpouring to his mother:

> I have spoken of finding oneself – I mean that one must escape from oneself in the sense of that phase that Jesus must have had in mind when he said that if you would find yourself you must first lose yourself, or words to that effect... The urge to slough off the stale accretions of habit + past history + environment, to start again as it were from scratch, to shed the old self with all its millstones + be 'born again', is surely a tacit admission that if a man has not found himself he must lose and find himself anew?

The arrival of 1948 found Henry still in Palestine, though his and the rest of the battalion's time there was now limited. The British would soon withdraw, leaving the Arabs and Jews to hopefully co-exist in peace, an outcome that – then as now – was actually rather hard to imagine. He reassured an anxious Winifred that, despite alarmist reports in the British press, he was not in any great danger and certainly not in the thick of any fighting. The country was, he said, for the most part, entirely peaceful and he had actually found the time to safely travel (in his new Jaguar) with several other officers to some marshes where it had been possible to shoot ducks. During the evening Henry had brought down two of the seventeen ducks that were hit. No doubt to Winifred's consternation, he then cheerfully informed her that his duck-shooting exploits had been accompanied by the distant sound of gunfire as an attack on a distant Jewish village was dealt with by unknown forces. It was only the ducks that were in danger, he told her reassuringly.

As January ran its course, Henry had concerns on several fronts. His fellow escapee, Albert Arkwright, was in the process of having his account of the Warburg escape proofread before publication, a prospect that was not to Henry's taste. He advised his mother, who had been in contact with Arkwright, that he did not like the idea of surnames and regiments being mentioned. He was, he said, 'against all forms of self-advertisement masquerading as art'. Despite Henry's reservations, the work was nevertheless published, including names.

Once the battalion was disentangled from its duties in the Middle East, Henry expected to get at least a month's leave and intended to use the time to look up old friends, including Archie Rose and the Balfour family. He was planning to visit Belgium and see the d'Oultremonts as well as getting back to Neath, where he hoped to lay the groundwork for some matches that the battalion rugby team could play against local teams in October 1948.

A possible career in music still appealed to him, though he confessed that the earlier reservations of the accomplished musician R O Morris had severely dented his confidence. He was determined to call upon Morris while on leave to attempt to obtain from him a final verdict on the prospects of earning a living by way of his musical talent. In the meantime, he was stuck with soldiering and took his former Commanding Officer Sammy Stanier and another senior officer on a 500-mile round trip in his Jaguar, visiting Beirut and Baalbek. He was also asking Winifred to help organise bringing his Jaguar and his pet dog, Jacko, back to the United Kingdom.

Henry's company (now reduced to only 35 men) moved to the police station in Nablus, where their work amounted to providing 'security for the government + police who are still nominally functioning – though the area is full of armed Arab troops who have come in from Syria + Transjordan + are only waiting for the British to leave Palestine before they invade and try to wipe out the new Jewish State. Since we are not strong enough to drive them out or prevent them from being reinforced, we maintain a kind of gentlemen's (or what the Jews would call a crook's) agreement, by which we leave them alone if they leave us alone + don't make trouble.'

In March, Henry enjoyed a period of leave. He travelled from the Baalbek area of Lebanon to Damascus and then on to Beirut before heading towards the Cedars, an area in the north of Lebanon where it was possible to ski. The trip proved problematic and his party was forced to stay in a small village after being snowed in – though this was no doubt a welcome change from the stifling heat of Palestine. He eventually enjoyed five days' skiing, and, on the return journey, the party stopped to view the famous Crusader castle at Krak des Chevaliers. Henry was able to happily describe his experiences in a letter to his mother, with the added bonus of being able to tell her that he hoped to arrive back in Great Britain the following month. His Palestinian travails would soon be over.

CHAPTER FOURTEEN
Inside Intelligence

WITH THE ENDING of the British Mandate in Palestine in 1948, Henry duly returned to Britain with his Welsh Guards comrades. In June he was chosen to command a 75-strong Welsh Guards contingent at the Trooping of the Colour on Horse Guards Parade. There was particular public interest in the 1948 ceremony since, for the first time since 1939, the soldiers would be wearing the full ceremonial uniform of red tunics and bearskins. The ceremony had been cancelled from 1940–46 and in 1947 simple battledress had been worn by those taking part. As it happened, the decision to return to the ceremonial uniform in 1948 held within it the seed of its own failure.

Around 250,000 spectators awaited the event in Whitehall and along the route on the morning of 10 June. There had been heavy rainstorms on the previous day and it had rained outside of London on the morning of the parade. It was fine, however, when a police car drove carefully through the assembled masses, using a loudspeaker to broadcast the unwelcome news that the ceremony had been cancelled "due to the weather". The Major General commanding the London District had been given an unfavourable weather forecast and, fearful of the damaging effects of rain on red tunics and other expensive military equipment, he had taken the decision to cancel the event, much to the disappointment of the crowd. The expected storms failed to materialise but by then it was too late to save the ceremony.

In 1948, Henry commenced 'special employment' with the War Office and continued in that situation until his retirement from the Army in 1956. The precise nature of his duties and the locations where he was employed are sketchy, but it is known that in 1952 he was based in West Germany, while in 1953 he was stationed in Klagenfurt in Austria.

After its defeat in the war, Germany had been occupied by the Allied powers as a process of de-Nazification took place and the country's devastated infrastructure was gradually rebuilt. The northern portion of western Germany was occupied by the British and included the cities of Hamburg, Hanover and Cologne. Also stationed within the British zone were military and administrative units from Belgium, Poland and Norway. The Americans occupied the southern area of western Germany, including the cities of Kassel, Nuremburg and Munich. The region to the west of the American sector was the responsibility of the French, centred on the city of Kaiserslautern. The eastern part of Germany was under the control of the Soviet Union and included the cities of Berlin, Leipzig and Dresden. The city of Berlin, although solidly situated in the Soviet zone, was treated as a special case and was itself divided into British, American, French and Soviet sectors. Post-war Austria had been dealt with in a similar manner, with the Soviet Union controlling the eastern part of the country while the central portion was held by the British in the south and the Americans in the north. To complete the picture, the western part of Austria was placed under the control of the French.

Relations between the Western powers and the Soviets soon became strained as political differences came to the fore in the post-war period. While Britain, America and France saw merit in helping the occupied areas under their control improve their living conditions and economy, the Soviets seemed more interested in merely collecting reparations from a defeated Germany. In 1948 the Western powers decided to unite their zones of occupation into a single economic unit and, in June, introduced a new currency. This move infuriated the Soviets, who decided that all air, road, rail and water links between western Germany and Berlin would be cut, causing huge supply problems for the non-Soviet controlled areas of Berlin. A risky battle of wills ensued in which the Western powers showed that they were not prepared to be browbeaten by the Soviets. Between June 1948 and May 1949 an astonishing 2.3 million tons of food, fuel, machinery and other goods were airlifted into non-Soviet controlled Berlin, largely by American airpower. These measures, coupled with economic sanctions that were imposed on the Soviet Union and its allies, saw the blockade being abandoned in May 1949.

It was into this troubled political landscape that Henry Coombe-Tennant found himself posted in 1952–53. It is likely that his 'special employment' by the War Office involved him in intelligence activities in both Germany and Austria. The North Atlantic Treaty Organisation (NATO) had been established in 1949 to provide a bulwark against possible Soviet aggression in Europe. The British forces in Germany and Austria gradually saw their role change from occupiers to comrades-in-arms of those occupied, as NATO forces took up positions on the border with East Germany with the aim of repelling any potential Soviet attack.

The British already had an intelligence-gathering operation in occupied Germany at the time of Henry's arrival, though it is not certain that he served within it. In 1947 the Intelligence Division, a body that reported to the Foreign Office (and then to the War Office from 1952 onwards), had stated that its main functions in post-war Germany were to ensure 'the security of the British Zone of Germany. This task embraces the investigation and combatting of all threats to that security, including those which emanate from foreign espionage and from subversive political movements of the left.' There was much to be done in defeating influence from the Soviet Union, but there was also a need to stifle any Nazi revival that might be attempted by surviving and influential former members of Hitler's Nazi Party.

Military intelligence duties in West Germany involved trying to determine exactly what the Soviets (and their Warsaw Pact allies) were planning. Post-war Communist activity in Greece and Italy, the Berlin blockade and the North Korean invasion of South Korea all helped to raise tensions and instil the fear that the worldwide advancement of Communism might eventually involve an invasion of Western Europe by the Soviets and their allies. It was vital, therefore, that NATO forces gather accurate intelligence on enemy intentions. Some of this could be obtained by simple observation of the enemy border area, though it was important that, wherever possible, information was also available on the positions of enemy reserves much further back in East Germany. Knowing where these units were could give an indication of where an enemy attack might be focused, allowing NATO to concentrate its forces on the threatened locations rather than stringing them out over the entire border. Location intelligence regarding enemy units would also help provide target information to NATO air and artillery formations as an attack developed. Despite the numerical superiority of the Warsaw Pact forces, plus the possible element of surprise, it was hoped that NATO forces could stop any enemy advance as far to the east as possible.

German soldiers who had been captured by the Russians during the Second World War were still being released from captivity in the early 1950s. On their return, these men were interrogated about what Soviet military resources they had seen during their journey to the west, in the hope that useful information on enemy concentrations could be acquired. It was also possible to monitor Soviet military radio traffic, decoding some messages and, where that was not possible, watching for changed patterns of enemy radio activity that might be an indication that something unusual was afoot. As an experienced soldier, it is very likely that Henry would have been required to examine such intelligence material and then try and determine if it gave any clue to likely Soviet intentions.

Henry's personal diaries for the period 1952–54 have survived, though perhaps unsurprisingly they fail to give much detail on his military and intelligence activities. One duty that he undertook on 14 February 1952 was to act as one of the four guardsmen who mounted the vigil by King George VI's coffin in Westminster Hall, one at each corner. Henry had, of course, met the King on at least two occasions during the war: when he had been presented with his Military Cross in 1943 and when he had had tea at Sandringham after breaking down in Norfolk. He later received a note of thanks from Her Majesty, the Queen, for his duty at Westminster Hall.

He visited Brussels, probably in connection with his NATO duties, though it is not clear. In his spare time he took part in a boar shoot and regularly visited the 'club' – presumably an officers' club – where he served on the committee and occasionally played bingo. He maintained his interest in skiing, visiting Davos and Klosters when on leave and enjoying the climbs up the slopes and the rapid descents. In August 1953, he attended the Bayreuth Festival where, over five days, he saw Wagner's *Ring Cycle* performed.

He established a friendship with Graham Beer, an MI6 officer who was stationed in Germany in the 1950s and who, like Henry, had studied at Cambridge University – though their time there did not coincide. It is possible that Henry was also a member of MI6 by this time, while appearing to be an Army officer. When Graham's son Charles was born in 1956, Henry became his godfather and attended his christening. Graham remembered that Henry was driving a Bentley while in Germany and – after bringing down a stag while hunting in the German forests – unthinkingly placed the unfortunate animal in the velvet-lined boot and ruined the lining.

By the beginning of 1954, Henry Coombe-Tennant was serving in Austria with the force that went by the designation of 'British Troops Austria' (BTA). As with British forces in Germany, the troops in Austria had morphed from occupiers to allies of the Austrians as NATO strove to discourage Soviet expansionist ideas. He was based in Klagenfurt and seems to have taken part in various BTA activities. He attended meetings of its ski club and observed and possibly took part in its skiing championships in February 1954. He also attended the BTA horse show, an event that he must have enjoyed given his long-standing affinity with horses and riding. He managed to squeeze in a trip to the United Kingdom in September 1954, where he had dinner with his brother Alexander before the latter got married at Westminster. As 1954 came to a close, so did Henry's involvement with the British forces in Austria. He returned to the United Kingdom and served there until his retirement from the Army in 1956. His mother Winifred was by that point 81 years old and in poor health. On 31 August 1956 she died at her home in Cottesmore Gardens, Kensington, with Alexander in attendance. The primary cause of death was certified as being bronchopneumonia, with arteriosclerosis being shown as a secondary factor.

Winifred had long anticipated the end of her days and, in July 1954, had given instructions as to what should happen on her death. She had expressed a wish that her final hours should not be spent in her home but that, logistics allowing, she should be admitted to a nursing home. Henry had pointed out at the time that this might simply not be possible and that a doctor might be reluctant to authorise removal from her home, which would give Winifred notice that the end was near. That was of little import to Winifred who, firm as ever in her belief in the survival of the human spirit after the death of its earthly body, assured her son that her death was something she would welcome. She had also agreed that Henry should not be sent for as her death drew near, as he wished to remember her as she had appeared in life. It was also her wish that her body be cremated and her ashes placed in the crypt of All Hallows by the Tower in London. Even though the family had left Neath as far back as 1931, news of her death was received with sadness in South Wales and a great many fulsome tributes were paid to her work and character. David Bell, the curator of the Glynn Vivian Art Gallery in Swansea – whose owner, the Swansea Corporation, Winifred had advised on possible purchases for the gallery over many years – noted:

> Wales has never been rich in patrons of painting but in her was born a gift for patronage which was never limited to the superficially successful nor tainted with snobbery. It was this enthusiasm as much as her more practical help which touched and benefitted so many artists in Wales. And it was this enthusiasm that gave Evan Walter[s] the power to paint the only picture he ever painted which leaves no room for regret – his last portrait of her and painted shortly before his death.

Swansea artist Alfred Janes stated:

> She has been linked for as long as I can remember with the encouragement of artists, particularly Welsh artists. At the time of her residence at Cadoxton, her home was a meeting place for many young painters. One of her greatest contributions to art was the introducing of young artists to each other in her most hospitable home, thereby setting up life-long friendships and relationships.

Her unstinting efforts on behalf of wartime prisoners of war – and especially Henry and his Welsh Guards comrades – were acknowledged by an officer of the regiment, who told Henry that his mother had been 'one of the best Welsh Guardsmen we have had...'

Memorial services were held in both London and Cadoxton. All Hallows by the Tower was the setting for the London service, conducted by the Reverend Tubby Clayton of the Toc H organisation, a long-time friend of the family. Henry and Alexander were present, as well as family, friends and representatives of the Welsh Guards, the Baptist Union and

Toc H. At Cadoxton, the service took place in Saint Catwg's Church, situated just a few hundred yards from the old family home and the church that the family had attended in former years. Alexander, as the elder son, read the lesson and also present were representatives of the Gorsedd of Wales, the Red Cross, Glamorgan County Council and a number of local dignitaries, tenant farmers and estate workers.

It seems that although his mother's extensive psychic activities under the guise of 'Mrs Willett' had remained a secret to all except a small circle of members of the Society for Psychical Research, Henry himself had become aware of this in 1944. At the time of his mother's death, Henry Coombe-Tennant was essentially an agnostic in terms of his religious beliefs. However, he was well aware of Winifred's firm belief that her spirit would survive the death of her earthly form and it seems that, shortly after her death, his interest had become piqued at to whether or not his mother's spirit could, in fact, be contacted. Henry was already a member of the Society for Psychical Research and he asked Mr W H Salter, a lawyer and psychical researcher who had been President of the Society in 1947–48, to make certain enquiries on his behalf. Salter had previously had some contact with Miss Geraldine Cummins, a well-known psychic medium, and wrote to her in August 1957. He stated that a member of the Society wished to try and contact his late mother, and asked whether she would like to take part in what was a 'peculiar' case.

Miss Cummins accepted and, with assistance from Henry, several samples of Winifred's handwriting were sent to her for perusal and for comparative purposes with any handwriting that might emerge during a sitting with her spirit via the process of automatic writing. Salter revealed the enquirer to be Major A H S Coombe-Tennant, a name that apparently meant nothing to Miss Cummins. Over the following 30 months, Miss Cummins produced 40 scripts, each supposedly the work of Winifred Coombe Tennant's spirit.

The scripts might be construed as Winifred attempting to convey to Henry, via Miss Cummins, elements of her life on earth that would gradually convince her son that it was indeed the spirit of his mother producing the communications. Christopher Tennant's death in 1917 while serving with the Welsh Guards was mentioned, as were the Balfours. Winifred's work as a magistrate was referenced as was the service of one of her sons (given as 'Henry' or 'Harry') during the Second World War. 'Cadox [Cadoxton] Lodge' was referred to, as well as Winifred's husband Charles and several of his family members. The origins of Winifred's psychical doings as 'Mrs Willett' were dealt with, and her sittings with Sir Oliver Lodge and Gerald Balfour were recounted. 'Winifred' also apologised to Alexander, telling him that she regretted thinking of him in less favourable terms than Henry and in taking less interest in him than his younger brother – of whom she had, of course, had such high expectations. She apparently concluded the 39th and penultimate session by saying to Alexander:

> Now I see it all so clearly, I find I love you dearly, but not with the selfish overwhelmingly possessive desire that I showed for Henry. Dear sons, I send you from the Hither World my true love in equal shares.

Those sceptical of the validity of scripts such as these will question whether the information supposedly coming from Winifred in fact came from Miss Cummins herself, possibly by simple fraud. Advocates of psychic or paranormal occurrences posit that such events can be explained by telepathy or a similar, but unexplained phenomenon. Some believe that the subconscious mind of the medium can draw on facts contained in remotely located books or even the mind of a living person. Was it possible that Miss Cummins had simply researched the family history in some manner? Had she had contact with acquaintances of the family and innocently gained knowledge in that way? Had she read accounts of Tennant family history many years earlier which resurfaced in her memory when approached by Mr Salter and Henry? This book is not the place to confirm or deny the truth behind the scripts. Numerous studies of such material have been published in recent years and examine the evidence in great detail.

It is worth noting, however, that Henry and Alexander did find some telling points and mannerisms in the scripts. Henry found the description of his relationship with his mother very accurate, and thought another passage was 'so true to my mother's style of expression that as I see it, I seem to see the words in her handwriting.' Alexander Coombe-Tennant asserted, regarding one long script, "That is one hundred per cent my mother!" Despite them being impressed by some of the family detail recorded in the scripts emanating from Miss Cummins, Henry nevertheless remained an agnostic for several more years. His attitude to religion was later to change suddenly, in circumstances cloaked in mystery.

Though firm facts are understandably scarce, it seems that after retiring from the Army in 1956, Henry Coombe-Tennant was certainly a member of the Secret Intelligence Service of the United Kingdom, specifically MI6. It is quite likely that he joined the Service in the early 1950s, though that cannot be confirmed. It has often been claimed that recruitment into Britain's secret intelligence services depended heavily on 'the old boy network', where a serving intelligence officer would give a former schoolmate a 'tap on the shoulder', before confidentially asking whether he was up for a certain type of work. In Henry's case, he certainly had the right credentials: good family background, educational history that took in Eton and Cambridge, membership of the 'right' gentlemen's clubs in London (e.g. the Athenaeum), daring exploits during the Second World War and post-war work in Army Intelligence. He had also previously met British MI6 agent Kim Philby, now infamous as a traitor, at Cambridge and possibly again while working for the Special Operations Executive in 1944.

Having joined the secret world of MI6, Henry was posted to the British Embassy at The Hague in the Netherlands, where he performed the role of Second Secretary, no doubt concerned with matters of military intelligence and probably other clandestine activities. He was certainly in post in The Hague when, in 1957, Barbara Walsh (Barbara Lloyd after her marriage) arrived and took up the post of his secretary. The Head of Section at that time was Maurice Whinney, a former RAF pilot who had been winkled out of that role in 1944 by an MI6 impressed by his aptitude in flying top-secret missions during which he trialled improved air-to-ground communication equipment.

Despite the passage of 60 years, and even with the Official Secrets Act now no longer applying to her, Barbara Lloyd still feels commendably unable to reveal what issues had occupied Henry and herself during their time with MI6 at The Hague. The secrets of 'The Office', as Barbara called her MI6 station, were to remain just that – secrets. She upholds the ideals of her grandfather, Colonel T J Kendrick, OBE, who was himself the MI6 Head of Station in Vienna during the Nazi era and was at one time arrested and interrogated by the German secret service before being released after diplomatic pressure from Great Britain.

Barbara Lloyd remembered her posting to The Hague as 'the most interesting job I have ever had'. Of working with and for Henry Coombe-Tennant, she noted:

> I can only say what a privilege it was to work for such an extremely intelligent, modest and remarkable man. He was the epitome of a true British gentleman. He was a very private person and never spoke about his personal life. I know that he was extremely musical, and on occasions would invite me to go with him to a concert. He was also extremely fond of horses and on more than one occasion invited me to the Concours Hippique in Rotterdam. Henry was very reserved, one might almost say 'enigmatic', but in the nicest possible way.

Henry Coombe-Tennant's arrival as an MI6 agent at The Hague in the mid-1950s coincided with the Cold War between the Soviet Union and its allies and the NATO Alliance countries. The role of MI6 was to advance and protect British people and British interests overseas by a variety of methods, and the Service provided the British Government with a worldwide covert capability. Intelligence could be gathered by a range of secret techniques or even simple human observation. In particular circumstances, operations could be mounted on foreign soil to detect or prevent serious crime and to defend the national security of the United Kingdom.

It is likely that Henry would have been involved in intelligence gathering during his time in post, though given the obviously secret nature of his work for MI6, it is impossible to know just exactly what he got up to. There were several issues that might have attracted his attention at the time. For example, the Netherlands and Indonesia were embroiled in a dispute over territorial claims to Dutch New Guinea, and for a period the Dutch made use of an informer in high Indonesian circles, sharing the information with their British counterparts. Additionally, as a key member of NATO, Great Britain was concerned to see Dutch military resources being potentially deployed to the Pacific when the more dangerous Communist military behemoth was so close to its border in Europe. Henry would have been well placed to evaluate the likely impact of such deployments on overall Dutch military strength and probably had contacts in its armed forces that he could express concern to, in the knowledge that his words agreed with MI6 in London – would filter up the Dutch chain of military command.

The British were also keen to have the support of the Dutch with regard to the issue of the Suez Canal. Even after the abortive invasion of Egypt carried out by British, French and Israeli forces in 1956, the Dutch still supported Britain in the United Nations Assembly. No doubt MI6 officers at The

Hague, possibly including Henry, would have been keen to encourage this very welcome support with a frequent exchange of information and by promoting the views of the British Government in London to key Dutch contacts.

Henry certainly made an impression while carrying out his duties at The Hague, to the extent that, on 22 March 1958, he was made an officer of the Order of Oranje-Nassau. This award was often granted to foreign diplomats for the manner in which they had undertaken their duties while in the Netherlands. Henry had the added advantage of having helped defend The Hook of Holland in 1940, an action that had facilitated the escape to Great Britain of Queen Wilhelmina. It is not clear if Henry's role at The Hook helped him gain the award almost 20 years later, but it certainly can't have done any harm. On leaving The Hague, Henry was ready to commence his final posting. This would see him head back to the Middle East, but this time to Iraq rather than Palestine. To form a picture of the Baghdad that he arrived in in 1959, it is necessary to first look at the bloody events of July 1958.

Britain had had a long relationship with Iraq, having invaded the country during the Great War and captured Baghdad in 1917. The post-war settlement resulted in Britain effectively imposing a monarchy onto the country, while taking little notice of the claims and aspirations of the various ethnic and religious groups that comprised the kingdom. The British Mandate came to an end in 1932, to be followed by independence, though the British continued to take a great interest in the country. By 1958 Iraqi oil was of increasing importance, while Britain supplied about 30% of the goods imported into Iraq annually, a record figure at the time.

There was a disconnect, however, between Iraq's growing economy and the lot of most of its population, who largely lived in poverty and lacked basic services. The Iraqi Parliament was usually packed with supporters of the ruling cabal and the elections of May 1958 were so obviously rigged that hostility towards the regime increased markedly. Many were unhappy at what they saw as the nepotism and corruption rife amongst members of the Iraqi ruling class. Another irritant was what was seen as British meddling and string-pulling in Iraqi affairs, something that the Government of the country seemed quite relaxed about.

14 July 1958 provided opponents of the Iraqi Government with an opportunity for enforced change. Elements of the Army had been given routine orders that involved them having to move through the streets of Baghdad, and the military took the chance to seize control of the radio stations and announce a revolution. The King and Crown Prince of Iraq, together with several family members, were killed by the rebels and the Prime Minister was apprehended on 15 July and similarly dealt with. Anti-British sentiment resulted in the British Embassy in Baghdad being attacked by an angry crowd, leading to the murder of a British Embassy official. In the aftermath of the revolution, over 100 prominent Iraqis who were suspected of being pro-British were interned, pending trial by a military tribunal. A former Iraqi prime minister, several high-ranking Army officers, senior officials and even a noted broadcaster were among the numbers detained. Several were subsequently executed by the new regime.

The nature of Henry's role in 1959 Baghdad is again hidden in the shadows that always surround intelligence agents. In the same way that his work in Germany and Austria had revolved around enemy intentions during the Cold War between East and West, it is likely that in Baghdad he would have been seeking intelligence on the activities of possible Communist sympathisers in the new Revolutionary Government of Iraq, as well as on those who agitated within a myriad of political organisations for further change within the country.

He would have been concerned to ensure that Iraq, at worst, remained broadly neutral in East-West relations, while trying to steer his Iraqi contacts away from a policy of closer ties with the Soviet Union. His previous military experience rendered him well suited to report back to London on the type and quality of military equipment that the Soviets were in any event supplying to the Iraqi armed forces and he also probably took part in low-level covert actions, possibly planting stories in the press that either helped the British or hampered their enemies. Forged documents or even poison-pen letters could be circulated in a manner that caused friction or confusion within Iraqi organisations seen as hostile or unhelpful to British interests in the area, while seditious literature could be distributed anonymously. Good old-fashioned bribery could also play its part, with particular individuals being bought off for the service of Great Britain, or by secretly funding organisations sympathetic to British interests.

It is likely that, after the 1958 revolution, Henry would have inherited an MI6-organised network of Iraqi informers and political sympathisers whose members needed to be discreetly questioned about how they saw the political situation unfolding in Iraq and what developments were likely to occur in the future. It is also possible that some of the previous MI6 contacts that Henry might have hoped to utilise on his arrival in the country would have been caught up in purges by the new Government in the wake of the bloody revolution. This could have been on the basis that they had previously been too close to the deposed Government, too friendly towards the British or, indeed, that they had been suspected of being agents of a foreign power. In that situation there would be an urgent need to rebuild the MI6 intelligence networks, which brought its own dangers. As the revolution of 1958 had not been foreseen by British agents on the ground in Baghdad, London would have been very keen to try and determine if it marked the genuine commencement of a new era or whether a still unstable situation was likely to flare up again, with unpredictable consequences for the future of Iraq and British interests there. And Iraq was still unstable: in 1959, the year of Henry's arrival in the country and a year after the revolution, there was trouble in both Mosul and Kirkuk, where it was common for so-called enemies of the new regime to be arbitrarily hung from lamp posts.

Another area of interest for Henry Coombe-Tennant in his MI6 role in Iraq would have been matters relating to the British Protectorate of Kuwait. In the 1950s, Britain imported 40% of its crude oil from the Kuwaiti oilfields, while the Emir of Kuwait had invested £300m in British banks in London. Ever keen to protect its commercial interests in Kuwait, the British Government paid lip service to supporting the idea of Kuwaiti independence, while dropping veiled hints about how dangerous such a move would be. Neighbouring Iraq viewed what it saw as British imperialism in Kuwait with alarm, and there was concern in British quarters that Iraqi military intervention could not be ruled out. Indeed, Henry predicted that an Iraqi invasion of Kuwait was likely at some stage, though his view was discounted at the time. In the event, there was no invasion in this period, though a British force was temporarily deployed to Kuwait as a precautionary measure in 1961, after Henry had left the intelligence services.

One thing is certain about Henry's time in Iraq: from his own writings it is clear that something happened there that caused him both physical and psychological suffering. In the aftermath of that traumatic but largely undocumented event, Henry's life underwent a significant change and by 1960 he was back in Britain and no longer in the employment of MI6. He was about to embark on a career change that came as a total shock to his family and led his older brother, Alexander, to advise him that he was about to squander his undoubted talents.

CHAPTER FIFTEEN
A Benedictine Monk

AS PREVIOUSLY DISCUSSED, one of the few things we know for certain about Henry's time with MI6 in Baghdad is that his experiences there had a life-changing effect on him. As he recorded in 1965:

> Six years ago in Baghdad I became involved in a sequence of events and experiences whose significance seemed to me to transcend their actual content... I don't wish to be questioned about these events and experiences. It will be sufficient to say that this was a period of profound mental and physical suffering, during which (if I may put it in this way) my own ego, which had for so long been the self-sufficient centre of my inner life, disintegrated. I have grown a new ego since, of course, though not a self-sufficient one, but at that time there was nothing to hold me together. I was in pieces, + if the pieces were to be re-assembled, a new principle of unity would have to be found.

In the absence of any other surviving evidence, it is impossible to say exactly what events had such a significant impact on Henry. There is a possibility that his work for MI6 led him into situations where he might have been temporarily subjected to extreme stress or even torture by unknown parties in a post-revolution Iraq, but that is pure conjecture. Whatever it was, it had a pronounced effect on his outlook and led him to seek answers in a religious context, a surprising move for someone who had, by 1959, been an agnostic for almost 30 years, despite a strong family background in Anglicanism.

He had, of course, been baptised in the local church in the village of Cadoxton where the family home had been in his youth, and was confirmed in 1926 while at Pinewood School. His parents each practised their religion in different ways. His mother Winifred was seen as being deeply religious, though she did not routinely attend any church services. His father Charles was a 'strict Sunday church-goer', attending church every Sunday, often reading the lesson and taking Henry and Alexander with him in their younger days.

Henry had found the experience of attending church as a young man to be unenjoyable. The fact that his father was not only 60 years older than Henry but also suffered from severe deafness made discussion on theological themes (or anything else, for that matter) very difficult. The local vicar was elderly and suffered from a speech impediment that made his sermons, already pitched at an intellectual level that was too lofty for a young Henry to understand, even harder to follow. To round off what was usually a dispiriting experience each week, Henry later noted that:

> I did not like the archaic language of the prayer book, the Victorian hymns and anthems, and the sentimental harmonies of the village organist. I was bored, and in the winter cold. I acquired a dislike of church services which, to be candid, I have never really lost.

Always of a serious and independent disposition, Henry had, at the age of 12 or so, struck out on his own in relation to his religious beliefs. During the period in which he was most interested in China, he had formed the opinion that religion should encompass both the Christian God and Buddha. He passed through a period of burning incense sticks in front of a statue of Buddha before this phase of his young life ran its course and his attention turned back to his studies, much to the relief of his mother and Headmaster. At Eton College in his early teens he had found that:

I did not like chapel services at Eton any better than those at my village church, and I resented having to go – once a day and twice on Sundays. However, I did from time to time get up early on Sundays to go to Holy Communion, which was voluntary. I think I ceased to do so at about the age of 17, and after I left Eton, I seldom set foot in a church until nearly 30 years later.

During his often dangerous wartime service he had never thought to thank God for things he believed had happened due to the exercise of his own powers rather than the kindly intervention of some greater being. He was fairly agnostic in outlook, keeping an open mind on the subject and never decrying those who sought solace in religious beliefs, but to him the concept of actions that were 'right' and 'wrong' had nothing to do with the existence of God. Henry's moral compass told him that one should do the 'right thing' irrespective of whether or not God existed and required such behaviour from those who sought entry to the Kingdom of Heaven.

He said: 'As an agnostic I had no belief or hope in life after death. But this did not lead me, as it leads some, to question the value of human relationships and right conduct. Even now... fear of Hell is not a serious factor in my life (though perhaps it ought to be), nor is the prospect of eternal bliss one that I find particularly stirring.' He adopted his usual, pragmatic and analytical approach to such issues, finding it hard to accept that religious behaviour was merely something that one did in church on Sundays, as an optional extra to how one treated others during the course of the week.

Never one to address issues in a half-hearted way, Henry seems to have sought a more immersive experience after his mental and physical trials in Baghdad. He wrote: 'I began the task that autumn [1959] by praying to a God in whose existence I did not believe. This remarkable performance seemed to work. I continued to pray, + also to think. I read some books about Christianity. I chose Catholic books, because I had often thought that if I ever turned to religion, it would be to the

Catholic Church, who seemed to know her own mind... At the end of the year I asked for instruction, and in May 1960 was received into the church.' This was achieved by the good offices of the Rector of the American Jesuit College in Baghdad.

Henry came back to England later in 1960 and, having left the employ of MI6, pondered his future. As Henry told his old comrade, Paddy Leigh Fermor, by letter in 1982:

> On returning to England, full of ½ baked ideas about becoming a priest, I bought a house in Leicestershire + had a winter's hunting, all the while feeling more + more sure that a cross roads, fork roads, turning point, watershed, or what have you was looming up. After a talk with Monsignor Warlock (now Archbishop of Liverpool) I visited Downside as a guest for 3 days + had various conversations, soaked in the atmosphere (special guests' atmosphere, of course, not the real thing!) + decided to return as a postulant in May. After 2 months as a postulant I had no further doubts. I was clothed as a novice in September 1961, professed in temporary vows in 1962 + in solemn vows in 1965, priested in 1966 and given a local Parish (Radstock) in 1969...

Downside Abbey, near Bath, was the home of the Community of St Gregory the Great and was the senior Benedictine monastery in Britain. The community had left France after the Revolution and had made its way to Downside by 1814. For a time, the 'monastery' and school were accommodated in existing buildings on the plot of land that had been bought by the community. Development of the complex began seriously with the building of what is today referred to as the 'old chapel' in 1823. In the latter part of the nineteenth century, a new monastery and associated buildings were constructed on the site. The episcopal motto of St Benedict was *Pax Inter Spinas* – peace among thorns – and perhaps Henry was finally seeking some peace after the turbulence of a world war and his work in intelligence in a very dangerous Iraq.

The decision to enter Downside Abbey was, however, one taken in a typically hasty manner by Henry, in a similar vein to his earlier choice to forsake academia and join the Army. It immediately undermined the plan that he had formulated to live the life of an independent gentleman in the village of Foxton, near Market Harborough in Leicestershire. As befitting a gentleman of independent means, in the latter part of 1960 he had engaged the services of a Dutch couple that he had met while working in The Hague. Mickey and Gladys de Lange would provide the necessary support to look after Henry's home and garden, as well as attending to his domestic requirements at Foxton. Following his abrupt change of plans, Henry still felt an obligation to the de Langes. With their services no longer being required for the Foxton house after only six months, he promptly bought them a house in Bristol and, in what was almost a role reversal, kept an eye on their welfare for the remainder of their lives from his new home at Downside Abbey. After Mickey died, he even drove to Bristol on a regular basis to attend to Gladys' garden as well as buying her a stairlift when she developed mobility problems.

While Henry was quite happy in his new setting at Downside and was now living well away from the cares of the everyday world, it was nevertheless a busy time. As he breezily told a member of the Balfour family in 1961, he was in his first year as a novice and had three more years before taking final vows. He likened the experience to life at the Guards Depot, where a guardsman was constantly attending to menial chores and working against time. At Downside he was involved in gardening, the polishing of silver, the setting out and putting away of sacred items, and study, in addition to attending the various religious services. It was very much a 'head in the clouds and feet firmly planted on the ground' experience.

In 1969, after being at Downside for several years, Henry (who had taken the monastic name of Dom Joseph Coombe-Tennant), was given charge of the parish of Radstock. This came as a great relief to him as dealing with a busy parish would neatly remove him from his previous role teaching the boys in Downside School, which he had found unappealing. As Jonathan Elms, a pupil at the school in the 1960s, recalled, Henry's arrival at the Abbey had caused something of a stir:

> He wasn't teaching much in my time (1962–66) as he hadn't yet been ordained, so that was an added cause of intrigue… Therefore there was a buzz about the mysterious Dom Joseph, because – unlike the others – he wasn't much in the school, and boys have vivid imaginations! We knew he'd had a 'good war', so didn't understand why he had nothing to do with CCF [Combined Cadet Force]. In those days, though, one never asked!

Another former pupil, Brian Mooney, stated that when he was at the school, Henry was "extremely good looking and somewhat patrician but without in any sense being snobby. He did get involved in the slightly high end of things… he only discovered about his engineered birth quite late in life and it came as a bit of a shock!"

Stephen Beale lived in the village of Stratton Fosse, in which Downside Abbey is located. He has fond memories and recalls that around 1966–67 Henry:

> …was affectionately known by us young lads in the village… as Father Joe. [He] ran our youth club, we didn't have anything else to do. He supervised games such as British bulldog, indoor soccer, board games, table tennis, etc., which he brought with him as we had none. Having taken 6*d*. for our entry, which our parents provided if they had it – if not, Father Joe would say that it's OK. Then he would sit at a table reading, occasionally looking over his glasses to make sure that all was well. We thought he was a very kind man as I remember and well respected by us all, but he had an authority which he rarely had to use, just his presence shone through to us.
>
> I can see through his life that he always had the ability to radiate his character to others around him and bring out the best in them without too much effort. He was a natural, in modern terms.

Paul Tracey came across Henry at Downside School in the late 1960s and saw him as a man who "greatly impressed me as a monk and as an individual", taking his role seriously and with great humility. The pupil was struck by the fact that 'Father Joseph' had virtually no personal possessions at the Abbey, his monastic cell containing only a bed, a shelf and a crucifix. His hair was always cropped short as a monk, meaning that he did not need a comb for some 30 years. Henry told Paul of the time when, newly arrived at the Abbey, the Abbott had directed him to clean up the mess after a boy had been sick in the Abbey church, an eminently suitable role for a novice. Henry, with a distinguished academic, military and diplomatic record behind him, found his new status highly amusing.

Paul remembers that – despite the hockey pitch frequently being waterlogged – Henry would arrive to supervise the mayhem dressed in his full monk's habit. His long-standing antipathy towards sport in general shone through:

> Joseph didn't seem to actively dislike hockey. He simply appeared not to see the point of it and therefore wanted to get the game over and done with in the shortest time possible. He never ran while refereeing and if the action, such as it was, took place at the opposite end of the pitch from where he was standing, his imposing figure would stride across the pitch to where the majority of the players were congregating. If he thought there had been an infringement of the rules, he would call for play to stop by raising his arm. I never recall his using a whistle. Joseph had a limited understanding of the rules of hockey and when he thought a rule might have been breached, he would call both teams together to discuss what had just happened and to decide the appropriate response. Invariably, no consensus was reached and Joseph would conclude that the fairest course would be to restart the game with a bully-off. The consequence of this was that the two teams ran fairly aimlessly around from one bully-off to the next, until Dom Joseph, hearing the distant sound of the Abbey bell, would end the match by saying 'I think that tea is starting.' I never remember anyone keeping the score.

Henry took a relaxed view of his pupils' activities, treating them as adults and turning a blind eye to their occasional smoking and drinking of alcohol, providing those frowned-upon pleasures were not enjoyed on school premises. He took a similar approach in his role as president of the school's shooting society, permitting its juvenile members – somewhat alarmingly – to have access to their guns whenever they wished. To facilitate this, he allowed them to retain the key to the gunroom amongst themselves. This practice backfired somewhat when several pupils left the school, having completed their studies, and Henry realised that he had no idea of the whereabouts of the key. He urgently despatched letters to several former pupils, so that the missing key could be promptly located and returned to his laid-back care.

At Radstock, Henry soon co-opted Father Dominic Mansi, also a monk at Downside Abbey, to help him with the young people of the parish. Father Dominic remembered: 'He specifically asked for me, as he said that I was good with young people. As a young monk, I was not much older than some of them, so that helped!' It was not all work and Henry's general ineptness at sport had not left him; Father Dominic noted: 'On Mondays, the traditional day off for the clergy, Fr. Joseph and I played golf together. I can remember Fr. Joseph teeing up to drive off and spending some time in taking stroke after stroke, trying to hit the ball. He was a person who did not give up easily. He finally hit the ball. But the ball disappeared. We searched and searched for it. Suddenly it began to rain. I put my hood up and Fr. Joseph did the same, then suddenly the ball appeared: it had been in his hood all along. We had quite a laugh about it when we reached the nineteenth hole.'

In 1973 he was sent to the parish of Malvern where, for a period, he enjoyed a little more independence than had been the case at Radstock, though he was glad to return to the latter as Curate in 1976, combining that role with the posts of Guest Master and Junior Master at Downside Abbey. He retained the latter two roles (or "burdens", as he referred to them) until 1979, after which his only concerns remained the parish of Radstock and the routine monastic chores, which he enjoyed. He noted in 1982, 'Most of my Parish work consists of visiting – occasionally advising, more often listening. I never thought I should be able to cope with Parish work, but you never know until you try.'

The pattern of monastic worship changed over the first two decades that Henry spent at Downside. When he first arrived, the Hours were all performed in Latin, though the demands of worship were simplified and reduced over time. As well as reducing the time spent on worship, the revisions also meant that there was less time for work in the choir and many elements were now sung in English rather than Latin. Henry missed the Latin; he still said his own Mass in Latin provided he was not on Parish duty or in the local convent.

Though it caused the raising of several pairs of monastic eyebrows, he regularly received the *Journal of the Society for Psychical Research* at Downside Abbey and still retained his interest in psychic affairs, a subject that had been so important to his mother. Indeed, despite the reservations of the Catholic Church on the subject of psychic research and spiritualism, he found the time to deliver a talk on the topic in June 1975 to the Malvern Women's Institute, giving the same talk at Downside School in February 1977. Probably informed by the activities of his late mother and also by his indirect dealings with the noted medium Miss Cummins in the aftermath of Winifred's death, he kept an open mind on the subject, telling his audiences that all claims of psychic activity needed to be very carefully examined before any firm conclusions were drawn. He certainly did not rule out the possibility of communication with the spirits of the dead. Interestingly, he mentioned in his notes for the talk some detail of the work of 'Mrs Willett' in psychical research, while never apparently revealing to his audiences that Mrs Willett was, in fact, his late mother.

While serving as a monk at Downside, he continued writing on philosophy and other topics, contributing articles on 'Philosophy as a Second-Order Activity' for the *Downside Review* of July 1969, and 'The Identity Theory and Christian Belief' for the *Review* of October 1976. He also drafted (for an unknown audience) an article entitled 'The Divisions of Being', which, he noted, was concerned 'with what Wittgenstein called the "philosophical grammar" of 4 pairs of technical terms belonging to the Aristotelian-Thomist tradition...', the terms being 'Matter and Form', 'Substance and Accident', 'Essence and Existence' and 'Potency and Act'. These were clearly not papers aimed at the casual reader but demonstrated Henry's continuing interest in serious philosophical discourse. In 1970, he sent his old Cambridge tutor, Charlie Broad, a 'Discussion Note' on 'What Persons Are' and received almost four foolscap pages of tightly written criticism in response.

Another aspect of Henry's character was his love of fine wine. On visits to his brother's home in Surrey, he would relish being allowed to enter the 'cave', where Alexander stored his wine collection. Henry enjoyed taking his time to examine the wines in the cave, accurately cataloguing each new addition with great care and attention to detail. Father Dominic of Downside Abbey remembered: 'During our time together in the parish [Radstock], Fr. Joseph was posted to Little Malvern. He loved working there and I often visited him. He opened doors for me into the world of wine and jazz. He would open a bottle of wine in the morning and we would drink it in the evening. One evening we drank a wine from Chile. I had hardly heard of Chile, let alone knowing that the country produced wine.'

On one occasion Henry played host at Downside Abbey to a visiting military chaplain and, as a 'thank you' for his hospitality, was invited to enjoy a lunch in Bath at the reverend gentlemen's expense. The chaplain made the fatal mistake of allowing Henry to choose the wine to accompany the meal. It seems that Henry studied the wine list and – to him, quite naturally

– went for quality, paying no attention to price. The lunch was a great success but the chaplain subsequently admitted that he had to spend several months exercising financial self-restraint in order to get his bank balance back in order.

Henry also enjoyed painting – landscapes in particular – and was not averse to having his efforts critiqued by friends with greater artistic talent than his own. He was advised by one informal critic to avoid too much "clear blue sky" with no clouds or features of interest in his paintings and another suggested recreating his promising watercolours of Greek scenes in oils. He retained his interest in music, composing at least one work that was performed in the Abbey. Chess was a lifelong interest and when he finally retired from parish work, his grateful parishioners presented him with a carved chess set as a farewell gift. Over the years he had set and had published in the press a great many chess puzzles that required completion within a small number of moves.

In 1979 a press furore over the exposure of Anthony Blunt – so much part of the establishment that he was a former Surveyor of the Queen's Pictures – as a Soviet spy would have rekindled Henry's memories of his days in MI6. Blunt had been part of the 'Cambridge Four' spy-ring that included Donald Maclean, Guy Burgess and Kim Philby, all of whom had fled to Russia before their traitorous activities were discovered. It seems that all four had been known to Henry at Cambridge University and he would probably have encountered some of them again later through the Special Operations Executive or MI6. There were strong suspicions that there were actually five members of the spy-ring and the identity of the final member of the group led to much contemporary speculation.

Even Henry's old tutor at Cambridge, Charlie Broad, was named as an unconvincing candidate, while Henry himself was apparently mentioned half-heartedly in some quarters, purely due to his having known Kim Philby and the others for some years. Henry bore no ill will towards Philby, remarking that if he happened to pass him in the street (unlikely, since Philby had already defected to Moscow by that time), he would ask him how he was. It was 1990 before John Cairncross was revealed as the 'Fifth Man' – though, in the shady world of espionage, some still harboured doubts as to whether the entire structure of the Cambridge spy-ring had been uncovered.

As the years advanced, Henry still remembered his wartime comrades with pleasure and affection. As well as corresponding with former Special Operations Executive agent Paddy Leigh Fermor in the 1980s, he had attended at least one informal Warburg Prisoner-of-War Camp reunion dinner organised by fellow former captive Tom Stallard. It took place in the Gore Hotel, London in 1959 and was attended by 17 former POWs, who enjoyed a meal of hare soup, roast teal and cheese accompanied by sherry, several fine wines and Old Nathaniel Port. Stallard himself had climbed over the wire at Warburg at the same time as Henry in 1942, though he had subsequently been recaptured near the Dutch border. Another attendee, Bruce Todd, hosted Henry on biennial visits to his home on the Greek island of Skiathos for over a decade during the 1970s and 1980s. As Henry said, 'Life in the Villa Maria with Bruce's very English friends is indeed seeing Greece from the outside – but he is a good host + I enjoy it.'

He was still attending regimental dinners in the early 1980s, meeting up again with old comrades such as his former commanding officer, Sammy Stanier. He participated in other regimental events, such as the Welsh Guards St David's Day Service of 1972, which took place at All Saints Church at Pirbright Camp, with Henry delivering the address. In November 1980 he gave the address at the Welsh Guards remembrance service in the Guards Chapel on Birdcage Walk in London. He posed the question of why those Welsh Guards comrades who had died in conflicts around the world (including recent losses in Northern Ireland) should be remembered in a religious service, continuing:

It isn't as though, in this age, we were still able to regard war as a religious exercise. Perhaps it was so regarded before the coming of Christ, + even afterwards at times (as in the Crusades). But modern war, with its terrible destructive power, has brought home to us the fact that, even when it is rightly fought for a just cause, war is a wasteful tragedy brought about by human error. It cannot be what God wants.

He concluded that there were circumstances, brought about by the actions of man, where God could require just men to temporarily act in a manner (bearing arms, for example) that was justified, even if it was contrary to the divine plan. He also asked the congregation to remember the fallen of other Allied nations and even to pray for the dead of those countries who had been Britain's enemies during the war.

The advancing years gradually took their toll and old comrades slowly began to disappear. Fellow Warburg escapee Rupert Fuller died in 1957, while Tom Stallard answered the final roll call in early 1983. In December 1983, John (Jack) Higgon, Henry's commanding officer in Boulogne in 1940, died. Henry, representing the Abbot of Downside (who had also been a prisoner of war), gave an oration at the funeral in Pembrokeshire and also read the address at a memorial service held in honour of his old comrade in the Guards Chapel, London in February 1984.

By summer 1986, Henry's own health was starting to be a concern. He began to suffer hip pain which reduced his mobility, and the consultant physician at the Royal United Hospital in Bath recommended prompt hip-replacement surgery as Henry was in considerable discomfort. Then, as now, lengthy National Health Service waiting lists meant that an immediate operation was impossible and paying for private surgery was beyond the means of the monastic community at Downside.

Alexander Coombe-Tennant visited Henry at Downside and was very concerned at the deterioration that he saw in the health of his brother, who was now 73 years old. Indeed, he made the Downside hierarchy well aware of his opinion of what he judged to have been neglect on its part in the care of a clearly ailing Henry. Smarting from Alexander's criticism, the Abbey authorities tried to restrict Henry's movements so that he did not further exacerbate his medical problems, though their advice fell on deaf ears and Henry took part in many activities at Downside, even if it meant that he had to almost crawl to the appropriate location.

His plight was eventually brought to the attention of the Director of Army Surgery at the Ministry of Defence in London and Henry's distinguished war service referred to, with a hope that something could be done to quickly assist a 'distinguished ex-soldier'. In the event, it was 20 March 1987 before Henry was admitted to the Royal National Hospital for Rheumatic Diseases – which was, by chance, conveniently located in Bath and thus not too far from Downside Abbey. Henry's nephews – Alexander's sons, Mark and John – recalled that their uncle rather enjoyed the surgical experience, listening intently to the medical discussions in the operating theatre since only a local anaesthetic was administered. His enjoyment was marred when, part way through the procedure, he was required to wear headphones so that music muffled the sound of the drilling and sawing, as well as the doctor's conversations.

The operation was a success but it was decided that it was inadvisable to replace the second hip, as it appeared that Henry's heart was showing some signs of weakness. Henry was still left with considerable pain in the other hip and with limited mobility, a fact that seemed to play heavily on his mind and resulted in a prolonged period of deepening depression. As one who knew him sadly noted, 'Always a quiet man, he now became close to a mute and withdrew into himself. Henceforth his mind was being driven by a flagging willpower and he appeared to have lost his zest for living... It still became pitiful to watch so brilliant a light being slowly snuffed out.' Baron Peyton of Yeovil was an old comrade who had been a prisoner of war in Laufen and Warburg with Henry. He was still in contact with Henry in the 1980s and recorded that 'the pain which he endured towards the end never diminished the grace and serenity which he carried everywhere with him.'

Even while in considerable discomfort, Henry still found it possible to make occasional positive contributions. In November 1988 he was contacted by Daphne Friele (nee Park) who had worked for the SOE at Milton Hall during 1944–45, while Henry had been there training as an Operation Jedburgh agent. Daphne had been instrumental in tracking down former 'Jeds' for a first reunion event in Paris – it is unclear whether Henry attended, though, given his health issues, it seems unlikely. While seeking out American Jeds, she had met Dr S J Lewis, a historian with the Combat Studies Institute at Fort Leavenworth, Kansas. Dr Lewis was writing an account of the activities of 11 Jedburgh teams that had been parachuted into northern France in the summer of 1944. His research included Henry's Team Andrew's exploits and aided by Ms Friele, after an exchange of correspondence, Henry and Dr Lewis met at Downside Abbey on 9 May 1989. Dr Lewis' account of the work of the Jedburgh teams was subsequently published in 1991.

Despite having spent almost 30 years at Downside Abbey, Henry remained at the heart of the Coombe-Tennant family. As his nephew Mark remembered:

> Henry was always an integral part of our family and frequently stayed with us in Surrey. He shared a profound brotherly love with my father, who he always called 'Cher' (as in the French) and my father in turn called him 'Dijon'. They would quite often speak to each other in French, and held one another's achievements in the highest regard. Their mother Winifred was of course a strong binding factor throughout their lives, and her activities in South Wales and subsequently in London and with the SPR [Society for Psychical Research] were ever-present. Henry was the 'Wise One' from the get-go.
>
> I recall Henry's superb piano playing, his chess puzzle skills, and his hours spent gardening or cataloguing my father's

dishevelled wine collection. Henry loved the peace of being in the countryside and used to pray in the attic, where many of his possessions reside to this day. As children we used to play with his guards' bearskin and ceremonial swords, his piano or his collection of 78 rpm classical records. Later he would correspond with us in school and tell cheerful stories about weddings that he had conducted, never phased at driving considerable distances in his mustard coloured Mini. Like many, Henry did not want to talk about his wartime experiences and felt simply that he did what he had to do given the circumstances. He was not seeking to be a hero, but was drawn into events that unfolded and was evidently highly skilful. Undoubtedly, he enjoyed the camaraderie of Army life and later in the community at Downside. He was invariably fascinated by colour television, compact discs, or whatever the future would hold, and was a pillar of the Coombe-Tennant family.

And what of 'The Plan', which Winifred Coombe Tennant, Gerald Balfour and the elite of the Society for Psychical Research hoped would see him develop into the new Messiah? He certainly had the intellect and his physical appearance was also noteworthy, as Jean Balfour had recorded in 1944:

> Many people thought he was the most beautiful human being they had ever seen, and it was probably true. He was extremely good-looking, tall, slender, and well-built, with dark-brown hair, very fine deep blue eyes and a real 'presence'.

He had impeccable manners, as befitting one of his social status and upbringing, but Lady Balfour found him somewhat withdrawn, only becoming animated when philosophy or one of his other academic interests was being discussed. She knew of the great things that were expected of him by Winifred Coombe Tennant and others in the inner circle of the Society for Psychical Research but, though he seemed to be an exceptional person, she thought he lacked the emotional enthusiasm and inner fire that was necessary if one were destined to become a great leader. If Winifred's belief in the practicality of Henry being helped forward by entities from the spirit world had any basis in reality, who can say how much additional effort on Henry's part would have been required? Henry undoubtedly gleaned information over the years on what his mother had intended his destiny to be, though it seems to have had very little impact on his behaviour. He had sometimes been a reluctant soldier but he had nevertheless stuck at it for 20 or so years, remaining in a tightly structured environment that left little scope for an expansive role in the wider world. His work with the intelligence services also kept him on a tight rein, while Downside Abbey was almost a retreat from the world at large. 'The Plan' had simply fizzled out, with a probably sceptical Henry doing little to help secure its realisation.

By the winter of 1989 Henry had reached the age of 76 and, with his physical condition gradually deteriorating, it was clear that the end could not be too far away. He was suffering from heart failure, due to the right ventricle of his heart weakening and no longer being able to effectively pump blood to his lungs. This would have tended, among other things, to increase his lethargy and tiredness, adding to the already diminished mobility due to his hip problem. To add to his difficulties, he developed bronchopneumonia, a dangerous condition for someone of his years, and it proved fatal. As one uncredited obituarist subsequently recorded:

> He died... in the small hours of 6th November 1989, while reciting prayers... His funeral took place a week later in the Abbey Church, with the Abbot, the Rt Revd John Roberts – who by a strange coincidence had been in the same wartime prison camp as Henry – concelebrating with other members of the Community. Many of the mourners had travelled a great distance and risked foggy and unpredictable November weather, determined to pay a final tribute and be present at the graveside of their dear old friend. The closing words of the Abbot's address were poignantly put: 'He was a good man; a dear man. And we shall remember him until one day when we shall meet him again.'

Henry was laid to rest in the monks' burial ground at Downside Abbey.

Sometime before his death, Henry had pondered the imponderable, telling his brother Alexander and his sister-in-law Jennifer:

> Why fear death? What is the point of being a Christian + going on about resurrection + the joys of Heaven if one can't face the prospect of death? If on the other hand one doesn't believe in life after death, it will be just like going to sleep + not waking up again, + the 'not waking up again' is obviously not going to be experienced, so why worry?

This echoed the pragmatic approach he had taken with his mother when, with his participation in the Second World War being imminent, she had tried to convince an agnostic Henry that his spirit would survive his death in battle, if that awful event were to transpire. He had left his mother in no doubt at that time that what happened after death was of no concern to him. To enter Heaven would be a joy, while if death resulted in only an unending darkness, then what was the loss to an individual if he simply ceased to be?

In his final hours, Henry would no doubt have been fortified by his Catholic faith and by his belief in the existence of an afterlife in Heaven. It is very tempting when considering his outlook to return to the words of his loving mother, Winifred, who had herself held such strong beliefs regarding the survival of the human spirit after the death of its earthly body. In 1908 prior to Henry's birth – Winifred had suffered the tragic loss of her daughter Daphne at the age of only 18 months. An apparently delightful child, Daphne had been lovingly known to family members as 'The Darling'. In the sad aftermath of Daphne's death, Winifred had told Christopher – her firstborn child, who was then still at school – that, many years in the future after their own deaths, they would all ultimately meet again in a new form and a new place. She had written, 'the Darling is still part of our lives, + she is still with us, though unseen... And you and I will find the Darling waiting for us [and] we shall cling to each other in the great joy of reunion.'

One can only imagine the unbounded happiness that would have occurred should Henry's spirit have departed his body in November 1989 to find the spirits of Winifred, Charles, Christopher and Daphne all patiently waiting to lovingly welcome 'The Wise One' as he crossed over the threshold to his new beginning. Then they would all truly have experienced 'the great joy of reunion.'

Select Bibliography

Arkwright, A S B, MC, *Return Journey – Escape from Oflag VIB* (Seely, Service & Co. Ltd., not dated).

Beavan, Colin, *Operation Jedburgh – D-Day and America's First Shadow War* (Viking, 2006).

Brutton, Philip, *A Captain's Mandate – Palestine 1946–48* (Leo Cooper, 1996).

Card, Tim, *Eton Renewed* (John Murray, 1994).

Colley, Dr M S and Colley, N L, *More than a Grain of Truth – The Biography of Gareth Richard Vaughan Jones* (privately published, 2005).

Cooksey, Jon, *Boulogne – 20th Guards Brigade's Fighting Defence – May 1940* (Leo Cooper, 2002).

Cormac, Rory, *Disrupt and Deny – Spies, Special Forces, and the Pursuit of British Foreign Policy* (Oxford University Press, 2018).

Crosby, M G M, *Irregular Soldier* (XB Publications, 1993).

Cummins, Geraldine, *Swan on a Black Sea – A Study in Automatic Writing: The Cummins-Willett Scripts* (Whitecrow Books, 2013 edition).

Daly-Groves, Luke, 'The Intelligence Division in Occupied Germany: the untold story of Britain's largest secret intelligence organisation', *Journal of Intelligence History*, 18:1, 2019, DOI: 10/1080/16161262.2018.1545824.

Dorril, Stephen, *MI6: Inside the Covert World of Her Majesty's Secret Intelligence Service* (Touchstone, 2002).

Downside Abbey Trust, *Downside Abbey Guidebook* (Downside Abbey Press, 2017 edition).

Ellis, Major L F, CVO, CBE, DSO, MC, *Welsh Guards at War* (Gale and Polden, 1946).

Fairbairn, W E, *All-In Fighting* (The Naval and Military Press – facsimile, not dated).

Falle, Sam, *My Lucky Life – In War, Revolution, Peace and Diplomacy* (Isis Large Print, The Book Guild, 1996).

Fitzgerald, Desmond, *A History of the Irish Guards in the Second World War* (The Irish Guards, London, 2000 edition).

Foot, M R D, SOE, *The Special Operations Executive 1940–46* (BBC Books, 1985 edition).

Glover, Michael, *The Fight for the Channel Ports* (Leo Cooper/ Secker & Warburg, 1985).

Hanbury, Peter, *A Not Very Military Experience* (privately published, 2000).

Hashimoto, Chikara, *The Twilight of the British Empire – British Intelligence and Counter-Subversion in the Middle East, 1948–63* (Edinburgh University Press, 2019 edition).

Hayes, Paddy, *Queen of Spies – Daphne Park, Britain's Cold War Spy Master* (Duckworth Overlook, 2016 edition).

Irwin, Lt. Col. (ret.) Will, *The Jedburghs – The Secret History of the Allied Special Forces, France 1944* (Public Affairs, 2005).

Jones, Benjamin, *Eisenhower's Guerrillas – The Jedburghs, The Maquis and the Liberation of France* (Oxford University Press, 2016).

Laker, Robert, 'Geneva in Motion: Winifred Coombe Tennant's Experiences at the Third Assembly of the League of Nations' (unpublished dissertation, Swansea University, 2020).

Lord, Peter, *Between Two Worlds – The Diary of Winifred Coombe Tennant 1909–1924* (The National Library of Wales, 2011).

Lord, Peter, *Winifred Coombe Tennant – A Life Through Art* (The National Library of Wales, 2007).

Select Bibliography

Monk, Ray, *Ludwig Wittgenstein – The Duty of Genius* (Vintage Books, 1991).

National Archives, The, *Special Operations Executive Manual – How to be an Agent in Occupied Europe* (William Collins/ The National Archives, 2014).

Neave, Airey, *Little Cyclone* (Biteback Publishing, 2016 edition)

Pritchard, Sydney, *Life in the Welsh Guards 1939–46* (Y Lolfa, 2007).

Reid, Miles, *Into Colditz* (Michael Russell Publishing Ltd., 1983).

Roy, Archie E, *The Eager Dead – A Study in Haunting* (Book Guild Publishing, 2008).

Stanier, Brigadier Sir Alexander, BT, DSO, MC, *Sammy's Wars* (privately published, 1998).

Stewart, Brian and Newbery, Samantha, *Why Spy? The Art of Intelligence* (Hurst and Company, 2020 edition).

Tucker, Keith, *A Scratch in Glamorganshire – George Tennant 1765–1832* (Historical Projects, 1998).

Waller, David, *The Magnificent Mrs Tennant: The Adventurous Life of Gertrude Tennant* (Yale University Press, 2009).

Index

As Henry Coombe-Tennant appears throughout this biography, his name has NOT been indexed.

Adair, Allan 194
Alington, Cyril 32, 34
Allen, Hugh 28–9
Antwerp 186–7
Arab Legion 206, 208, 215
Arandora Star, SS 40
Ardennes 152–4, 156, 160, 166, 169–70, 186, 188, 190, 201
Arkwright, Albert S B 103, 108–10, 113–15, 119, 125–7, 129, 131, 135, 137, 139, 141, 145, 216
Armitage, Henry St John B 213
Arques 32
Ashton, Teal 215

Bader, Douglas 199
Baghdad 230–2, 234, 236–7
Balfour, Arthur 13, 205
Balfour, Betty 14–15, 17
Balfour, Gerald 13, 15–18, 22, 24, 30, 39, 226, 249
Balfour, Jean 202, 249
Baring, Rupert (Lord Revelstoke) 91
Beale, Stephen 239
Deasley-Robinson, A C 39
Beckwith-Smith, Merton 55
Beer, Charles, 222
Beer, Graham 222
Beijing 47
Beirut 217
Belgium 48, 67–8, 74, 109, 120–1, 129, 134, 136, 144–5, 161, 164, 166, 177, 180, 186, 201, 216, 219
Bell, David 224
Bemelmans, Tita Ada 124–6, 180

Biarritz, SS 74–5
Bilbao 134
Blunt, Anthony 244
Bordeaux 135
Bottomley, A C 41
Brackenbury, Revd F F 24
Bright, John 10
Broad, Charles D 43–4, 52–3, 55, 58, 243–4
Bruce, D 181–2
Brussels 129–30, 134, 136–7, 165, 180, 186, 194, 222
Buckingham Palace 65, 141, 196, 203
Burgess, Guy 244
Butler, James R M 43

Cadoxton 14, 22, 35, 224–6, 235
Cadoxton Lodge 9–10, 16, 19, 26, 35, 38
Cairncross, John 245
Cambridge University 41–4, 48, 52–53, 55–6, 58, 222, 244
Canada 43–4, 46
Cannicott, Stanley 149
Canterbury, SS 71
Catterick Camp 61
Cavell, Edith 134
Chamberlain, Joseph 10
Changchun 47
Chelsea Barracks 64–5, 195–6
Chetwode, Sir Philip 88–9
China 26, 30, 38, 42, 46–8, 57, 235
Churchill, Clementine 91
Churchill, Winston S 144, 201
Clarendon, Lord 89, 93, 141

256

Index

Clayton, Revd P B (Tubby) 48, 224
Comet Line 122, 131, 133–4, 150–1
Consett 50–1
Coombe Tennant, Charles 9–10, 35
Coombe Tennant, Winifred 9–20, 22–7, 29–30, 32–4, 36–43, 45–6, 48–50, 52, 54, 56–60, 62, 84–8, 90–4, 97, 100–102, 139, 141, 216–17, 223–6, 235, 242, 248–9, 251, 251–2
Coombe-Tennant, Alexander 11, 15, 17, 20–1, 36–8, 40, 42, 53–4, 57–8, 62–3, 84, 141, 223–7, 233, 235, 243, 246–7, 251
Coombe-Tennant, Jennifer 251
Coombe-Tennant, John 247
Coombe-Tennant, Mark 247–8
Copland-Griffiths, F A V 64
Crete 199
Croft, Lord 92
Croix Scaille 169
Cross-Correspondences 12
Cummins, Geraldine 225–7, 242

d'Oultremont, George 131
d'Oultremont, Edouard 131, 150–1, 153, 157, 162
Dalian 47
Dalton, Hugh 144
Damascus 217
Davies, Victor 85
Davison, William 92
de Bollardière, Jacques P 153–6, 159–62, 166–7, 170, 173, 175–6
de Gaulle, Charles 143, 153
de Jongh, Andrée 134–6
de Jongh, Frédéric 135
de Lange, Gladys 238
de Lange, Mickey 238
De Pree, John Bourlon 112–13
Dean, Donald John 80
Dössel 94, 110
Douglas-Hamilton, Nigel 43
Downside Abbey 237–243, 246–51
Dunkirk 68, 74–5
Durham 49–50

Edward, Prince of Wales 44
Eindhoven 178
Eisenhower, Dwight D 142–3, 181
El Alamein 154

Elizabeth II / Princess Elizabeth 196, 222
Elms, Jonathan 239
ENSA 203
Eppink, J H 118
Eton College 29, 31–8, 40–4, 53, 63, 227, 235–6
Exercise Ferret 206

Fairbairn, William 149–50
Feraille-Warnon, Elisabeth 130
Fermor, Patrick Leigh 199–201, 237, 245
Few, M E 100
Fisher's Hill 14, 17, 24
Fox-Pitt, William A L 55–7, 60, 75, 80
Friele, Daphne 248
Fuller, Rupert J 109–15, 119, 123, 127, 129, 131–3, 135, 137, 139, 141, 145, 151, 246

Geneva 20, 87–8, 90–2, 94, 198
George VI 66, 141–2, 196, 222
Gibraltar 40, 63–4, 138, 205
Gilroy, C B 96
Gladstone, William Ewart 10
Glubb, John B 213
Glynn Vivian Art Gallery 10, 38, 224
Goch 190, 193
Goethals, Antoine 129
Granta magazine 48
Greindl, Jean 131
Groenen, Michel 125, 180
Groenen, Solange 124
Gubbins, Colin 143–4
Gurney, Edmund 16

Haganah 208
Hague, The 68, 70–2, 228–30, 238
Haifa 206
Hanbury, Peter 77–8, 81–3
Harpoon Force 69, 71, 73
Harrison, Frank 151–4, 157–8, 162–3, 201–2
Hautes-Rivières 172
Hawick 203
Haydon, J C 69, 71–3
Heber-Percy, Cyril H E 69, 71,73–4, 191–2, 204
Helbert, Lionel 21

257

Hennessy, George 60
Higgon, J H V (Jack) 75, 79, 81–3, 246
Highgate Cemetery 35
Hills, J D 43
Hitler, Adolf 42, 62, 66–7, 142, 187, 191, 221
Holland 67–70, 73–4, 111, 118, 120, 144–5, 152, 230
Hook of Holland 70–4, 152, 230
Hope-Jones, William 34
Horrocks, Brian 189

Institute of Pacific Relations 46
Irgun group 208–9

Janes, Alfred 228
Japan 46–7, 142
Jebel Rum 213–14
Jeddah 211–12
Jerusalem 205, 208–9
Johnson, Albert 'B' 136
Jones, Gareth 42–3, 57
Juliana, Princess/Queen of the Netherlands 72

Keith, HMS 80
Kendrick, Thomas J 228
Keynes, John Maynard 54–5
Kilkenny, John 148
Kleve 190
Knox, Alfred 92
Kœnig, Marie Joseph P F 181
Kreipe, Heinrich 199

Laufen 83–4, 87, 89, 92–4, 96, 248
Law, Andrew Bonar 88
Law, R K 88
Lawrence of Arabia 212–13
League of Nations 10, 20, 205
Leonard, Gladys O 18, 33
Lewis, A R (David) 65
Lewis, S J 248
Liège 127–30
Liégeois, Elisabeth 130
Lille 131, 133
Little Malvern 241, 243
Llewelyn, Desmond 96
Lloyd George, David 10, 19, 26, 42, 60, 91

Lloyd, Barbara (née Walsh) 228
Lodge, Oliver 13–14, 18, 226
Louvain 187, 189
Lyttelton, Edward 34
Lyttleton, Mary 13

Maclean, Donald 244
Madrid 138
Maid of Orleans, SS 71
Malcolm, HMS 72
Manchukuo 57
Mansi, Dominic 241, 243
Maude, Chris 201–2
Mecca 211
Metula 206–7, 210
MI6 9, 222, 227–9, 232–4, 237, 244
Milton Hall 147–48, 150, 248
Mona's Queen, SS 74
Mooney, Brian 239
Moral Sciences Club (Cambridge University) 48, 54–5
Morris, R O 215–17
Moss, Bill Stanley 199
Moulson, Ronnie 105, 114
Murray, William Grant 10, 38
Myers, Frederic W H 11–13, 16

Nablus 214, 217
Namur 187
Narvik 153
Neath 9–10, 35, 37, 216, 224
Nichols, John S 197, 201
Nijmegen 179–81, 190, 194
Norway 66–7, 153, 219
Nothomb, Jean-François 136
Nouzonville 170, 172–5

O'Connor, Richard N 178
Oflag IV C (Colditz) 92, 198
Oflag VI–B (Warburg) 94, 139
Oflag VII C/H (Laufen) 84, 89
Oflag VII–B (Eichstätt) 102
Old Dean Common Camp 73
Operation Agatha 209
Operation Citronelle 153–4, 156, 160–1, 163–6, 169–74, 176
Operation Grenade 190
Operation Jedburgh 144–5, 148, 156, 248
Operation Olympia 105–6, 112–13

258

Index

Operation Veritable 190
Operation Vicarage 197

Palestine 204–5, 207–10, 214–15, 217–18, 230
Paris 11, 66, 133–5, 165, 176, 248
Pearce-Serocold, George 10
Peyton, John 247
Philby, Harold A R (Kim) 227, 244–5
Pinewood School 24–7, 30, 53, 235
Pirbright Camp 56, 58, 245
Playsted, Dorothy 23
Plowden-Wardlaw, James 48
Porter, T C 34
Porthcawl 40
Pym, Leslie 92

Radstock 237–8, 241–3
RAF Tempsford 156
Reid, Miles 200–1
Reid, Pat 92
Richardson, Mary Clarke 10
Ritschdorff, Jeanne 129
Ritschdorff, Mathilde 129
Roberts, John 250
Rohmer, Sax 26
Roosevelt, Franklin Delano 143
Rose, Archie 46–7, 52, 54, 216
Rouen 32
Royal College of Music 28–9, 215
Royal Institute of International Affairs 46
Royal Naval Volunteer Reserve 48
Russia (USSR) 66, 88, 142, 244

's-Hertogenbosch 191
SAARF 196–201
Salle-Coolen, Catherine 126
Salter, William S 225, 227
Sandringham 196, 222
Saudi Arabia 210–11, 213–14
Scott-Moncrieff, Robert 99
Searle, Kenneth 103–5, 107–8, 114
Shenyang 47
Shirley, W 24–30
Sidgwick, Henry 16–17
Sittard 183
Society for Psychical Research 11–12, 16, 225, 248–9
Southey, R J 204, 206

Special Operations Executive / SOE 9, 143–5, 148–9, 199, 227, 244–5, 248
St Jean de Luz 135–6
Stallard, Tom 245–6
Stanier, Alexander (Sammy) 58, 64, 66–7, 75–9, 217, 245
Stanley, Henry Morton 10
Stirling, David 199
Stobs Camp 203–4
Straight, Whitney 45
Switzerland 34, 52–4, 59, 88, 93, 110–11
Sykes, Eric A 150

Ta'if 211–12, 214
Tavender, Miss 18–20, 22
Tennant, Christopher 10–11, 15, 17–19, 32, 53, 62, 84, 226, 251–2
Tennant, Daphne 11–12, 14, 16, 251–2
Tennant, Dorothy 10
Tennant, Eveleen 11
Tennant, George 9
Tennant, Gertrude 10, 37
Thomson, Joan 45, 49, 52, 59, 61
Thomson, Joseph John 45, 49, 52, 59
Threipland, William Murray 61
Tiberias 206–7, 209–10
Tindall, Kenneth 21–4
Toc H 48, 224–5
Todd, Bruce 245
Todd, Leonard 33–6
Tongerlo 125, 180
Tow Law Camp 50
Tower of London 65–6, 203
Tracey, Paul 240
Transjordan 214, 217

Ukraine 57
Ulster Monarch, SS 195

Venetia, HMS 80
Venomous, HMS 80
Vienna 228
Vigor, G St V J 69
Vimy, HMS 80

Wadi Rum 213
Wakeham, Roy 28–9, 31

259

Walsh, Barbara – see Lloyd, Barbara
Walters, Evan 10, 224
Warburg 94–103, 110–11, 115, 135, 139, 147, 216, 245–6, 248
Warlock, Derek 237
Webb, L A R 182
Wellington Barracks 58
West Downs School 11, 21–4
Whinney, Maurice 228
Whitshed, HMS 80
Wild Swan, HMS 80

Wilhelmina, Queen of the Netherlands 72–3, 230
Willett, Mrs 12, 225–6, 242
Williams, A J 85
Williams, Kyffin 10
Winchester College 11, 17
Windsor 66
Windsor-Lewis, James 77, 79

Zhangjiakou 48

Also from Y Lolfa:

£6.95
Memoirs of a soldier who fought with the
Welsh Guards during the Second World War.

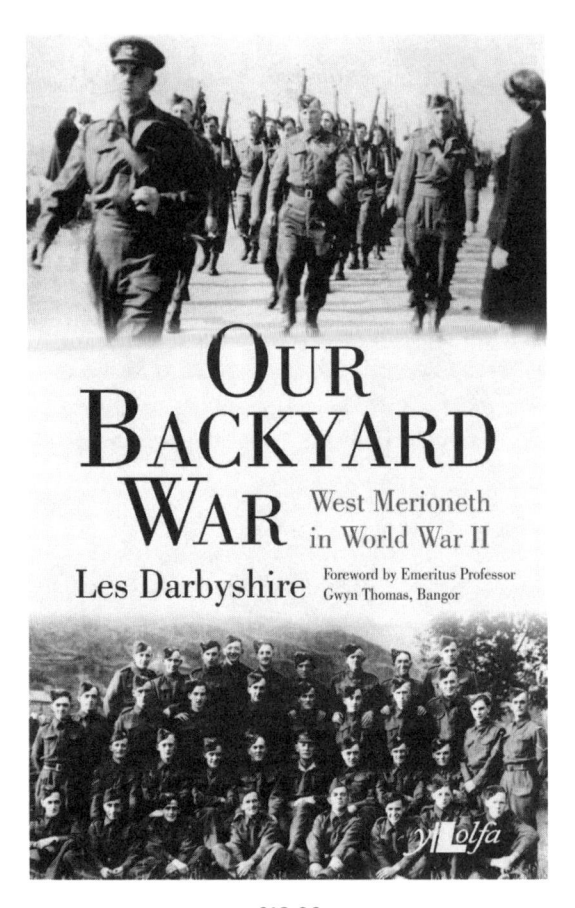

Our Backyard War

West Merioneth in World War II

Les Darbyshire

Foreword by Emeritus Professor Gwyn Thomas, Bangor

£12.99

Recollections from those who lived and trained in the western area of Merioneth during the Second World War.

GWYN JENKINS

A WELSH COUNTY AT WAR

ESSAYS ON CEREDIGION AT THE TIME OF THE FIRST WORLD WAR

y olfa

£9.99

A social and cultural history of the impact of World War I on everyday life in one Welsh county.

CYMRY'R RHYFEL BYD CYNTAF

GWYN JENKINS

'Yr wyf yn llawn arswyd am y dyfodol.'
Lloyd George, Awst 1914

£9.95

Perhaps the definitive history of the First World War from the Welsh perspective, recording the experiences of soldiers, sailors, nurses, munitionettes, pacifists and many others from all over the country. (in Welsh)

The Welsh at Mametz Wood
The Somme 1916
Dr Jonathan Hicks

£12.99

The story of the horrific First World War battle for Mametz Wood in July 1916, including personal accounts from soldiers on both sides and photographs published for the first time.

The Welsh at Passchendaele 1917

DR JONATHAN HICKS

y Lolfa

THE FOLLOW-UP TO THE NUMBER ONE BESTSELLER, *THE WELSH AT MAMETZ WOOD*

£14.99

A detailed study of the Welsh soldiers who fought in 1917 at Passchendaele, where hundreds of thousands were killed or wounded. With previously unpublished photographs.

WALES
AND THE FIRST AIR WAR 1914–1918

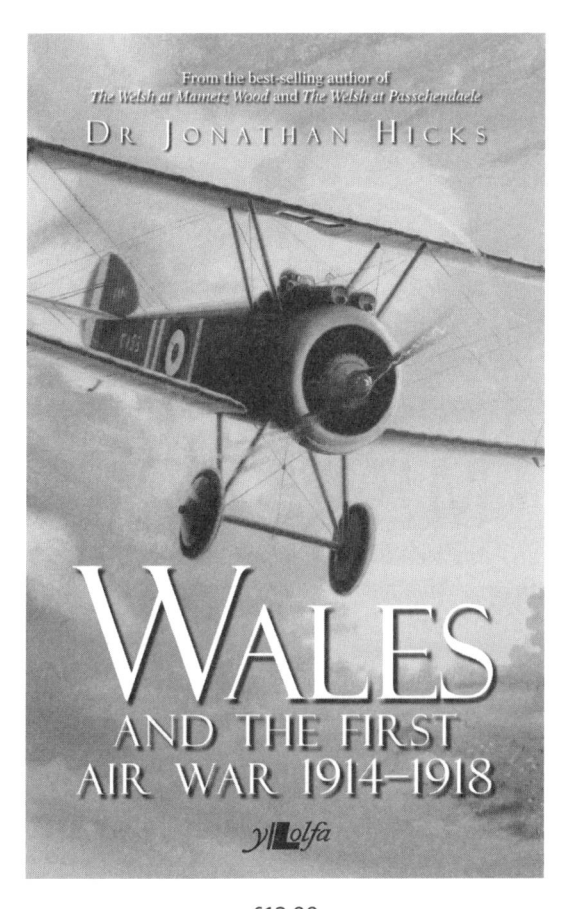

From the best-selling author of *The Welsh at Mametz Wood* and *The Welsh at Passchendaele*

DR JONATHAN HICKS

y Lolfa

£12.99

An account of Welsh involvement in the Royal Flying Corps, Royal Naval Air Service and Royal Air Force during the First World War.

DR JONATHAN HICKS

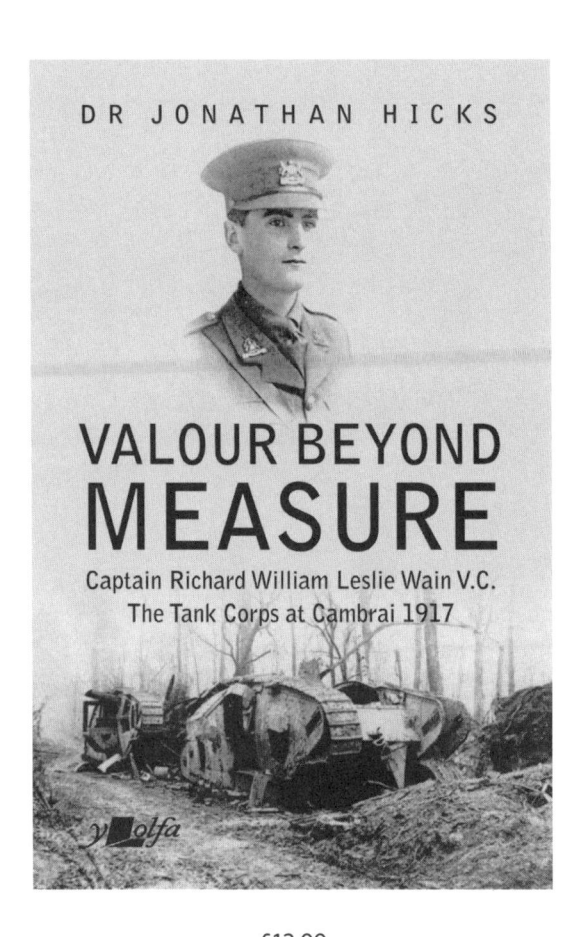

VALOUR BEYOND MEASURE

Captain Richard William Leslie Wain V.C.
The Tank Corps at Cambrai 1917

£12.99

Biography of First World War hero Richard Wain from Penarth, Glamorgan, also tracing the history of the Tank Corps and its contribution to the winning of the war.

Wales and World War One

Robin Barlow

£14.99
A comprehensive history of Wales'
involvement in the First World War.

A Haven from HITLER

"Kate Bosse becomes a figure of huge moral and symbolic significance."
– Simon Brooks, *Planet*

A young woman's escape from Nazi Germany to Wales: the story of Kate Bosse-Griffiths and her family

Heini Gruffudd

y Lolfa

Welsh Book of the Year 2013

£9.95

The moving story of Kate Bosse-Griffiths' escape to Wales from the horrors of the Holocaust in Nazi Germany.

Evacuee

From the Liverpool Blitz to Wales

Barbara Warlow Davies

£7.99

The remarkable story of an English-speaking four year old's evacuation from the Liverpool blitz to Ceredigion during the Second World War.